BANNED!

A Review of Theatrical Censorship in Britain

BANNED!

A Review of Theatrical Censorship in Britain

———

RICHARD FINDLATER

MACGIBBON & KEE

FIRST PUBLISHED 1967 BY MACGIBBON & KEE LTD
COPYRIGHT © RICHARD FINDLATER 1967
PRINTED IN GREAT BRITAIN BY
THE GARDEN CITY PRESS LTD
LONDON AND LETCHWORTH

BANNED!

A Review of Theatrical Censorship in Britain

The matter of theatre censorship may seem a small matter when compared with what is going on in Vietnam or Rhodesia or with the problem of the balance of payments. But it is not. No issue of artistic freedom is ever small or unimportant. Do not let us muddle on any longer with this; do not let us say that because it works in a liberal fashion, therefore we shall tolerate it. It is an affront to the freedom of artists. It must be abolished. In present hands it may operate in a liberal way; in other hands it may not. As an institution it is wrong. As an institution it is false and it must go.—LORD WILLIS, speaking in a debate on theatre censorship in the House of Lords, 17 February 1966.

Law alone can give us freedom.—GOETHE

★　★　★

INSIDE the precincts of the Palace of St James, just around the corner from the busbied guardsmen on sentry duty, in a four-storey eighteenth-century house with a worn brass plate by the white portico and a liveried porter in the tiny hall, are the headquarters of the senior officer of the Household of Queen Elizabeth II, the Lord Chamberlain. His office in Stable Yard has the air of an exclusive ancient club, with a continuous tradition of over four hundred years behind it; but bitter argument has flared up around it for generations, and in the past sixty years in particular it has been the intermittent target of books, petitions, pamphlets, articles, questions in the House, several abortive Bills, and two Parliamentary committees, as well as a couple of unofficial ones. It has been by far the most controversial section of the Royal Household: but not because of its services to Her Majesty.

Down below the Yard the house's Tudor cellars are bursting with a unique theatrical library, which overflows into spare corners upstairs—as well it might, because it includes a copy of every play, sketch, opera libretto and pantomime script publicly performed in Britain in the last half-century. In a sombre apartment on the first floor, now an office but until recently a waiting-room, hung with portraits of Queen Victoria and Prince Albert and equipped with albums of royal photographs of the

1890s and even later periods, some of the leading dramatists of their time have braced themselves to debate the future of their plays. Now they wait in a little ground-floor snuggery, with a chintz-covered sofa and prints of Windsor Castle, to argue the case for a phrase, a situation or even a whole play. For there is only one legal route to the stage for an English author, and it lies through this palace annexe. Before any new theatrical text by a living writer can be publicly performed it must be sent here by a manager for the approval of the Lord Chamberlain, with a fee of two guineas (for anything over two acts). The fee is for reading: you don't get your money back if the Lord Chamberlain refuses to approve your typescript, but without his licence no new work can be publicly staged in Britain by paid actors before a paying audience— whether it is a translation of Aristophanes, a new *Mother Goose*, a Britten libretto, an Osborne play, or a Bart musical. Every writer is his own censor; every manager and theatre owner censors the drama, in different ways; and the public applies its own working censorship: these kinds of control are unavoidable and indestructible. But, in addition, the British playwright still has to obtain *official* permission before his work can be staged, from Camerarius Hospitii as the Chamberlain was known in Tudor times.

About eight hundred scripts a year come to this hushed warren of rooms, where the Lord Chamberlain and his men—doing their legal duty under the Theatres Act of 1843—serve as loyal arbiters of what is too indecent, profane, blasphemous, seditious, treasonable, in poor taste, or just excessively un-English to be presented in a theatre. He can ban any play or part of a play, 'either absolutely'—says the law—'or for such time as he shall think fit': as long as he believes it is necessary for 'the preservation of good manners, decorum or the public peace so to do'. Every word and every bit of 'business' must have the sanction of the Chamberlain before it is seen by an audience. Even after he has issued a licence, he can change his mind and veto a line, a scene, or indeed the entire play. Against his verdict there is no appeal. As censor of the stage he is above Parliament and outside the law.

The theatrical responsibilities of the Lord Chamberlain do not end there. When you take your seat in a London theatre, you are usually— whether you like it or not—under his official protection. For he not only vets the nation's drama but he also licenses the capital's playhouses. On stage and off, in both text and building, his safety precautions must be observed. Officially, he ensures that there are enough exits in case of fire; that a safety curtain is lowered and raised during every performance;

10

that the scenery is fireproof, and the seats are fixed to the floor; that the ventilation and sanitation are up to standard; that naked flames are not wantonly exposed to view. In fact, the inspection and general hard labour are done by the Greater London Council, but it is the Lord Chamberlain who is still legally in charge, who issues the Central London playhouses with their permits to keep open, and who can, in law, close them all down.

To the administration of this key post in the British theatre the current Chamberlain, Lord Cobbold, P.C., G.C.V.O., brings a long experience of uncontroversial public service, certifiably free from any professional connection with the stage—in the tradition of the job. Educated at Eton and King's, married to a daughter of the Earl of Lytton, Cameron Fromanteel Cobbold entered the Bank of England in 1933 as Advisor, and within sixteen years became its Governor, a post he held until 1961. He is a member of the Athenaeum and White's. In 1962 he was chairman of the Malaysia Commission of Enquiry.

None of these experiences, however, qualified Lord Cobbold for the absolute and arbitrary power which he was given over the English drama in 1963, at the age of fifty-nine, when he succeeded the Earl of Scarbrough as Lord Chamberlain. He is the censor of our stage because the Queen then gave him a white staff, which has represented the authority of the Lords Chamberlain ever since the Tudor ones used it to keep order at Court. When a Chamberlain resigns or, in practice, when a sovereign dies the white staff is broken in half (nowadays, for everyone's convenience, it unscrews in the middle, and the Chamberlain keeps half as a memento). Lord Cobbold, in fact, *inherited* the task of censorship as one of the secondary chores which has been attached for generations to the office of Lord Chamberlain at the Court of St James.

As head of the Royal Household, chairman of the Household Committee, and senior courtier of Queen Elizabeth, the Lord Chamberlain has a great deal of other anxieties besides the theatre. He is the organizer of royal levées, investitures, and garden parties; he arranges the reception and entertainment of foreign royalties and heads of state; he is the Queen's official emissary to the House of Lords; he supervises the administration of several royal homes; he carries out the Queen's wishes in filling such royal jobs as the Poet Laureate, the Keeper of the Jewel House, the Queen's Watermen, the pages of the backstairs and the chamber, the Gentleman Usher of the Black Rod and many other figures

11

in the Court hierarchy. He examines the credentials of people who want to be presented at Court or to get into the Royal Enclosure at Ascot. He controls the warrants by which tradesmen can put 'By Royal Appointment' on their vans and shop-fronts. He watches out for disrespectful, non-royal use of the royal insignia: as in the case some years ago when he stopped a magician and his wife, who called themselves 'Magic's Royal Couple', from showing a miniature crown on their writing paper and advertisements, and from using on stage a crown of tin and cotton wool and an orb of aluminium and diamanté. He keeps an eye on the well-being of the six hundred royal swans, and the maintenance of the royal art-collections. He is the organizer, in sum, of all ceremonial affecting the Royal Family, outside such occasions as the crowning or burial of a sovereign, when the Earl Marshal takes over. His prime duty, in fact, is to the Queen and her family. The Chamberlain must wait upon the throne, and the theatre must wait upon the Chamberlain, as it has done for over two hundred years.

But *why* must it? Is he indispensable? Do we need a censor at all, let alone a palace one? For generations English novelists, poets, cartoonists, biographers, journalists and, more recently, television writers and performers have indulged, unhindered, in what to the Lords Chamberlain of their day must have appeared to be downright pornography, blasphemy, libel, sedition, obscenity and treason. The drama has always, until recently, lagged far behind. Dramatists have been denied a freedom taken for granted in the other arts and subjected to the arbitrary personal decisions of a Court official and his clerks. Many plays have been banned; thousands have been mutilated; nobody knows how many have been withdrawn on the Chamberlain's advice, or left unfinished, or never begun, because of his existence, and the taboos he maintains. Liberty of expression in matters of religion, politics, and sex, still far from complete, has been slowly and painfully increased against the opposition not only of the censor but of nearly all the managers and a vociferous section of public opinion. It is not surprising that for the last sixty years the people in the house in Stable Yard have stirred up so much argument and that so many people outside it still demand that the Lord Chamberlain's censorship of the stage should be abolished.

As I write, a Parliamentary investigation into his censorship is expected to begin. It has been heralded several times during the last twenty years, as in 1949 and 1958. The most recent promise was made early in 1966, and it now seems likely that a report should be issued before the sixtieth anniversary of the *last* committee which sat in 1909. That one had a distinguished cast which included many of the leading writers, actors, and managers of the day. It resulted in a report of half a million words. But this had no visible effect at all, except to make the operations of censorship, for a while, even less sensible, consistent and efficient than before.

The next report, when it comes, may clear up the mess; or it may be equally confused and equally ineffectual. Will that really matter? Is the censorship of the stage of any importance? After all, anything goes these days—or so many people believe: some think that it has gone too far. Certainly there has been a radical change in the tolerance of the Lord Chamberlain's Office, and words, situations and themes are openly staged that were unthinkable in the theatre ten or even five years ago (although they were often thinkable—and viewable, too—in print, on the TV screen, in newspapers and in real life). The gentlemanly censors in Stable Yard have small relish, it seems, for the benevolent despotism which they are obliged to exercise. The Court official who was once the ogre of serious British drama seems to have faded almost completely away. Why not leave him alone, some people ask, in spite of his meddlesome past? Why vex his ghost?

Yet there is nothing spectral about the surviving power of the Lord Chamberlain, even though the present tenant of that ancient office does not choose to exercise it at full stretch in the theatre. Although he is a reluctant censor, he is a censor nevertheless, with an absolute authority which is still intact—and will *remain* intact if many influential voices, in and out of the theatre, are heard in Whitehall. Although the Chamberlain has relaxed the severity of his scrutiny and reduced the number of his taboos, it is still impossible for a serious writer to be certain that he can explore freely on the stage themes and situations which he can often discuss without any veto in any other medium and which dramatists in many other countries can openly discuss in the theatre. And narrower-minded successors to Lord Cobbold and his aides might yet change the climate of censorship—and of English drama—without anyone being able to prevent them.

That, I submit, is one reason why the study of our theatrical censorship is not only a matter of digging up the past, but is relevant to the present and the future of the English stage. This book contains a good deal of exhumation, achieved with the help of earlier books to which—with other valuable sources and generous helpers—grateful acknowledgments are paid in a final note; but the digging has been done not only to bring the record up to date, but also for the amusement of the general reader. The tale I have to tell is one of corruption, injustice, petty tyranny, humbug, waste, ignorance, bigotry and superstition. Yet it is also a funny story, part of one of the most extraordinary, entertaining and instructive chapters in English cultural history. And the story is not over yet although the first Lord Cobbold may be the last Lord Chamberlain to censor the stage . . .

2

There is no poorer excuse for a censorship than history.—MORRIS ERNST and WILLIAM SEAGLE: *To the Pure . . .*; 1929

* * *

SOON after the secular drama began to push its way slowly and stubbornly into the periphery of English life about four hundred years ago, it was recognized by responsible people that this sort of thing could not be allowed to spread unchecked at the bottom of society without expert pruning from the top. If God, the King and the social order were to receive their due meed of acquiescence, the men in charge of the machinery of State realized that the theatre had to be kept in its place. From a different quarter came the Puritan demand that it should be abolished altogether, or should, at least, be purged of its more glaring and infectious improprieties. This dual attitude towards the indispensability of theatrical censorship has confused the argument about it ever since the Reformation. An official censor began to interfere in the drama around the time that the first professional theatre opened its doors in London, in 1576. Established by the Crown, entrenched by political finagling, reinforced by the support of both the trade and the Puritan belt, and, in due course, sanctified by tradition, his office has remained in power generations after its equivalents disappeared from other areas of the national culture, unshaken by the recurrent quarrels about its authority and supported by the steadfast English conviction that the theatre can't, really, be trusted on its own.

From the start, in the reign of Henry VIII, censorship of the professional stage was concerned with protecting both State and Church against religious and political heresy and the more frequent affliction of embarrassment, rather than with questions of good taste or bad language. That concern is still its basic function four hundred years later, whatever the squabbles on the surface may be. The censor's office, then, was established as an annexe of the royal palace; it is still there today. The centre of political power has moved half a mile away, across the park to Whitehall and Westminster, but the State still retains the old shield against anti-royal and anti-Christian behaviour on the stage.

15

Theatrical censorship was originally imposed as part of the attempt to stamp out Catholic resistance to the Reformation and to establish a settled loyalty to the Defender of the Faith, Henry VIII, as head of both Church and State. During the sixteenth century—as Dr Glynne Wickham has made plain in *Early English Stages*—Church and State deliberately 'censored out of existence' the vigorous religious theatre of the Miracle Cycles, with its 'living demonstration of Catholic doctrine'— or, as the Protestants saw it in post-Reformation times, the maintenance of idolatry and superstition. The King's assumption of supreme authority over the Church, and his displacement of the Pope, involved such revolutionary disturbances in religious and political thinking that a gag had to be put on the new secular theatre which followed in the wake of the Miracles, and which was still, in Puritan eyes, tainted by Catholic associations. Conflicts of opinion over religion were inevitably connected with divisions over succession to the throne. As Dr Wickham says:

The drama of our own times so rarely reflects anything but the most superficial of current topics that it may require an effort of serious imagination for us to realize that the drama of the sixteenth century was adult enough to reflect in detail the quickly shifting religious and political issues of the day. As one of the most inflammatory instruments of propaganda known to the age, it invited the attention of the lords temporal as well as its traditional controllers, the lords spiritual.[1]

The stage was feared as a political platform and as a religious pulpit, especially—as Dr Wickham points out—because of 'the acute proximity of the audience to the actors and the convention of direct address'.[2] Moralists feared it because of the acute proximity of the playhouses to the brothels and of the playgoers to each other, as a breeding-ground of disease, absenteeism, and general lewdness. These fears had some substance. Allegory and parable, moreover, were familiar conventions of thought; and 'it was more natural for spectators to assume that what they saw and heard was an emblem in which truth was to be divined than that text, acting, costume and setting represented an exact copy or image of the actual world'. Physical violence and even public riot, moreover, were much more easily triggered off than they are today. Swords were worn and often used; while the dangers of plague made tempers worse. In the eyes of the State all this meant an urgent need for controlling the professional companies, centralizing them under royal patronage, and

[1] *Early English Stages*, Vol. 1 (1959).　　　　[2] Ibid., Vol. 2 (1963).

censoring their themes and their texts: but the Crown had to fight both Church and City for the commanding role.

It was in 1543, four years after the dissolution of the monasteries, with 'An act for the advancement of true religion and for the abolishment of the contrary', that the content of the drama was first regulated—in a negative sense—by the State. Any plays which challenged the authorized religion were, together with books, ballads, songs 'and other fantasies', to be 'abolished, extinguished and forbidden'. This was an incidental feature of the Act, which approved of plays 'for the rebuking and reproaching of vices and the setting forth of virtue', as long as they did not 'meddle with interpretations of Scripture' that clashed with the official doctrine 'set forth or to be set forth by the King's Majesty'.

Edward VI repealed this law when he succeeded to the throne in 1547; and as a result, polemics by Protestant propagandists were widely performed with State approval, and inflamed the feelings of Catholic audiences by attacks on the Mass and the Eucharist. In order to keep the peace, new measures of control had to be taken. So in 1549 a royal proclamation prohibited *all* plays throughout the country for a period of three months, because most of them were said to 'contain matter tending to sedition and contemning of sundry good orders and laws'. Two years after that, in 1551, another royal proclamation ruled that actors of plays or interludes in English must have a special royal licence, signed by half a dozen members of the Privy Council, even in order to play for their patron in his own house. In the same year, printers were directed to apply for permission to print plays. When Queen Mary came to the throne in 1553, she reaffirmed that neither the printing nor performance of plays was allowed without a royal licence. And so on . . .

Who was to do the censoring? That has always been the nub of the problem. It was solved for books in 1556 by giving the Stationers Company the exclusive monopoly of printing, in return for the State service of suppressing heretical and seditious works. This licensing system continued, in effect, until 1695. But censorship of the stage proved more difficult to regulate. Both City and Church wanted to have the last word, but the Crown held out and kept control. In 1559 Elizabeth gave supervisory powers to municipal officers in the towns and to the Lord Lieutenant or two J.P.s in the shires, ordering them to prohibit all plays 'wherein either matters of religion or of the governance of the estate of the commonweal shall be handled, or treated; being no meet matters to be written or treated upon, but by men of authority, learning and wisdom, nor to be handled before any audience but of grave and discreet persons'. A similar argument is still piously pursued today. Yet this curb was not enough. Against the theatre the State used Poor Law regulations, Star Chamber orders, an Order in Council authorizing the general demolition of playhouses (never implemented till the Restoration). Above all, it used the Master of Revels. This Court official was selected as the first effective censor of the professional stage in England, working under the jurisdiction of the Lord Chamberlain.

For the Master, as for his twentieth-century successors, censorship was only a sideline of active service to the Throne. The Revels Office, officially instituted in 1545, was concerned with the theatrical pleasures of the monarch, and its Master also sifted applications by outside companies (professional and amateur) to perform at Court, co-ordinated the backstage work of the other royal departments involved, and supervised both theme and content. The first official Master, Sir Thomas Cawarden, was appointed for life at £10 a year as *Magister Jocorum, Revelorum et Mascorum omnium et singulorum nostorum, vulgariter nuncupatorum Revelles et Maskes*, a nomenclature which served, in its range, as the model for the powers of his successors. In 1574, the Master's powers outside the Court over the professional stage were inaugurated with the historic patent granted by the Queen to the Earl of Leicester's players, who were authorized to perform regularly in London on weekdays, and to tour throughout the realm—on condition that all their plays should be 'seen and allowed' by the Master, 'for the time being'. (Two years later they opened the first professional playhouse, the Theatre.) During the long term of office enjoyed by Edmund Tilney, who took over the post in 1578 and made the most of it till his death in 1610, the Master of the Revels exercised wide and increasing power over the theatre, although, with a vagueness which characterizes the history of the whole institution, there was no mention of his function of censorship in the patent appointing him in 1579. Soon after he took control, the Queen gave Tilney the power to press into service any painters, embroiderers, glaziers, joiners, tailors, armourers, feather-makers, skinners, sadlers, basketmakers and other craftsmen he required; to requisition any transport or materials necessary for 'any exploit, workmanship or piece of service' required by the Revels Office; to commit any resisters to prison, for as long as he thought fit; to set at liberty any Revels employees arrested by anyone else during any project. He was empowered to command all players and 'their playmakers' to present their plays before him, or his deputy, and to 'order and reform, authorize and put down, as shall be thought meet or unmeet unto himself or his said deputy, on that behalf', and to send them to prison for as long as he thought fit, 'if any of them, whatsoever they be, will obstinately refuse'. From its beginnings the English dramatic censorship was associated with arbitrary, personal suspension of freedom, protected by the Crown; although, as in later years, the tyranny in practice was somewhat less ferocious than it looked on paper.

It was the Martin Marprelate controversy of 1589 which really established the power of the Revels Office. Disturbed by the energy with which the theatre in taking the Church's side against the militant Puritans had handled religion and politics, and eager to placate the growing anti-theatrical opposition in the City, the Privy Council decreed that the Archbishop of Canterbury should nominate 'some fit person well learned in divinity' to collaborate in censoring plays with Tilney and a representative picked by the Mayor of London—a concession to both Church and City, which rescinded Tilney's powers as granted in 1581. This triumvirate was briefed to 'strike out or reform such parts and matters as they shall find unfit and undecent to be handled in plays, both for Divinity and State'. If the actors failed to deliver up their 'books' for judgement and abide by the verdict, they would not only be severely punished but also prohibited from exercising their profession 'forever hereafter'. Like many savage-sounding Tudor edicts, this became a dead letter; but it confirmed the Master of Revels as a big wheel in the theatre, perhaps because, as Dr Wickham suggests, he refused to give up the powers granted in 1581 without substantial compensation; more than the Church or City would pay. The two advisors soon dropped out; the Church in general lost authority in this field; the City's claims were bypassed; and by the time Shakespeare was established as an actor in London, Edmund Tilney was in practice the day-to-day arbiter of the drama.

Every play had to be sent to him for his approval, at a fee of five shillings. This was gradually, over six years, raised to seven shillings, which was in 1598 an extortionate price, in relation to the Elizabethan author's average income of £6 to £10 a play. When he was sure that, as far as he could see, there was no offence in the script, after instructing the author to make any necessary cuts and revisions, the Master signed the 'book' of the play, and the company kept that as its licence. He made as much money as he could by thinking up new extensions of his power; by selling permission to break the laws—as in the dispensations he gave companies to act during the forbidden period of Lent; by licensing playhouses, and increasing his fees from 10s a week to £3 a month. He also received £100 a year from the Queen.

The Revels Office and the Master's home were originally in part of the old Blackfriars priory, then moved to Warwick Inn; but in Tilney's career they were in Clerkenwell, in the ancient priory of St John, where a suite of thirteen rooms (plus kitchen, stable, garden, etc.) went with the job. Here, for much of Elizabeth's reign, were stored the royal tents and armour, all the tackle which the Court required for a 'progress' through the realm or for a royal hunt, and the rich velvets and satins for the great masques at Whitehall. In the world of Elizabethan show business the censor also served as a kind of royal accountant and quartermaster. The Office of the Revels requisitioned all the necessary material and equipment for the Queen's entertainment, the masks, costumes and ornaments from the Wardrobe, the Office of Works and other departments of the Tudor stage, engaged tailors, painters and carpenters, maintained a careful check of the properties' cost and condition and submitted the bills to the Treasury. Throughout the autumn and early winter the Master supervised preparations for the Christmas season of entertainments at Court. Not only the players and playmakers, but also acrobats, bear-baiters and royal fools came under his watchful eye.

The Master was not, however, his own master. The monarch sometimes directly intervened and the Privy Council did not finally recognize his authority until late in the 1590s. Even in 1601 it was instructing the Lord Mayor and the justices of Middlesex to censor plays; and the Lord Chamberlain occasionally granted a licence without consulting the Master. For the Office of the Revels as a department of the royal household came under the Lord Chamberlain's supervision together with the rest of an intricate Tudor hierarchy which included the Privy and the Outer Chamber, the Mint, the Armoury, the Jewel House, with such functionaries as the Harbingers and the Yeomen of the Guard, the Esquires of the Body and the Sewers of the Chamber, the Astronomer and the Mole Taker, the Carvers, the Gentlemen Pensioners and the musicians. Unlike his successor today, the Lord Chamberlain was then also engaged, indirectly, in theatrical management. Not only did he organize masques and diversions, and visit Clerkenwell to 'hear' a play and correct its author, but he also had his own company of actors. The Lord Chamberlain's Men were the best in the land: their fellowship included the greatest dramatist in the history of the world. One Lord Chamberlain (Lord Hunsdon) formed the troupe in which William Shakespeare spent nearly all his working life (it was later known as The King's Men). Two more (Lord Pembroke and his brother, Lord Montgomery) were the patrons to whom the First Folio was dedicated. The Elizabethan censor, indeed, was regarded not so much as an enemy of the theatre but rather as its ally. It was to the Master of the Revels, the Lord Chamberlain, the other noble patrons of acting companies, and the Queen herself that Shakespeare and his contemporaries looked for protection from the growing Puritanism of the middle class, expressed in the crusading hostility of local authorities, most of all in London. While the Court promoted the drama, the City wanted to suppress it. All the theatres opened in London from 1576 to 1616 were built outside the City's control—either in 'liberties' inside the limits, like Blackfriars, or beyond the boundaries. Royal censorship, moreover, was restricted by and large to matters of 'Divinity and State'. The Master of the Revels was on the watch for any insult to a foreign power, any attack on the Established Church or the Tudor administration, any slight to the Queen and Court. But the Elizabethan censor, unlike most of his successors, did not believe that the *moral tone* of the theatre was his business. The old priory at Clerkenwell was not an assize of stage ethics, public propriety and good taste. If Edmund Tilney had applied the moral standards of the past two hundred years, the Elizabethan drama would have been shredded into insignificance. A characteristic interference is Tilney's order to the authors of *Sir Thomas More*: 'Leave out ye insurrection wholly, and the cause of it.'

Two historians of the stage censor, Frank Fowell and Frank Palmer,[1] deduced in 1913 that Shakespeare and his contemporaries 'are not likely to have been seriously thwarted' by the Master of the Revels, and that his effect upon 'the important drama' of the Elizabethan theatre was 'probably slight'. Virginia Gildersleeve, author of *Government Regulation of Elizabethan Drama*, suggests that it would not have been 'materially different' without his supervision. True, Shakespeare himself does not appear, from the scanty evidence available, to have suffered directly from the censorship. After the first production of *Henry IV Part I*, he was ordered to change the name of a character, Sir John Oldcastle, which he had taken from a previous play, as the powerful Oldcastle family objected. Complying, he created Falstaff. Once his company was briefly under suspicion: when *Richard II* was staged by the Lord Chamberlain's Men at the instigation of the Essex conspirators on the eve of their rebellion in 1601. But with his colleagues he was rapidly cleared and, indeed, played at Court before the Queen two weeks later on the eve of Essex's

[1] *Censorship in England* (1913).

21

execution. The deposition scene had been cut when the play was published in 1597, and was not included in a printed text until five years after the Queen's death. Yet it was not prohibited on the stage. That, overtly, is all. He may have suffered from the censor's meddling; we do not know. But it seems unlikely that it prevented him from writing controversial plays: and although he can be described (by John Wain) as 'an intensely political writer',[1] it does not appear that he had a smothered partisan concern with religion or politics, against the grain of official opinion. It may be, as critics have proposed, that his work conceals explosive allegories about his own society: that, like Tourneur and Massinger, he was dramatizing contemporary England in foreign disguise. Here is one argument.[2] *Hamlet* was written about the time that James I came to the throne of England. Like the Prince of Elsinore, the new King had a murdered father and a mother who married the reputed murderer; and he himself had been entertained at Elsinore some years earlier. Yet Hamlet is not all Stuart. The King—it is suggested—is represented by four characters, and 'by covering his tracks in this way, Shakespeare was free to express a great deal of what he saw and felt about the impending reign.'[3]

Well, perhaps. We cannot know for sure. Yet, as L. C. Knights has said, 'even where the political interest is most coldest' in Shakespeare's plays, 'it is never exclusive or, as it were, self-contained. The implied question, what does this political action or attitude mean, is invariably reduced to personal terms.' There was no counterpart in his time, after all, for today's permanent opposition of intellectuals on the left of the established order: Shakespeare shared with many of his contemporaries a genuine belief in this order. He appeared to celebrate, rather than to deny it, not only out of expediency but from conviction too. As a dramatist, in many ways, he enjoyed a far greater freedom than any of his successors, even those of today. It was indeed too great for later generations. For over two hundred years his plays were bowdlerized and 'improved'; some were never staged at all, or were shelved for long periods; and this was the censorship imposed on theatrical practice by managerial and public taste, rather than by an official arbiter.

It was not only the sexual candour and the bawdy language, taken for granted by the Elizabethan censor and the Elizabethan audience, which

---

[1] *The Living World of Shakespeare* (1964).
[2] 'The Natural History of Censorship', by Claire Russell and W. M. S. Russell, in *'to deprave and corrupt . . .'* (1962).   [3] Ibid.

would have been unthinkable for any dramatist to attempt (or any manager to stage) throughout the eighteenth and nineteenth centuries. Shakespeare and his contemporaries were also allowed to take liberties with recent history, to put relations of the royal family on the stage, to dramatize—up to a point—controversial political events, and even to savage the morals and manners of princes and their parasites, as long as these targets were safely Italianized or treated with some other hypothetical alienation effect—all in a way that is still forbidden by the Lord Chamberlain today. They could practise a kind of theatrical *journalism* which is now impossible, unbothered by official protection for people in the news, unless they had powerful friends at Court, or by codes of good taste and moral delicacy. Yet Shakespeare's apparent immunity from interference and the Master of Revels's relative freedom from moral humbug should not lead one into too rosy a view of the pre-Restoration censorship because—in the words of Fowell and Palmer—it '*merely* insisted' (my italics) that the dramatist 'should kiss the hand of royalty and not rattle the people's chains on the stage'.

Other dramatists were pressed harder, perhaps because they went further. Tom Nashe had to escape from London to avoid prison for 'very seditious and slanderous matter' in *The Isle of Dogs*, in 1597: the Privy Council closed the theatres and ordered them to be destroyed, but three of them reopened later that year. Samuel Daniel came under suspicion because his *Philotas* was thought to be a disguised drama about Essex's rebellion, and Sir Fulke Greville destroyed the manuscript of a play about Antony and Cleopatra in case it might be misunderstood by the censor as an allegory about Essex and the Queen. George Chapman had to leave town because he introduced the Queen of France into a play in 1608—*The Conspiracy and Tragedy of Charles, Duke of Byron*—which was banned after a protest from the French Ambassador. Three actors were jailed and licence to print was given only after intensive lobbying and heavy cutting. Thomas Kyd was arrested and tortured on suspicion of sedition. Thomas Middleton had to accept heavy alterations in several plays, and was on the run for a time after the rousing success of his *A Game at Chess* in 1624. In this piece, passed without cavil by the censor, he ventilated popular delight at the failure of the plan for linking the thrones of England and Spain in marriage, representing the *dramatis personae* under the thin disguise of chess pieces, and savaged the Spanish monarchy and the Catholic Church. After this 'perfect piece of literary political art' (T. S. Eliot) had actually run ten days and created an international incident, the Privy Council ordered the play to be closed, and its author and cast to be 'examined' and arrested if necessary. The Bishop of London prohibited the performance of *Sir John Van Olden Barnevelt*, probably by Massinger and Fletcher, which presented the story of a Dutch national hero's revolt against Spanish oppression, within three months of his execution. Later it was 'reformed' by the Master, who cut large sections where 'the voice of protest against despotism and eulogy of political liberty rang out too unmistakably'. The Privy Council ordered the Master of the Revels to prevent, 'upon his peril', the performance of a play about a French marshal for whose death King Louis XIII was held responsible; and on another occasion it vetoed the production of an attack upon the Dutch atrocities in the East Indies (commissioned by the East India Company). Massinger had to revise and cut *Believe As You List*, because it originally presented the deposing of the King of Portugal by the King of Spain (he altered all the names at the Master's instructions); and the King of England took immediate exception to Massinger's *King and Subject*, which appeared to include a camouflaged attack upon his own methods of administration. One passage in particular roused Charles's indignation. It was in a speech by Massinger's fictional monarch, which included such lines as these:

> Moneys ? We'll raise supplies what ways we please,
> And force you to subscribe to blanks, in which
> We'll mulct you as we shall think fit.

Reading the text at Newmarket the King wrote on it: 'This is too insolent, and to be changed.' Shirley's *The Ball* was nearly banned because, according to the Master, 'there were divers personated so naturally, both of lords and others of the Court, that I took it ill'.

Ben Jonson, in particular, suffered from official interference. He spent two months in prison because of his role as actor in and part-author of *The Isle of Dogs*. The King sent him to jail again eight years later with Chapman and Marston for writing *Eastward Ho*, because it poked incidental fun at the Scottish courtiers who had followed James I to London. He was forbidden to write a reply to *Satiromastix*, Dekker's attack on him. He had to alter central characters in both *A Tale of a Tub* and *The Devil is an Ass*, because courtiers complained that he was smearing them in public caricature. He was summoned before the ecclesiastical Court of High Commission to account for profanity in *The Magnetic Lady* but when it was found that the cast had inserted oaths in the text, the Archbishop of Canterbury pronounced that both Jonson and the censor were innocent. He was arraigned before the Privy Council for suspected 'popery and treason' in his Roman tragedy *Sejanus*. Publication, however, was allowed when he added a pious explanation that the play was a warning to traitors who dared to conspire against a monarch. Yet towards the end of his life Jonson himself aspired to be the censor. King James gave him the double reversion of the Master of the Revels: that is to say, he was next but one in the queue.

It seems safe to agree with Fowell and Palmer that the pre-Restoration censorship gave English dramatists 'practically unlimited freedom in the selection and treatment of their subjects, *so long as the existing order of things was not menaced*' (my italics). They were free as long as they supported, or appeared to support, Church and State and Crown. No controversy about the Establishment was permitted to excite the commonweal. Although some ungrateful actors and authors clearly still believed it was their job to hold the mirror up to nature, the relative inefficiency of the censorship enabled them to push a certain amount of camouflaged 'dangerous matter' past the Revels Office on to the stage, and, as Virginia Gildersleeve says, 'the drama of the period abounds in apparently unrepressed portrayals of weak and vicious kings who meet avenging death, and of intriguing and pernicious favourites'. It is impossible to conceive that a contemporary equivalent of *The Revenger's Tragedy*, with its lacerating scorn for a royal court and even a stab at its official religion, could be licensed today. But on the whole the theatre, without coercion, was already firmly committed to one side in the coming struggle. Not only its freedom but its survival depended upon the supremacy of the Court, for the Court's enemies were the theatre's enemies, too. When they rebelled against the King, they closed all the playhouses and even ordered their destruction—the final censorship. Moreover, in this restriction of his liberty the dramatist was in the same boat with the novelist, the preacher, the poet and the pamphleteer. In Shakespeare's time the theatre was not—as in later centuries—singled out for censorship by the State, and enforcement was often noticeably inept. According to Fowell and Palmer, 'even orders to desist from acting were often ignored, and only flagrant cases appear to have been enforced for more than a day or two'.

Yet the censorship in the early seventeenth century played a significant part in narrowing the range of the drama and assisting in the contraction of the popular theatre of Shakespeare's heyday, until a national institution became the plaything of an aristocratic clique. Under orders from his royal employer, the Master of the Revels promoted what

Dr Wickham has described as 'the steady weakening of the relationship between the realities of religious, political and social life in England and the reflection of them upon the stage'. The censorship of the stage in Tudor and Stuart times helped to mould the attitude of the majority of English people to the theatre and to its censorship right up till the present day.

3

The instinct of the drama . . . to mix itself up with politics is incorrigible.
—SIR EDMUND CHAMBERS: *The Medieval Stage*; 1903

* * *

WITHIN a few years of his accession to the throne in 1603, James I—working through the Master of Revels—tightened the Crown's control of the theatre. He took out of the nobility's hands the right to license a troupe of their own: all three leading London companies (including Shakespeare's) were absorbed into the Royal Household by royal patents, which also protected their playhouses and accorded them the right to play outside London (without much competition) in any town or university. As liveried servants of royalty, actors were immune to arrest—except by the Lord Chamberlain's warrant. The drama in the next few years moved more rapidly towards its isolation from the national life as a privileged royal appendage, satisfying Court taste and avoiding Court taboos, under the erratic tutelage of the Lord Chamberlain and his agent, the Master of Revels. These helped to kill the genuinely popular theatre of Shakespeare's day; although they were, of course, assisted—on the other side of the fence—by those stalwarts who believed that 'popular Stage-plays . . . are sinful, heathenish, lewd, ungodly, spectacles, and most pernicious corruptions'; and that 'the profession of Play-poets, of Stage-Players, together with the penning, acting and frequenting of Stage-plays, are unlawful, infamous and misbeseeming Christians'.[1]

Under King James, however, this unholy trade enjoyed unprecedented prosperity, and the Revels Office took its share. In 1610 Tilney's nephew Sir George Buck succeeded to the job, and in his time—when the Office was moved from Clerkenwell to St Peters Hill, near Blackfriars, where it stayed till 1641—he extended the censor's powers in an even more arbitrary fashion than his enterprising uncle. He charged a fee (£20) for permitting the erection of a new playhouse; he raised the fee for licensing a play from seven shillings to a pound—preposterously high, when you

---

[1] *Histro-mastix, The Players Scourge*, by Thomas Prynne (1633).

consider that by 1640 a dramatist's maximum reward was £20; and he assumed, apparently on his own authority, the right to license plays for the press. His methods are illustrated in a surviving script of *The Second Maiden's Tragedy*. One line referred boldly to breaches in the class barriers: 'There's many a good knight's daughter is in service.' The censor changed 'knight' to 'man'. In another passage a wicked king drives a lady to suicide, to escape a fate worse than death, and he then exclaims sadly:

Hadst thou but asked the opinion of most ladies,
Thou'dst never come to this!

Out of chivalry, no doubt, Sir George altered 'most' to 'many'. Among the dangerous passages whose deletion he commanded was the second line below:

To end the last act of thy life in pandarism
(As you perhaps will say your betters do).

But the regime of Sir George—who went mad but lingered on in office—became notoriously lax, and it was with the arrival of Sir Henry Herbert in 1623 that the Master of the Revels reached the zenith of his power. Sir Henry, who bought his way into the censorship for the bargain price of £150 a year, had many friends at Court. Not only was he a brother of the poet George Herbert and the philosopher-diplomat Lord Herbert of Cherbury, but he was also a kinsman of the Lord Chamberlain, and it was at the Herberts' family seat, not long after he bought the job, that he was introduced by the Chamberlain to the King, who knighted him on the spot.

Explaining his principles of censorship to the Star Chamber, Sir Henry declared: 'The design is, that all profaneness, oaths, ribaldry and matters reflecting upon piety, and the present government, may be obliterated, before there be any action in a public theatre.' In practice, he changed 'By Jesu' to 'Believe me', 'Faith!' to 'Indeed', 'By heaven' to 'By these hilts', and showed that he was especially tender about the susceptibilities of his Welsh fellow-countrymen and kings' mistresses. Sometimes his royal master had to check his zeal. In 1634 the King called Sir Henry into his room one morning, 'went over all that I had crossed in D'Avenant's play-book', and ruled that in this play, *The Wits*, such expressions as *faith*, *death* and *slight* were 'asseverations only and no oaths', and were accordingly to be passed. The Master of the Revels obediently submitted to the royal will, but noted unrepentantly that he still 'under favour' conceived them to be *oaths*.

Sir Henry Herbert, however, was driven not so much by conscience as by greed. From the first he set out energetically to exploit the cash value of theatrical censorship. He re-established the right to license all printed plays and he ordered the resubmission of old plays at a pound a piece, 'since they may be full of offensive things against Church and State, ye rather that in former times the poets took greater liberty than is allowed them by me'. Sometimes he licensed books of verse, too. He claimed the right to license public games such as billiards, ninepins and fencing; he demanded fees from rope-dancers, quack-doctors, organists and dancing-masters. The proprietor of a waxworks, a showman with an opossum, a Dutchman with two dromedaries, all had to pay tribute to the censor of the stage. From the actors he claimed a monthly fee for allowing them to play at all. He sold them dispensations to work during Lent. He demanded from the King's Men the proceeds of two special performances a year, and a booking fee at every London playhouse. He exacted an annual fee from the musicians for permission to play in the theatre. He was paid bonuses for special services. Thus, the King's Men paid him £5 in 1627 'to forbid the playing of Shakespeare's plays by the Red Bull company'. He introduced the custom of paying him for the play, whether it was licensed or not, and he adopted a cavalier attitude towards the text which later censors imitated. Thus, in the year the Civil War broke out, Sir Henry noted: 'Received of Mr Kirke, for a new play, which I burnt for the ribaldry and offence that was in it, £2.' He was paid, on one occasion at least, £4 for licensing an old play, and the manager also gave Lady Herbert a pair of gloves, which—the Master noted with approval—'cost him at least twenty shillings'. Yet that was exceptional booty. Sir Henry was happy to charge £2 for 'allowing' a new play and a pound for an old one. The censor's fees thus increased by eight hundred per cent in only sixty years, and have remained at the same apparent level for the last 320 years.

Although Sir Henry Herbert was not the first man to discover that censorship can pay, nobody else appears to have openly boasted that it could bring in £4,000 a year. That was the extravagantly round figure (worth around £40,000 today) quoted by Sir Henry at the Restoration, when he waged a small civil war to get back his authority over the drama. Charles II swore him into the Mastership in 1660, but not long afterwards the King made nonsense of the appointment by an act which influenced the history of the English theatre for the next two hundred years. In 1662 and 1663 two courtier-authors, Thomas Killigrew and Sir William D'Avenant, were granted royal patents which gave them the authority to establish two playhouses in London and to enjoy a joint monopoly of the legitimate drama. To the fury of Sir Henry Herbert, Lincoln's Inn Fields and Drury Lane were allowed to be their own censors, charged with expunging 'any matter of profanation, scurrility or obscenity' from plays ancient and modern, to ensure that these 'might serve as moral instructions on humane life'—an ironical prelude to the era of Restoration comedy. Sir Henry was not going to stand for that, especially from D'Avenant, 'a person who exercised the office of Master of the Revels to Oliver the Tyrant', as he said. He petitioned the King; he sued D'Avenant twice for licensing fees which, he claimed, belonged to him; he sued actors for playing without his permission; he tried to close a theatre, the Cockpit, which he had not licensed; he extended his claims to the licensing of village wakes and lotteries. Powerful support came in 1661 from the Lord Chamberlain, who ordered local authorities throughout the kingdom to suppress all plays which had not received Sir Henry's licence. And it was the Chamberlain who, in 1662, arbitrated between the Master of the Revels and one of the patentees. Leaving D'Avenant in the lurch, Killigrew decided later that year to come to terms with the belligerent Sir Henry. He agreed to give the Master all the licensing fees due in the past two years from his company of players (£2 for every new play and £1 for every revival), plus a present of £50, agreed to pay the costs of his legal actions, and promised to help him in re-establishing the dominion of the Revels. Having won his battle and his perks, Sir Henry then sub-let the censorship to two deputies, and promised the reversion to Killigrew. When he died in 1673 Killigrew took over officially as Master, and was succeeded by his son Charles, who stayed in power for over forty years.

During this period from 1660 to 1700, when actresses were permitted to appear for the first time on the public stage, the English censorship still allowed actors and authors a margin of freedom which has never since been equalled, in one field at least. Licences were unhesitatingly granted to plays which were so far from being the 'innocent and harmless divertisements' which the royal patent charged the managers to provide that most of them were shunned by later generations as a sink of filth and obscenity, and for a time disappeared completely from the stage. One of them, *The Parson's Wedding*, was by the censor himself: even in 1913 Fowell and Palmer found it 'too coarse' for quotation.

30

Sexual innuendo in gesture and dialogue was a commonplace. Venereal disease was treated 'half as a joke, half as a glory'. Prostitution and even incest were all licensed as fit matter for the drama. Off-stage copulation thrived, and the dirty joke reached a kind of theatrical apotheosis. It is only in the last forty years, indeed, that the leading Restoration comedies have been revived and acclaimed as among the finest in our dramatic literature; and it is certain that had any dramatist between 1710 and 1910 attempted to take the liberties sometimes enjoyed by a Rochester, Shadwell or even Dryden, his plays would have been cut to shreds. Perhaps even now no writer would dare base a comedy on the central situation used in *The Country Wife*—a man who pretends impotence, through syphilis, as a way of bedding other people's wives in perfect security. Yet there was no protest, it seems, from the audience: the tiny Court clique and its dependents, who were the main patrons of the theatre, lapped it all up. The moral outrage came from those who *read* the plays later. The middle classes, the merchants, and the apprentices stayed away from the theatre. For twelve years there was only one open in London, and for forty years—from 1660 to 1700—only two; and even so the audience was small. Compare this with the dozen and more playhouses of Shakespeare's heyday and the wide range of society for which they catered.

The censors were not asleep. They ordered the revision or prohibition of many plays, especially after 1678—the year of Titus Oates and the Popish Plot. But their conscientious objections were generally roused only by political and religious offences, and often only after the plays had reached the stage. Nathaniel Lee's *Lucius Junius Brutus* was banned after the third performance because the censor detected, under the Roman trappings, 'very scandalous expressions and reflections upon ye Government'. Thomas Shadwell's *The Lancashire Witches* (1681) was savagely cut because he ridiculed an Anglican cleric as well as Catholic priests. Suspicions of anti-Catholic propaganda brought trouble for Dryden's *The Spanish Friar*, which was passed by Charles II but banned in 1686 by James II, who was offended by the title-role, Dominick. When the play was revived for Queen Mary, we hear, 'Some unhappy expressions put her into the greatest disorder, and frequently forced her to hold up her fan and often look behind and call for her palatine and hood, or anything she could think of.'[1]

Dryden's *The Duke of Guise* was banned for six months, and his

[1] Quoted in *Censorship in England* (1913).

prologue to Fletcher's *The Prophetess* was prohibited after the first performance, because it included, said Cibber, 'some familiar metaphorical sneers at the Revolution itself, and as the poetry of it was good the offence was less pardonable'.[1] John Crowne's *First Part of Henry the Sixth* was passed by the Revels but 'stifled by command' in 1681 after it reached the stage, he protested, because he introduced 'a little vinegar against the Pope', in an attempt 'to expose Popery and Popish Courts'. His *City Politics* was held up in the Lord Chamberlain's Office, until Crowne used royal influence to get it acted. Nahum Tate's *Richard II* was subjected, to 'a positive Doom of suppression, *without examination*', he complained, although 'every scene is full of respect to majesty and the dignity of courts'; it had to be turned into *The Sicilian Usurper*. Edward Howard's *The Change of Crowns* did not reach the stage until twenty years after it was written, because the Master of the Revels then 'saw political spectres in it that never appeared in the presentation'.[2] John Banks came under the official veto for three plays—*Cyrus the Great*, *The Innocent Usurper* (about Lady Jane Grey) and *The Island Queens* (about Mary Queen of Scots), banned for twenty years. Beaumont and Fletcher's *A Maid's Tragedy* was banned for a time by Charles II's Lord Chamberlain; perhaps because, Cibber suggested,

> a repenting mistress, in a romantic revenge of her dishonour, killing the king in the very bed he expected her to come into, was showing a too dangerous example to other Evadnes then shining at court in the same rank of royal distinction. . . .[3]

The fact is that the Restoration theatre, in general, was a Stuart toy, walled off from the life of the nation as a whole, mirroring the tastes of the King and his Court. Its censors vetoed any apparent attack upon the monarch's political or religious sympathies or upon the personalities of his friends and parasites. With morality—especially sexual morality—they had no concern at all.

The squabbles of Herbert and the patentees undermined the authority of the Revels Office, and the Killigrews' doubling of dramatic censorship with the management of a Theatre Royal destroyed it. The effective censor became, increasingly, the Lord Chamberlain. For a hundred years he had been the overlord of the Revels Office, and now that its Master was engaged in show business on his own account, his aristocratic superior intervened more frequently to enforce the royal will in

---

[1] *An Apology for the Life of Colley Cibber* (1740).   [2] Ibid.   [3] Ibid.

regulation of the stage. This was all the more necessary because the actors were liveried members of the royal household, and the London theatre was an adjunct of the Court. It was the Lord Chamberlain who ordered the arrest of actors for absenteeism, for disorderly conduct, for undue mobility of labour in moving between the two patent theatres; who suspended all performances at Drury Lane for a time because an actor who had drawn upon a gentleman was allowed to appear on the stage; who instructed Sir Christopher Wren to see that something was done about the dirty seats in the pit; who forbade actors to wear stage costume outside the theatre, and ordered the Master of Revels to see that they were punctual; who presided over disputes between managers and actors; who even took control of a company, when Charles and Thomas Killigrew were in the thick of a private war. He was known to have commanded a manager to reinstate an actress, restore her previous roles, and give her an exclusive dressing-room—*with a chimney*. Anyone who could do that was clearly the top man.

Actors and authors alike increasingly ignored the Master of Revels, who appealed to the Chamberlain; and he, in 1696, issued an order that no plays must be acted until they had been sent—'and that in due time' —to the Master. Several had been acted recently without a licence at both theatres 'wherein many things ought to be struck out and corrected'. The Chamberlain sternly instructed Killigrew to be 'very careful in correcting all obscenities and other scandalous matters and such as any ways offend against ye laws of God and good manners or the known statutes of the kingdom'. A year later came another directive, commanding the deletion of all scurrilous sentiments and expression of profanity. The wind of change was blowing.

Yet in 1695 the official censorship of books had ended. The Commons refused to renew the Act of 1633, and thereafter a man could write and publish what he pleased—subject, of course, to the laws of the land. There were heavy penalties for blasphemy and sedition; there were big disincentives to radical expression in print; but State censorship was over.

There was a growing revulsion not only outside the theatre and the Court, but in the audience, too, against the ethical tone of the drama. This reaction was vented violently by the Rev. Jeremy Collier in his celebrated attack in 1697 upon 'the immorality and profaneness of the English stage'. The explosive impact of his crusading book—filled with a Puritan disgust at the stage itself—was a symptom of shifting social attitudes.

33

Even more significant, perhaps, than Collier's book was the change in dynasty. With the disappearance of the Stuarts in 1688, the climate had altered. William III took a different view of the drama, and he applauded Collier's attack. In 1698 he proclaimed that 'notwithstanding an Order made 4 June 1697 by the Earl of Sunderland, the Lord Chamberlain of His Majesty's Household, to prevent the Profaneness and Immorality of the Stage, several plays have lately been acted containing expressions contrary to religion and good manners'—and something must be done. Further reminders to both the managers and the Revels Office were issued in 1703. In 1711 came an announcement from Queen Anne that 'the orders we have given for the reformation of the stage, by not permitting anything to be acted contrary to religion and good manners, have in great measure had the good effect we proposed'.

The targets of royal censure were thus extended to include *immorality* and *bad manners*. That may have reflected a sector of national taste in the early eighteenth century, among the increasingly powerful middle classes; and in particular a reaction against the old aristocratic codes— with all their moral and religious assertions. Certainly the militant Puritans were on the warpath again.

Yet without new measures of control the deliberate vulgarity and brutality of the Restoration era disappeared; and in the first thirty years of the eighteenth century the theatre enjoyed more relative liberty than ever before, or since. About 1715 Colley Cibber and his Drury Lane associates decided to defy the petty tyranny—or 'zealous severity', as Cibber called it—of the ageing Mr Killigrew, then in the fortieth year of his censorship. Cibber had already suffered from the Master's heavy hand, for Killigrew had expunged the whole first act of his version of *Richard III*, and had refused to grant the author 'the small indulgence of a speech or two, that the other four acts might limp on with a little less absurdity . . . No, he had not the leisure to consider what might be separately offensive. He had an objection to the whole act, and the reason he gave for it was, that the distresses of King Henry the Sixth, who is killed by Richard in the first act, would put weak people too much in mind of King James, then living in France; a notable proof of his zeal for the government'.[1] It was with the greater readiness, then, that Cibber called upon Mr Killigrew; pointed out that under the new patent granted by George I, the managers of the Theatre Royal—like D'Avenant and Killigrew *père*—were their own censors; and that they refused

[1] *An Apology for the Life of Colley Cibber.*

34

to pay the Master of the Revels any longer for licensing plays which, often enough, he had not even read. Thereafter Killigrew and his successors squeezed what fees they could from censorship, but their revenue was sadly reduced. The authority of the Revels Office lapsed.

In that new climate of commercial expansion and intellectual freedom, the dramatist shared for a time some of the liberty that the journalist and pamphleteer had begun to take for granted. Vetoes were often made at the instigation of people or institutions who had the ear of the Court, but they could sometimes be answered by simple evasive strategy. It was not, in fact, under the apparent pressure of any national demand for moral regulation that a new system of theatrical censorship was established in 1737. This was primarily designed to keep politics off the stage, and, in particular, to safeguard the dignity of one politician—the Prime Minister of England. It seems characteristic of the humbug which has haloed the censorship for centuries that the immediate need for its establishment was presented to Parliament as the protection of the public, not of Robert Walpole, that is, as a case of national morality rather than of party politics.

In the era of Swift and Addison, when the party warfare of Whigs and Tories promoted some vigorous journalism in the expanding press, a certain amount of political satire also reached the stage. In plays, as in ballads and pamphlets, the Government was justifiably regarded as fair game, and cautious sniping at it sometimes proved to be both permissible and profitable. One reason for the immediate and persistent popularity of *The Beggar's Opera* was its attack upon the 'great men' of the time. Although John Gay wrote in broad and generalized terms about 'statesmen' and 'courtiers', contemporary audiences gleefully recognized the targets in George II's Court and Walpole's Cabinet. On the first night in 1728 the smiling Prime Minister joined in the applause, but in private he could not have been amused by the Lord Chamberlain's failure to notice the dangerous thoughts of this 'Newgate pastoral' (which Swift and other Opposition writers had encouraged). To ban such a success, Walpole must have decided, would now be bad policy. Yet its licensing is not likely to have given him much confidence in the censorship.

Before the year was out, John Gay discovered the truth of the warning in his own song:

When you censure the age
Be cautious and sage,
Lest the courtiers offended should be. . . .

In December he submitted to the Lord Chamberlain a sequel to *The Beggar's Opera* by the name of *Polly*. Transported to the West Indies the highwayman-hero Macheath blacks his face, changes his name to Morano and turns to piracy. Within a few days Gay learned that *Polly* was banned by the Lord Chamberlain—'without any reasons assigned,' said the indignant author, 'or any charge against me of my having given any particular offence'. No reasons were necessary. Walpole had no desire to be pilloried again on the stage, perhaps as a blackface pirate, and so, as a diarist testifies, he 'resolved . . . to make use of his friend the Duke of Grafton's authority, as Lord Chamberlain, to put a stop to the representation of it'. He did not attempt to prevent Gay from *publishing* the work. The Lord Chamberlain's authority did not extend to print. There was no official censor of books and newspapers and in any event Walpole no doubt believed, with theatre censors throughout the ages, that what might be dangerous to stage was safe to read. Yet the banning of *Polly* roused a small political storm, for the author's cause was pleaded and publicized by many powerful friends of Gay and enemies of Walpole. The Duchess of Queensberry was an ardent supporter of *Polly*. According to Sir Walter Scott, 'she offered to read it to His Majesty in his closet, that he might be satisfied there was no offence in it. George II escaped from this dilema by saying that he should be delighted to receive Her Grace in his closet, but hoped to amuse her better than by the employment she proposed'. When the Duchess began to canvass for subscriptions to Gay's book, the King was not amused. He banished her from Court, and the Duke resigned his appointment as Admiral of Scotland. Yet gossip reported that seven or eight other duchesses in Gay's cause were competing to see 'who shall suffer martyrdom on his account first'. To buy *Polly* was, for the moment, a political gesture. The Lord Chamberlain's ban also saved Gay from a theatrical flop, for although *Polly* was only a feeble follower to *The Beggar's Opera* it brought Gay more money as well as a good deal of glory. (It was not staged until fifty years later, in 1777—with amendments.)

Gay gave Walpole no more trouble. Within three years he was dead. But by then a far more dangerous opponent in the theatre had arrived to challenge the Prime Minister's dignity. It was in 1730—the year after the *Polly* affair—that Henry Fielding scored his first successes on the London stage. All were, characteristically, presented in a theatre which existed in defiance of the law, for this Little Theatre in the Haymarket had daringly opened its doors ten years before without a licence from the Lord Chamberlain or a patent from the Crown. In *The Author's Farce*

Fielding hit out boldly at current vogues in entertainment, sounding a sharp note of social criticism ('If you would ride in a coach, deserve to ride in a cart' was a typical shaft). This note was heard again in *Rape Upon Rape*: or, *The Justice Caught in His Own Trap*, when Fielding, in later life himself a magistrate, added the law to his targets ('If you cannot pay for your transgressions like the rich, you must suffer for them like the poor'). But his biggest success in that triumphal year of 1730 was *Tom Thumb*, which proved so popular that he expanded it to three acts and presented it in 1731 under a new name—*The Tragedy of Tragedies or, The Life and Death of Tom Thumb*. In this brilliant burlesque Fielding was primarily concerned with theatrical satire, but he never lost sight of the wider social context in his work and Londoners at once recognized a disguised attack upon Walpole among the fusillades against Dryden, Rowe and Lee.

Fielding left no room for doubt about his political sympathies, later that year, in *The Welsh Opera: or, The Grey Mare the Better Horse*, where some of the top people of the age were boldly ridiculed. Walpole was attacked for both his public and his private morals, and the King and Queen appeared as Squire Ap-Shenkin and his wife, with stage servants who bore the names of the Queen's favourites. The impact of this ballad-opera was strengthened when it was staged as an afterpiece with *The Fall of Mortimer*, an edited old tragedy which showed a man ruling England with an insatiable appetite for plunder, intriguing with the Queen, selling places to the highest bidder, paying for his own luxury by corruption and oppression. Although the man's name was Mortimer, there was no doubt about the contemporary parallel which the audience was meant to draw.

By now, Walpole was naturally getting restive again under this ruthless barrage from the stage, and Fielding received his first warning. In June he enlarged and sharpened the satire of *The Welsh Opera* under the title of *The Grub Street Opera*, in which 'The Roast Beef of Old England' first appeared. It was announced by the theatre but was, apparently, never staged. The Government had intervened—'presumably,' says a biographer of Fielding, 'in a quiet manner through the Lord Chamberlain'.[1] In the following month *The Fall of Mortimer* was indicted as a 'false, infamous, scandalous, seditious and treasonable libel against His Majesty's Government'. A high constable appeared at the Haymarket with a warrant for the actors' arrest and although in

---

[1] *Henry Fielding: his life, work and times*, by F. H. Dudden (1952).

some mysterious way they were never brought to trial, threats of legal action became a familiar interruption of backstage life.

For a time, Fielding abstained from political warfare. For Drury Lane, which was linked with the Court party, he wrote farces, ballad-operas and comedies, one of which was dedicated to Robert Walpole, whose failure to respond with patronage may have been one reason for Fielding's later return to the attack. After three years of relative political passivity, he presented some mordant election scenes in *Don Quixote in England*, and nailed his colours to the mast by dedicating the piece to Lord Chesterfield, who had recently been dismissed from Court. Then in 1736 Fielding took the decisive step of entering theatrical management back at the Haymarket. With this own company and his own plays he set out to mount a personal offensive against the Establishment. His farces, complained his enemy and rival Cibber, 'seem'd to knock all distinctions of Mankind on the head . . . Religion, laws, government, priests, judges, and ministers, were all laid flat at the feet of this Herculean satirist.' Fielding did this in the knowledge that any moment his theatre might be closed, because it infringed the official monopoly of the drama held by Covent Garden and Drury Lane.

When Fielding began his stage career the patent theatres had tolerated their competitors, but now they were jealously on the alert and had recently taken legal action against companies at both the Haymarket and Goodman's Fields. Perhaps Fielding gambled on the inefficiency of the law and on his own cash-value at the box-office. Perhaps he was reassured by his own relative immunity, up to date, from the censor's interference. But certainly it was a monumental gamble and it started off with a bang. For in *Pasquin* Fielding not only presented a number of the personal 'smears' which delighted playgoers in that tiny, intimate world of Georgian London, but he also attacked political corruption and legal idiocy with gaily satirical audacity. It ran for nearly seventy performances, a rare achievement then. And nothing happened. Encouraged, Fielding made plans for his next Haymarket season. The year 1737 was a decisive year for him, and for the English theatre.

By this time Robert Walpole had had enough. For sixteen years he had been in power, and he knew that his power was slipping. Opposition to his ascendancy was growing and widening; it had reached his own Cabinet and the Court; he had even begun to talk of resignation, while the King and Queen discussed the possibility of dismissing the once all-powerful Minister. In such a climate, when the ground beneath his feet was crumbling, he could no longer brush off the mocking ridicule of

Henry Fielding. To serve as a theatrical Aunt Sally might not be dangerous in the hour of his ascendancy, but every palpable hit at the Haymarket now chipped another little piece off his pedestal. Within a few years Fielding had shown, as Fowell and Palmer say, that the stage 'might easily become the most trenchant and dangerous critic of politicians', and his most dangerous demonstration yet came in February 1737, when he opened the Haymarket with *The Historical Register for the Year 1736*. For here Fielding gave the most outspoken exposure of corruption in contemporary politics ever to be seen on the English stage, and at the heart of it was Walpole, flimsily disguised as Quidam, the fiddler, who makes people dance to his tunes by bribery. Fielding announced, moreover, that he was going to enlarge and redecorate the theatre, and to use it as a platform for satire: 'If Nature hath given me any Talents at ridiculing Vice and Imposture, I shall not be indolent nor afraid of exerting them, while the liberty of the Press and Stage subsists.' It was time, the Prime Minister decided, for the muzzle. By May, his chief organ, the *Daily Gazetteer*, published an open letter warning Fielding that action was likely by the Government if he continued. A series of letters urging the control of the drama appeared. Fielding's 'lack of restraint . . . could scarcely be allowed to continue', says a contemporary apologist for the Act of 1737, John Loftis[1]: 'it is less surprising that the Government took action . . . than that it tolerated for so long such a large body of dramatic abuse directed pointed and personally at the Chief Minister of State'.

Moves had already been made in Parliament to amend the stage censorship. One Bill was introduced in 1733, without making headway. Two years later Sir John Barnard introduced another 'to restrain the number of houses for playing of interludes and for the better regulation of common players of interludes'. His main concern, prompted by the report that a new theatre was to be opened in St Martin's-le-Grand, was with the public decency. Echoing the Puritans' complaints of the previous century, Sir John—a Lord Mayor of London—declared that there were already too many playhouses, and that they corrupted youth, encouraged vice and damaged trade. Public controversy about the building of theatres had been roused in 1729, with the opening of the one in Goodman's Fields, and the new Covent Garden which opened in 1732 helped to fan the flames of Puritan opposition. At first the House jeered at his Bill, until it was suddenly championed by Walpole.

[1] *The Politics of Drama in Augustan England* (1963).

Parliament was astonished at the Prime Minister's emergence in the unlikely role of moral crusader, but his ulterior motive was soon revealed. He wanted to introduce a clause extending and ratifying the powers of the Lord Chamberlain to licence plays. Sir John, however, disapproved of the Lord Chamberlain as well. That official's authority, he said, was already too great and was exercised with 'wanton' irresponsibility. And he snubbed Walpole by withdrawing his Bill.

On that occasion Walpole had misjudged his tactics, but now—two years later—he made no mistakes. First of all, he armed himself with an invulnerable *moral* excuse. It was not as an enemy of political liberty that he approached the House, but as a champion of decency. He announced that the manager of the theatre in Goodman's Fields, Henry Giffard, had brought him the manuscript of a new anonymous farce submitted for production. This was called *The Golden Rump* and was based on a recent lampoon in an Opposition journal. It was—so Walpole and his agents implied—from the hand of Fielding; and apart from being treasonable it was so indecent that Giffard had thought it his duty to notify the Prime Minister! Walpole did not reveal that for this public-spirited disclosure Giffard was paid the sum of £1,000. Yet there seems little doubt that the opportune discovery of this farce so soon after the opening of *The Historical Register* was arranged between the manager of Goodman's Fields and the Prime Minister of England. Did *The Golden Rump* ever even exist? It is said that copies were circulated judiciously in Parliament. Did one of Walpole's agents write it? Only Horace Walpole seems to have seen a copy. Nobody can be sure precisely what went on in those mazes of Georgian intrigue but it is clear that having touched off the fuse of righteous indignation Walpole rapidly drafted a Bill and pushed it through the House.

The time had come, he decided, to protect the public from these excesses of theatrical liberty. The man to shoulder this heavy burden was clearly his old friend, the fifty-four year old Duke of Grafton. As Lord Chamberlain he had a traditional right to interfere in the drama, and as an intimate of Walpole he could be told when to do it. But since, as Walpole knew to his cost, the Duke was apparently incapable of recognizing sedition and libel when he saw it, and, according to Lord Waldegrave, 'usually turned politics into ridicule, had never applied himself to business and as to books was totally illiterate', someone else would be needed to carry out the work. First of all it was necessary to give Grafton statutory powers over the stage.

The aim of Walpole's Bill was superficially innocuous. Instead of

40

making a new law, it set out 'to explain and amend so much of an Act made in the twelfth year of Queen Anne, entitled "An Act for reducing the laws relating to rogues, vagabonds, sturdy beggars and vagrants; and for the more effectual punishing such rogues, vagabonds, sturdy beggars and vagrants and sending them whither they ought to be sent", as relates to the common player of interludes'.[1] Under the new Bill any common players acting for money ('hire, gain, or reward') in a place where they had no legal settlement, or without royal patent or a licence from the Lord Chamberlain, were—like fencers and bearwards —to be 'deemed rogues and vagabonds' and liable to imprisonment. No theatrical performances were allowed in any part of Britain except in the City of Westminster and its liberties and the places of royal residence. Thus, the only theatres officially permitted to exist were Drury Lane and Covent Garden, the two 'patent houses' in London, which were confirmed in their monopoly of the drama. No new operas or plays or additions to old plays could be performed without the permission of the Lord Chamberlain, to whom they must be submitted, not by the author, but by the manager or theatre owner at least fourteen days before the performance. Failure to obey meant a fine of £50 and, much more important, the loss of the theatre's licence, which would 'become absolutely void to all intents and purposes whatsoever'. Moreover, the Chamberlain was given the power to prohibit the performances of all plays, operas and theatrical entertainments 'as often as he shall think fit'. In other words, he could close down the theatre whenever he had a mind to do so.

This Bill was introduced at the end of a Parliamentary session, when many M.P.s had already left London for the country. It was brought in—as Lord Chesterfield said—'at a very extraordinary season, and pushed with most extraordinary dispatch'. Walpole presented it on 20 May. By 6 June it had reached the third reading and within a month it had been given the royal assent (10 Geo. II c. 19). Three days later, the theatres closed down in Goodman's Fields, Lincoln's Inn Fields and the Haymarket (and also in York and Bristol). With them closed *The Historical Register for 1736*, the theatrical future of its author, and the English drama's unfettered freedom of speech.

Control of the stage was now vested by law in one official of the royal household, and a few months later Walpole's plans were fulfilled when

---

[1] The Act's definition was 'No new interlude, tragedy, comedy, opera, play, farce or other entertainment of the stage, or any part or parts therein, or any new prologue, or epilogue.'

two men were sworn in as members of the Lord Chamberlain's staff to serve as censors of the drama, though there was no statutory warrant for their appointment. They were William Chetwynd, appointed as Licenser of the Stage at a salary of £400 a year, and Thomas Odell, who was paid £200 a year as his deputy. Curiously enough, Odell was the man who had helped to rouse the anti-theatrical opposition by building the theatre in Goodman's Fields. He had sold it to Henry Giffard, and it is scarcely surprising to find that Giffard was tacitly allowed, after the Act, to present a company at Lincoln's Inn Fields, with plays performed 'gratis' between two parts of a musical concert, an evasion at which the Lord Chamberlain winked, and later to reopen for a time the illegal house in Goodman's Fields. What is more, Odell had been the author of unsuccessful satires in the Fielding mould such as *The Patron: or The Statesman's Opera*. Unlike the Duke of Grafton, he and the mysterious Chetwynd knew what to look for.

On the face of it the Licensing Act of 1737 restored the system of the previous century, with a Licenser of the Stage instead of a Master of the Revels as the effective censor, under the supervision of the Lord Chamberlain. But in fact the balance of power was very different, and both dramatists and actors had been better off under the empirical, inefficient rule of the Revels. Compared with such Masters as Tilney or Herbert, the new 'Licensers of the Stage' were subordinate jacks-in-office. But they were *full-time* censors, which meant that they had more time for meddling in theatrical affairs; and their master, the Lord Chamberlain, no longer exercised his authority as only one of several channels of the royal will, but as an absolute arbiter with a supremacy established by law.

Walpole did not fetter the theatre without meeting strong opposition in both Houses, but only one Parliamentary protest has been preserved. It is the great speech by Lord Chesterfield which has become the *locus classicus* for the enemies of censorship, for it still sums up with masterly eloquence the basic case against the Chamberlain. In one respect Chesterfield was proved to be wrong: he predicted that Walpole's next move would be to establish an official censor of the press. Yet he was right in pleading—though the argument seems unfamiliar even today—that the stage was one of the sentries 'posted by the constitution of a free country', and that Walpole's Bill was designed not only to restrain its licentiousness but its liberty too. Why, he asked, was any new law needed?

Our laws are sufficient for punishing any man that shall dare to represent upon the stage what may appear, either by words or the representation, to be blasphemous, seditious or immoral . . . If the stage becomes at any time licentious, if a play appears to be a libel upon the Government or upon any particular man, the King's courts are open . . .

Walpole's Bill, he warned, would 'prevent every man of a generous and free spirit' from writing plays. It encroached not only upon liberty but upon property, for 'wit' was a kind of property: often the only property of those who had it. 'It is, indeed, a precarious dependence,' said Chesterfield. 'Thank God! we my Lords have a dependence of another kind; we have a much less precarious support, and therefore cannot feel the inconvenience of the Bill now before us; but it is our duty to encourage and protect wit, whosoever's property it may be . . .' Yet wit was to be 'excised' under the new Bill—'and the Lord Chamberlain is to have the honour of being chief ganger, supervisor, commissioner, judge and jury'. Chesterfield summed up his case in a plea that has become famous:

If poets and players are to be restrained, let them be restrained as other subjects are, by the known laws of their country; if they offend, let them be tried, as every Englishman ought to be, by God and their country. Do not let us subject them to the arbitrary will and pleasure of any one man. A power lodged in the hands of one single man to judge and determine, without any limitation, without any control or appeal, is a sort of power unknown to our laws, inconsistent with our constitution. It is a higher, a more absolute power than we trust even to the King himself; and therefore I must think we ought not be invest any such power in His Majesty's Lord Chamberlain.

That was a fine speech, but it had no effect upon the Bill's passage through Parliament, and it had no immediate impact upon the public, for at that time Parliamentary reporting was still illegal. When news of what Walpole had achieved spread through the town, popular resentment was expressed. One journal (*The Craftsman*) was suppressed for a time because of its outspoken criticism of the Act. A French observer, the Abbé le Blanc, noted that the Licensing Act caused 'a universal murmur in the nation, and was openly complained of in the public papers. In all the coffee-houses of London it was treated as an unjust law, and manifestly contrary to the liberties of the people of

England.' In the following year, a journalist noted: 'It is well known that the act for putting the Stage under a Regulation (as the Phrase was) went against the Grain of the Publick—they declar'd against it, but had not Interest enough to hinder its passing.' But Walpole's tactics and timing minimized the influence of the champions of theatrical freedom, and his Bill became law before people knew what had happened. Playgoers expressed their feelings six months later, on the Covent Garden production of the first plays to be licensed under the new Act—Sir Hildebrand Jacob's three one-acters, *A Nest of Plays*. They were furiously booed off the stage, and their first night was their last. In October 1738 there was another popular outburst when the New Haymarket—closed to English actors—was opened, with the Lord Chamberlain's 'authority', to a troupe of *French* players. As one journal said:

> When the Bill appeared for their playing, with the Word *Authority* placed at Top, the Publick was stung to the Quick, and thought themselves to exert that Liberty they enjoy, and to resent the Affront put upon them by the Chamberlain . . . When the Act passed, we submitted, and tho' it was reported that a foreign Company of Actors would be sent for, we did not believe it; for we could not suppose that, while the Discontent occasioned by the Act was fresh in everyone's Memory, a Chamberlain would grow so wanton with his new Power, as to insult the Publick in this Manner.

The first-night audience began by singing Fielding's 'The Roast Beef of Old England', in a chorus of patriotic protest, while they waited for the curtain to rise. When it did go up, they saw the French visitors between two files of Grenadier Guards with fixed bayonets—and pandemonium broke out. Watched by the French and Spanish Ambassadors, the entire house demanded that the troops should be withdrawn. Yielding to popular pressure, the Guards retreated. And some time later, after howling down the actors and the magistrate who threatened them with the Riot Act, the audience was victorious. The curtain came down, and the season was abandoned.

Yet that, it seems, was all. There were no other popular demonstrations, no parliamentary campaigns, no sustained attacks in the press. Walpole had won. It is significant that the principal individual victim and target of the Licensing Act—Henry Fielding—gave up the struggle almost at once. Two more works from his pen reached the stage. One, an afterpiece called *Miss Lucy in Town* (1741), was banned for a short time *after* it had been passed by the Lord Chamberlain's Office, because some courtier had complained of libel. His comedy, *The Wedding Day* (1743), was at first banned because of its 'immorality'; but, a few weeks later, it was staged at Drury Lane after Fielding had agreed to changes by the censor, including the deletion of what a recent American historian describes as suggestive, passionate and physiological references.[1] Although he had discovered a theatrical genre in which his talents found full play, he made no public protest against the Act once it was law, and he made no attempt to evade or defy the censor. He turned his back on the servitude of the stage, and chose the freedom of the novel. Yet he had established a claim to be, in Shaw's words, 'the greatest practising dramatist, with the single exception of Shakespeare, produced by England between the Middle Ages and the nineteenth century'.

[1] *The London Stage 1660–1880, Part 3, 1729–1747*, edited by Arthur H. Scouten (1961).

4

We do not like it to be called 'censorship'.
What do you call it?
The examination of plays.

—The Hon. SIR S. C. B. PONSONBY-FANE, K.C.B., Comptroller of the
Lord Chamberlain's Department, before the 1892 Committee.

* * *

SHORTLY after the Act of 1737, the Lord Chamberlain's office moved
to a house which was especially built for it on the site of Prince Henry's
Riding Stables in Stable Yard. From this house the Lords Chamberlain
attempted for the next hundred years with sporadic zeal to apply the
Act by restricting the drama, at least in London, to only three playhouses: the two 'patent houses' of Covent Garden and Drury Lane all
the year round, and the Haymarket during the summer. Opera enjoyed
a separate, licensed home at the Italian Opera House. In spite of the
Act the number of provincial theatres slowly but steadily increased,
although special acts of Paraliament and royal patents were necessary;
and in 1788 J.P.s were empowered to license performances as long as
they were not continued for more than sixty days, or within twenty
miles of London, or within ten miles of any royal residence. In London
itself the check on the development of the stage helped to keep the
market for drama artificially small; and, in time, it distorted the patterns
of theatrical architecture, economics and dramaturgy. Indeed, one
recent historian—John Loftis, in *The Politics of Drama in Augustan
England*—has even suggested that it was the power it gave to the Lord
Chamberlain as licenser of buildings, not as the censor of plays, that
was the most significant aspect of the Act of 1737. But then Mr Loftis
believes that the imposition of censorship was a good thing: 'It is less
surprising that the Government took action in 1737 . . . than that it
tolerated for so long such a large body of dramatic abuse directed
pointedly and personally at the chief Ministers of State.'

Soon after the Act was passed, actors and managers began to dodge
its regulations with an ingenious repertoire of evasions. Not so the
authors. The right to act in unlicensed showplaces was successfully, if

46

spasmodically, exercised: the veto on unlicensed *plays* was never really challenged. Why? Perhaps because there was no apparent pressure of new drama from below; but also because managers were not willing to risk too much at once in defiance of the law. If they staged a classical piece or a farce the Chamberlain generally turned a blind eye. If they encouraged a Fielding, their doom was too predictable. So theatrical entrepreneurs and star soloists advertised 'rehearsals' for which you obtained tickets 'gratis' at a 'private' house, so that the performance was—on the face of it—not for 'hire, gain or reward', or 'concerts' by a 'school of actors', or issued invitations to take 'tea at 6.30' or 'a dish of chocolate'. People bought peppermints or toffee at an exorbitant price from a neighbouring shop, and were 'given' tickets in return. Later the Lord Chamberlain licensed buildings for 'music, dancing and public entertainments', as distinct from stage plays, under the Disorderly Houses Act of 1751 (25 Geo. 2), which gave saloons and, later, music-halls a precarious stake in the nation's show business and the chance to try their own evasions.

The Chamberlain often appeared to acquiesce in these ludicrous dodges, although he pounced on an offender every now and then to show that he treated seriously his job of protecting the monopoly in the legitimate drama. The term 'legitimate' as a word for 'straight' plays derives from the 1737 Act; because until 1843 the drama of words alone, without music, ballet, pantomime or spectacle, could only 'legitimately' be staged in the patent houses. But towards the end of the eighteenth century he had to deal with the problem of a growing number of theatres claiming licences for musical performances, ballets of action, spectacle, pantomime, horsemanship, and 'burlettas'—which were later empirically (not officially) defined as plays with 'not less than five pieces of vocal music in each act'. These were such theatres as Sadler's Wells, the Surrey, Astley's, the Coburg, the Olympic and the Lyceum. All sometimes staged straight plays under absurd subterfuges: 'Perhaps the commonest of all was to have a piano tinkling continually, in a transparent attempt to give the performance a legal standing.'

For five years after they came to power the new censors stoked up the fires of debate by petty tyrannies but were sometimes oddly blind to the 'sedition' under their noses. For instance, they banned the historical tragedy of *Edward and Eleanora*, presumably because its author James Thomson—better known as the poet of *The Seasons*—was under the protection of the Prince of Wales, then at war with his royal father; and in the play Edward's royal father, surrounded by evil advisers, seemed plainly intended to evoke George II of England. Eight suspicious lines looked to the Lord Chamberlain's men like inspired filial propaganda against the King. In the opening scene one character demands:

> Has not the royal heir a juster claim
> To share his father's inmost heart and counsels,
> Than aliens to his interest, those who make
> A property, a market of his honour?

And the dead Henry III is apostrophized by his son in a way which the living George II might—so the censors thought—take amiss:

> O my deluded father! little joy
> Hadst thou in life, led from thy real good
> And genuine glory, from thy people's love,
> The noblest aim of kings, by smiling traitors!

Edward and Eleanora had to wait nearly forty years for production. It dragged with it into complete oblivion another historical play *Arminius* (1740), whose author William Paterson had copied out for Thomson the text of *Edward and Eleanora* submitted to the censor. When the Lord Chamberlain's men saw the same handwriting on *Arminius* a few months later they at once refused it a licence. Yet they left immune Thomson's tragedy *Agamemnon*, although this was nothing less than 'a flagrant attack upon Queen Caroline and Sir Robert Walpole'.[1] By the time Thomson completed it, early in 1738, Queen Caroline's death had neutralized the play, but, when produced, the political allusions were 'greatly applauded'.[2]

It is among the more baffling curiosities of the censorship's history, that not long after the Act a man who should, however inaccurately, be dubbed the English Aristophanes began his successful career in defiance of the law, and continued it with relative immunity. As a writer and an actor, Samuel Foote satirized and mimicked prominent contemporary personalities, yet—most of the time—neither they nor the Lord Chamberlain took action. After an initial intervention by the police, who stopped a performance and dispersed the audience, Foote was rarely troubled. His targets were personal rather than political: fashionable doctors, actors and actresses, a judge, an auctioneer, a

---

[1] *James Thomson*, by Douglas Grant (1956).
[2] *Memoirs of the Life of David Garrick*, by Thomas Davies (1780).

preacher, men about town, city characters. He flourished not only as an actor but as a manager at the Haymarket, and in 1766 he was given a patent and the right to use the 'royal' label on condition that he rebuilt the theatre. Foote dedicated a number of pieces to various Lords Chamberlain, with whom, says his biographer Percy Fitzgerald, 'he appears to have been on intimate footing, and, as they protected him as far as they could, it is no wonder he was grateful'.[1] Yet one Lord Chamberlain, Lord Hertford, was obliged to ban Foote's *A Trip To Calais*, because it presented on the stage Elizabeth Chudleigh, *soi-disant* Duchess of Kingston, a celebrated adventuress of the time; and this attack embroiled Foote in a lingering, savage and suicidal vendetta which wrecked his career. But it was his own folly, and not the censorship, which was to blame.

The Lord Chamberlain's most controversial interference with the drama in these salad days of the new censorship was the banning in 1739 of *Gustavus Vasa*, a historical tragedy by Henry Brooke. Although performed without incident in Ireland, over which the Chamberlain had no jurisdiction, it was refused a licence here because of 'some strokes of liberty which breathed through several parts of it', and, more particularly, because the Vice-Regent of Denmark and Norway was thought to be a lampoon of the Prime Minister of England: its picture of corrupt Sweden might well have been identified with the Opposition's view of England under the Whigs. Brooke at once published the play with a protesting preface ('Patriotism is the great and single moral which I had in view'), and, like Gay's *Polly* ten years before, it had an immediate success in print, making the author a reputed profit of between £800 and £1,000. It also brought into action the heavy artillery of Dr Johnson, in his pamphlet *A Complete Vindication of the Licensers of the Stage from the Malicious and Scandalous Aspersions of Mr Brooke . . . with a proposal for making the Office of Licenser more extensive and effectual*, ascribed to 'An Impartial Hand'.

How dare the author of *Gustavus Vasa*, exclaimed Dr Johnson with deadpan irony, question the wisdom of the censor? 'Let me be forgiven if I cannot speak without temper of such insolence as this: is a man without title, pension or place, to suspect the impartiality or the judgement of those who are entrusted with the administration of public affairs?' Brooke had said, in his preface to *Gustavus Vasa*, that he had 'waited often on the licenser, and with the utmost importunity entreated

---

[1] *Samuel Foote*, by Percy Fitzgerald (1910).

49

an answer'. That, said Dr Johnson solemnly, was most improper conduct, due no doubt to Mr Brooke's 'erroneous notion that the grant of a licence was not an act of favour, but of justice: a mistake into which he could not have fallen, but from a supine inattention to the design of the statute, which was only to bring poets into subjection and dependence, not to encourage good writers, but to discourage all'. Mr Brooke had also asked for reasons why his play was banned. Reasons?

What is power, but the liberty of acting without being accountable? . . . The advocates for the licensing act have alleged, that the Lord Chamberlain has always had authority to protect the representation of a play for just reasons. Why then did we call in all our force to procure an act of parliament? Was it to enable him to do what he has always done? to confirm an authority, which no man attempted to impair, or pretended to dispute? No, certainly: our intention was to invest him with new privileges, and to empower him to do that without reason, which with reason he could do before. We have found, by long experience, that to lie under a necessity of assigning reasons, is very troublesome, and that many an excellent design has miscarried by the loss of time spent unnecessarily in examining reasons.

There was, suggested Dr Johnson, a great future ahead of the Chamberlain's Office. It offered, after all, 'a gainful and reputable employment to a great number of the friends of the government . . . it might be sufficient honour for any poet, except the laureate, to stand bare-headed in the presence of the deputy of the deputy's deputy in the nineteenth subordination'. There were plenty of jobs for the boys, in 'the great work of drawing up an *index expurgatorius* to all the old plays', for these were 'crowded with passages very unfit for the ears of an English audience, and which cannot be pronounced without irritating the minds of the people'. And that was only the beginning. The seminaries throughout the kingdom should be suppressed at once, and it should be a crime 'to teach to read without a licence from the Lord Chamberlain'. How else, Johnson asked, could we ensure 'decent submission to our superiors, and that proper awe of authority which we are taught in courts?'

* * *

With that trumpet-blast of irony from the Great Cham, however, the censorship of the stage settled into relative obscurity and tranquil ignominy. 'People are always fond of what is forbidden,' Lord Chester-field had warned, 'your prohibition will prove a bellows, which will blow up the fire you intend to extinguish.' But the censorship took care, after the first year or two, not to blow too hard. For the next century and a half it provoked no major riots or scandals. No outstanding dramatists were openly martyred, and no great plays were overtly suppressed. Few were written, although for that sterility the Lord Chamberlain cannot take *all* the blame. The best dramatists of the century—Sheridan and Goldsmith—wrote only five plays between them, and do not appear to have been inhibited by the censorship. Characteristically, Sheridan bowdlerized one of the Restoration comedies most ferociously attacked for its indecency by Collier—Vanbrugh's *The Relapse*—under the title of *A Trip To Scarborough*. Similar treatment was applied to Farquhar, Congreve and others. Yet his own view of such emasculating work may be reflected in *The Critic*, where Dangle, invoking the 'nicety' of the audience, says:

'No double entendre, no smart innuendo admitted; even Vanbrugh and Congreve obliged to undergo a bungling reformation!'

'Yes,' says Sneer, 'and our prudery in this respect is just on a par with the artificial bashfulness of a courtesan, who increases the blush upon her cheeks in an exact proportion to the demonstration of her modesty.'

The 'prudery' increased as the century wore on towards the age of Bowdler. By 1790 Congreve and Vanbrugh, if acted at all, were 'acted almost without dialogue', so heavy were the cuts.[1] Some 'perfectly innocuous' plays, Professor Nicoll testifies, were damned for supposed indecency. The London audience was extravagantly alert for any hint of immodesty—or unpatriotic sentiment. They applied their own censorship. The Chamberlain's Office appeared to do little of its own. The kind of trivial interference that happened occasionally was this; in 1761 a farce, *Register Office*, was abandoned at Drury Lane during rehearsals because the censor demanded the deletion of two characters, Lady Wrinkle and Mrs Snarewell, apparently on moral grounds. 'Un-fortunately for the author,' noted the Rev. John Genest, historian of the stage, 'these were by far the best parts in his piece—Lady Wrinkle applies to Gulwell (a rascal who keeps a Register Office) to get her a stout handsome footman—some hints are given why she is so particular as to the person of her servant, but nothing is said which could justify

---

[1] *History of the English Drama*, III, by Allardyce Nicoll (1952).

the Licenser in striking out the character—he ought to have been ashamed of himself . . .'[1] It was acted seven years later, with a few alterations. In 1771, when it was reprinted, the author omitted Lady Wrinkle completely.

An open instance of the underlying deterrent for any author who tried to use the drama, however modestly, in the spirit of Fielding was provided by Charles Macklin, the Shylock of the century and one of its outsize figures both on and off the stage. In 1770, at the age of seventy, he sent to Samuel Foote a play *The Man of the World*, which contained a deliberate attack on the Prime Minister, Lord Bute, as a corrupt and humbugging Scottish politician, Sir Hector Mackcrafty. The Lord Chamberlain banned it. He had, indeed, says Macklin's latest biographer,[2] 'no alternative'. 'The matter of the play was palpably objectionable. Foote was notorious for his razor-sharp political impersonations, and George III not infrequently attended the theatre.' Nine years later Macklin sent a second version to Covent Garden, in which Sir Hector was rechristened Sir Pertinax Macsycophant, and from it he deleted many political satirical passages, such as this : 'Scotchmen, Sir, wherever they meet throughout the globe should unite and stick together as it were in a political phalanx—For, Sir, the whole world hates us, and therefore we should love one another.' But it was still rejected. 'The Lord Chamberlain has refused to license a comedy of mine,' he said, 'being seasoned too high respecting venality.' It was not until Macklin was eighty-one, two years later, when the political climate and the Scots concentration of power at Court had changed, that the Chamberlain relented and the play—teeth drawn—remained in the repertory, as a popular favourite, for the next half-century.

Like all censors, the Lord Chamberlain's men worked in the dark. Not all their victims exposed their sufferings to the public, and no leading writers challenged the institution in open fight. There was little support for protests like Macklin's: 'It is dangerous to give the people an occasion to think, that satire or ridicule is shut out from the Theatre, in every vice or folly respecting the Ministers, and open to every mode of attack upon the friends of liberty, or those who are called so.' But although the censorship was tolerated as a regrettable necessity, the censors themselves were not altogether immune to criticism. There was, indeed, room for improvement. While Lords Chamberlain came and

---

[1] *Some Account of the English Stage* (1832).
[2] *Charles Macklin*, by William W. Appleton (1961).

went at Court, two men only sat in authority over the theatre for nearly sixty years. They were John Larpent and George Colman, and their reigns in the censor's throne are speckled with a lunacy which helps to account in part for the puerility of the English drama during that period.

Take Mr Larpent, the Examiner of Plays from 1778 to 1824. It is not surprising, perhaps, that he should have banned a play about the adventures of the Pretender, Kotzebue's *The Wanderer*; or that *King Lear* should have been kept off the stage for years, during the madness of George III, because of Shakespeare's bad taste in presenting to the common gaze the figure of a royal lunatic. But what is one to think of an arbiter of dramatic literature who objected to the word 'gammon' in a farce because he had a friend of that name in Hampshire; and who expunged from another play the line 'Bring my grey hairs in sorrow to the grave' because, he said, it was *profane*? Many authors submitted to the idiotic 'improvements' of Mr Larpent; few protested; but in 1809 he had the misfortune to meet a conscientious objector—Theodore Hook, then a rebel of twenty-one. The night before it was due to be performed, Hook was told that the Lord Chamberlain had banned his two-act farce *Killing No Murder*—without giving any reasons. Hook at once went on the warpath.

> I set off in search of the gentleman who had strangled my literary infant in his birth, and to find him I referred to the Red Book, where I discovered that John Larpent, Esquire was *clerk* to the Privy Seal Office, that John Larpent Esquire was *deputy* to John Larpent Esquire, and that the deputy's *secretary* was *John Larpent Esquire*. This proved to me that a man could be in three places at once, but on inquiry I found that he was even in a fourth and fifth, for it was by virtue of none of these office he licensed plays, and his place, i.e. his villa, was at Putney.

There Mr Larpent explained to Mr Hook that the Government did not wish the Methodists to be ridiculed. (He was himself a strict Methodist, and had built a tabernacle of his own.) But on being challenged by the author he agreed to license *Killing No Murder* if certain slighting references to preachers were deleted. Hook agreed, and in place of them inserted some clumsy hits at Mr Larpent himself, in the following kind:

> having advertised the farce of *The Devil to Pay*, old Justice Carpat,

who between you and I was a bit of a shoemaker—hearing as how it contained some personal reflections on the cobblering profession—stopped the performance and theatened to send us all to the stocks.

Weak as they were, such gibes were applauded energetically at the Haymarket, where the farce enjoyed an unusually long run, thanks to the censor. When it was published, with the bits which had offended his Methodist conscience included as an appendix, it went into six editions.

Larpent's attitude to the manuscripts in his charge is significant: he considered them as his private property. When he left the Chamberlain's Office he emptied the cellars, taking with him not only every piece submitted to him in forty-six years of censorship but also many plays from previous regimes. This irreplaceable collection of plays—many of them never printed—is now in the Henry E. Huntington Library in the U.S.A. By a happy accident for historians of the stage, it was bought *in bulk*, but it is extraordinary that the Licenser of the Stage should have been allowed to commit larceny on such a grand scale, or that so pious a Methodist should not have realized that he was pilfering the property of the nation. But then, of course, they were only plays.

Rake followed bigot when Larpent (who died at eighty-three) was succeeded in 1824 by George Colman, but the censorship now became stricter than ever before. Generally known as 'Colman the younger', to distinguish him from his dramatist-father, the 'Examiner of all Plays' was himself the author of twenty-five plays, several of them box-office successes, and had been a highly erratic manager of the Haymarket, whose affairs he once conducted from prison. By Regency standards some of his plays were reckoned to be 'licentious' in tone and language. Early in his career, in 1797, one had been banned by the Chamberlain; and when he himself at sixty-two became censor, he unctuously admitted that he had been a 'careless, immoral' author. In private, too, Colman had achieved some notoriety, and his tastes had won him the *entrée* to Carlton House, where he became one of the Prince Regent's favourites. It was no doubt with his royal friend's help that he stepped into Larpent's shoes. But if Prinny hoped that this would relax the moral codes of the drama he was soon disappointed, for Colman outstripped his Methodist predecessor in his eagerness to reform the ways of authors, and to suppress anything which, as he said, 'may make a bad impression on the people at large.'

Oaths and expletives, for instance, were soon scored out in red ink.

54

'I think nobody has gone away from a theatre the better for hearing a great deal of cursing and swearing', he solemnly told a Royal Commission in 1832, and so he made sure that *damme* never polluted the drama again. Colman's piety, too, was prodigious. 'I conceive all Scripture is much too sacred for the stage, except in very solemn scenes indeed, and that to bring things so sacred upon the stage becomes profane', he said. Not only did he delete any reference to *gods, heaven* and *hell*, even when the words occurred in lines chanted in a cathedral, but *Providence* and *Lud* were also offensive in his eyes. While Colman worked for the Lord Chamberlain, nobody was allowed to speak the word 'angel', because— he declared—an angel was a character in Scripture and must not be profaned by taking its name in vain on the stage. When the word 'thigh' was adjudged indecent, and 'holy virgin' was banned, it is not surprising that Colman forbade a near quotation from *Hamlet*, 'I'm like a goblin damned', because of its bad language!

He was also, of course, on the alert for any trace of political heresy. A few months after his appointment he found it, in a tragedy about Poland called *Alasco*, by Martin Archer Shee. So heavy were Colman's cuts that the enraged author withdrew his play from rehearsal and published it, deletions and all, with heavily sarcastic footnotes. In correspondence with the management, the Examiner of Plays had explained the dangers of *Alasco* in its entirety:

> Although the ferment of the times had greatly subsided, still plays which are built upon conspiracies, and attempts to revolutionize a state, stand upon ticklish ground; and the proposed performance of such plays is to be contemplated with more jealousy when they portray the disaffected as gallant heroes and hapless lovers. Thus drawn, *ad captandum vulgus*, their showy qualities and tender distresses of the heart throw a dazzle and an interest round their sedition . . .

To protect Crown and State from the insidious perils of Mr Shee's blank verse, Mr Colman cut from the play invocations to the God of Truth, the God of Mercy, dangerous words like 'despot', and such passages as these:

> *Our common wrongs—our country's wrongs, unite us.*

> >   *For your country*
> > *Fight and be free!*

Some slanderous tool of State,
Some taunting, dull, unmanner'd deputy.

Far from censuring such idiocy in his own 'unmanner'd deputy', the Lord Chamberlain of the day, the Duke of Montrose, was so much on Colman's side that he took the unusual step of registering an opinion in public. Replying to a protest from Mr Shee, the Duke explained why the censorship was a good thing:

> Whilst I am persuaded that your intentions are upright, I conceive that it is precisely for this reason—though it may not strike authors—that it has been the wisdom of the Legislature to have an Examiner appointed, and power given to the Chamberlain of the Household to judge whether certain plays should be acted at all . . .

Not surprisingly, Shee decided to abandon the drama for painting: he was later knighted and became President of the Royal Academy. But the *Alasco* affair was another reminder to authors—especially those of 'upright intentions'—that politics in any national dress was forbidden territory in the English drama and that to write anything at all serious for the stage exposed them to the humiliations of a single censor. It was staged a few years later at the Surrey, outside the Chamberlain's territory, without any of his cuts—and without any repercussions.

Colman himself showed his mettle again in the following year, when Miss Mary Russell Mitford, the quiet, retiring author of *Our Village*, had the temerity to write a play about *Charles I*. The very mention of regicide made the censor pale, and Colman felt that he was 'unable to take the responsibility of sanctioning its performance', although Miss Mitford was a devout Royalist.

> The fact is that the subject of this play and the incidents it embraces are fatal in themselves; they are an inherent and incurable disease; the morbid matter lies in the very bones and marrow of the historical facts, and defies eradication . . . I give Miss Mitford full credit for the harmlessness of her intentions, but mischief may be unconsciously done, as a house may be set on fire by a little innocent in the nursery.

Accordingly, the 'little innocent's' incendiary piece was referred to the Chamberlain himself, and he decided that it was unfit for public consumption in the reign of George IV. Playgoers should not be reminded that kings were quite so conspicuously mortal. Six years later the next Lord Chamberlain, the Duke of Devonshire, still maintained, when approached by Miss Mitford, that *Charles I* was too dangerous to stage; yet in 1834 it was presented at the Victoria (now, the Old Vic) without incident of any kind. Neither censor nor Court then made any attempt to intervene.

No other *causes célèbres* decorated George Colman's twelve years in power, but he continued to show a crusading zeal which contrasted oddly with his own early plays. When critics pointed out the contradiction, Colman declared: 'I was in a different position at that time. I was a careless immoral author, I am now an examiner of plays. I did my business as an author at that time, and I do my business as an examiner now.' It was good business, too. For Colman exploited the cash-value of censorship with a greed that soon became a byword in the theatre. He attempted, for instance, to wring from actors two guineas for every new song or glee or 'other musical interpolation' on a benefit night. He exacted the same fee from a manager when a public lecture on astronomy was given. Usually the actors, authors and managers paid up. They knew on which side their bread was buttered. He made at least £200 a year in fees. But sometimes he went too far. When Colman tried to extract licence fees for every one of the French plays presented at the Opera House in 1829, the manager appealed above his head to the Chamberlain, the Duke of Devonshire, who vetoed Colman's plan. When, in 1827, he savaged *Ben Nazir, the Saracen*, the Hon. George Lamb protested to the Chamberlain, who sent for Colman. Colman told the Duke that 'he need not give himself the trouble of reading the piece, for he had cut out every objectionable sentence', but the Duke was determined to judge for himself, and then informed Colman that he saw no objection to those parts that had been expunged, and ordered them to be restored. The next Chamberlain, the Duke of Montrose, also decided against his Examiner and for Charles Mathews, who refused Colman's request to submit a copy of his one-man entertainment for licensing, as it was largely given from memory, but agreed to submit a specimen *in performance* to the Chamberlain in person. Mathews won his case, for the Duke asked him only to give 'something as a slight sketch'. Colman also failed, after an initial success, to license oratorio. He pursued this 'not for the sake of the fees', he explained smugly, but 'because I think they may be immoral things'.

In general, Colman behaved as if he, not the Chamberlain, was in control: 'I am a sworn officer of the Crown, and no deputy of the Lord Chamberlain.' He told the 1832 Committee that his appointment was for life, or so he understood. When asked if the Chamberlain could dismiss him, he actually said: 'No, I should demur to that; I do not know what power the Lord Chamberlain has to displace me; such a thing was never thought of.' One result was that the Committee made the following recommendation: 'it should be clearly understood that the office of the Censor is held at the discretion of the Lord Chamberlain, whose duty it would be to remove him, should there be any just ground for dissatisfaction as to the exercise of his functions'. There were signs that the Chamberlain did plan to 'remove' his Examiner, but before that could happen Colman died. He had been, as his friend Planché said, 'either in pursuance of instructions or of his own mere motion, the inaugurator of a more rigid system of supervision . . . drawing on himself continual expostulations from managers and authors, animadversions in the public journals, and fits in abundance'.[1] The cause was certainly not in a directive from the Lord Chamberlain. Colman's record as censor was summed up by a less friendly critic: 'An inordinate fear of the devil, working on a mind reduced to the last gasp of imbecility, could alone originate such a ludicrous, yet injurious abuse of paltry power.'[2] As his latest biographer says, he was 'one of the most narrow, humourless and puritanical censors in the history of the English theatre.'[3]

Admittedly, Colman lived in an age of increasing prudery, in its attitude to the theatre, even towards Shakespeare. 'Barefaced obscenities, low vulgarities and nauseous vice so frequently figure and pollute his pages that we cannot but regret the luckless hour he became a writer for the stage', declaimed one critic in 1806. Thomas Bowdler—whose notorious family edition of the Bard first appeared in 1818—liquidated Doll Tearsheet, cut the last verse of the Willow Song in *Othello* and deprived the audience watching the Nine Worthies in *Love's Labour's Lost* of the joke about the kiss of Judas, because it was a 'very improper' reference to 'one of the most serious and awful passages in the New Testament'. Yet even Bowdler was content to use 'Heaven' without a blush. Colman, in fact, did not merely reflect the common prejudices and bigotries of the time, but he smelled danger where there was none. He attempted to regulate the drama to fit the taste of the most conservative, most frightened and most bigoted English minorities.

[1] *Recollections and Reflections*, II, by J. R. Planché (1872).
[2] *New Monthly Magazine*, XI.
[3] *George Colman the Younger*, by Jeremy F. Bagster-Collins (1946).

Like many of his successors, he overdid it. That is one of the occupational dangers of being a censor.

Complaining of 'the insipid levelling morality to which the age is tied down', Charles Lamb said—in 1808—'Our audiences come to the theatre to be complimented on their goodness.' As with other censors, Colman's attempts to enforce the compliment to the public's morality became an insult to their intelligence. So was the system, upheld by the Chamberlain's Office, which allowed two London theatres to penalise the others—an absurd and unjust protection of privilege summed up by the story that Delpini, a clown at the Royalty, was sent to prison in the 1780s because he spoke 'legitimate' words, without musical accompaniment, in the course of a pantomime. The words were 'Roast Beef!' Shades of Henry Fielding!

5

Zara: This is a Lord High Chamberlain
        Of purity the gauge—
        He'll cleanse our Court from moral stain
        And purify our Stage.

Lord Dramaleigh: Yes—yes—yes
        Court reputations I revise,
        And presentations scrutinize,
        New plays I read with jealous eyes
        And purify the Stage.

Utopia Limited, by GILBERT and SULLIVAN; 1893

★ ★ ★

COLMAN'S controversial excesses damaged the status of the Examiner-ship of Plays, though not the institution of censorship itself. After his death the rake-off was cut (only five shillings was demanded to license a song); the Examiner was not allowed to invent new impositions; and he was required to do more work for less money. Yet a more substantial reason for the slump in the Examiner's prestige was the increase in the Lord Chamberlain's authority, effected by the Theatres Act of 1843 (the 6 & 7 Vict.).

This Act, which still governs our stage today, repealed Walpole's Act of 1737 and other measures relating to theatrical control. It was the somewhat belated result of the 1832 committee of enquiry in which Edward Bulwer (later Lord Lytton) took a leading role, and was known accordingly as Bulwer's Act; and it fulfilled his hopes for greater freedom by abolishing the official monopoly of the 'patent' theatres. Every playhouse had still to be licensed by the Lord Chamberlain or the J.P.s or it had to have the authority of a royal patent. But from now on all theatres had the open right to stage 'legitimate' drama. Yet the Act failed to achieve another of Bulwer's ambitions—the abolition of the censorship. 'A censor upon plays seems to me as idle and unnecessary as a censor upon books', Bulwer had said in Parliament. 'I am at a loss to know what advantages we have gained by the grant of this almost unconstitutional power.' He argued that 'the public taste, backed by the vigilant admonition of the public press, might, perhaps, be more safely trusted for the preservation of theatrical decorum, than any ignorant and bungling censor'. But Parliament was so far from sharing his views that it gave this ignorant and bungling censor renewed authority over the drama, and no Chesterfield arose to defend the freedom of the stage. A few protests were made. Lord Campbell attempted to introduce a clause limiting the Lord Chamberlain's interference, unrestricted in the original Bill, to cases where it was necessary 'for the preservation of good manners, decorum and of the public peace'. But it was pointed out that the Act was designed not to limit but to *extend* the Chamberlain's jurisdiction, and the Lord Chancellor recommended the use of this clause under a formula which left the censor's authority almost as unlimited as before. Under clause 14 of the Act the Lord Chamberlain was confirmed in his power to prohibit the performance of any stage play, old or new—or any act, scene or part of it—in any theatre in Britain, either absolutely or for as long as he thought necessary, with one new proviso—'whenever he shall be of opinion that it is fitting for the preservation of good manners, decorum, or of the public peace so to do'.

In spite of some protests from the Chamberlain's Office, which favoured wider powers, his authority to license *buildings* was restricted to the Cities of London and Westminster; the areas which in 1843 were the boroughs of Finsbury, Marylebone, Tower Hamlets, Lambeth and Southwark; Windsor and other places of royal residence. Instead of issuing different licences for 'stage plays', burlettas, spectacles, etc, the Lord Chamberlain now decided to give the same annual licence— at a maximum fee of ten shillings a month—to all theatres within his authority: the Act added ten theatres and seven saloons, bringing the total to twenty-four. In the provinces, local J.P.s were empowered to license theatres at a maximum fee of five shillings a month.

But the Chamberlain's power to license *plays* was unlimited. A copy of every new 'stage play', every new addition to an old 'stage play', and every new prologue and epilogue intended to be produced and acted 'for hire', must be sent to his office at least seven days before its proposed performance (halving the time specified in the 1737 Act). 'Stage play' was widely defined as 'every Tragedy, Comedy, Farce, Opera, Burletta, Interlude, Melodrama, Pantomime or other Entertainment of the Stage, or any Part thereof'. To present a play, or any part of it, which the Lord Chamberlain had 'disallowed', anywhere in

61

Britain or in any theatres he named, meant a fine of £50 and—here, as in 1737, was the real deterrent—the loss of the theatre's licence. As the Chamberlain was empowered to close down either a theatre licensed by him or a patent theatre at any time, either under Clause 14, or because of 'riot and misbehaviour', or on 'such public Occasions as to the Lord Chamberlain shall seem fit', he was established in absolute authority over both 'stage plays' and the nation's key showplaces—with no provision for any appeal against his actions. Ireland was outside his jurisdiction. But in England the shackles which Walpole had riveted on the theatre were now reinforced by Melbourne.

For the first time the Examiner of Plays was given a vague statutory recognition. The Act said it was lawful to charge fees for the 'Examination' of plays according to a scale fixed by him, 'such Fee not being in any Case more than Two Guineas' and that the fees should be paid 'to the Lord Chamberlain or to some Officer deputed by him to receive the same'. Although, as we have seen, Colman had protested before the committee of inquiry that he was a 'sworn officer of the Crown, and no deputy of the Lord Chamberlain', the official view of the Examiner's status was indicated by the Speaker:

> The Lord Chamberlain is the person to whom the public look . . . I do not say he does so, but he ought not to shelter himself in any way behind the Examiner. The Examiner is nothing but an assistant—a clerk in his office—who does the drudgery for him, and should advise him.

Yet although this 'clerk' never quite regained the cash or kudos that Colman had enjoyed, it was he, rather than the Chamberlain, who ran the machinery of censorship. Chamberlains came and went with Ministries. Some were in power for a few months, none for more than seven years. But their 'deputy' censors might be in effective control for as long as twenty-five years at a time. During Victoria's reign there were eighteen changes of Lord Chamberlain but only five changes in the Examinership of Plays. Until the end of the century the five Examiners of Plays carried out their duties, under the nominal supervision of a string of Lords Chamberlain, without any spectacular injustice, notoriety or challenge to their authority, and without the financial extortions of previous incumbents. The Examiner earned a salary of £300 to £400 p.a., plus fees for the plays. He usually read about two hundred scripts a year, and received a guinea for one or two acts, two guineas for three acts or over, and five shillings for a song.

For twenty years, from 1855 to 1875, he was required to be the Inspector of Theatres as well. 'I am fallen on evil times', wrote one Examiner when this happened. 'I am paid no more, indeed rather less, than my predecessors in the Examinership, but I am set to do as much work as the whole series, since there was a censor, ever performed. I descend into the bowels of the earth: I mount upon such pinnacles as Satan stands on in *Paradise Regained*: I inhale evil smells; I cross dangerous places: 'sometimes I fall into the water and sometimes into the fire', and all for £500 a year, besides injuring my mind by reading nonsense and perilling my soul by reading wickedness . . .'[1] He was William Bodham Donne, a former librarian of the London Library.

It was an unhealthy job, too. 'I have been sick and dizzy half a dozen times a day', Donne wrote. 'I have imported into our own house several varieties of biting and stinging insects.' Looking back in 1870, he said, 'When I began acting as the Devil's archdeacon . . . in 1857, twenty Theatres then occupied me for more time, and required, beside curses, far more ink and paper than thirty-five do now.' Mr Donne was not even given an office: 'though the Lord Chamberlain ought to find me one in St James's Palace, he won't or can't, because the Duchess of Cambridge occupies the best rooms'. It was also a thankless job. Donne found himself the target of violent abuse in the press. ('Little did I think to live to be one of the most celebrated and unpopular men of the day.') At one time the theatre managers, firm champions of the censorship from Fielding to Osborne, began to lobby for the abolition of the Chamberlain's powers over the stage; not because he interfered with the freedom of the drama, but because he put them to expense and trouble in improving the safety and comfort of their buildings.

* * *

The Chamberlain's control of theatrical safety and comfort in London developed gradually. He ordered one theatre to be surveyed as early as 1812. He obliged the Covent Garden proprietors to deliver an architect's report on the building's safety in 1828 before he would allow it to open, even though it was not, as a patent theatre, licensed by him, and in the same year he asked the Surveyor of His Majesty's Works to make a structural survey of all the theatres in his jurisdiction. This did not touch on 'accessory arrangements affecting the security and

---

[1] *William Bodham Donne and his Friends*, edited by Catharine B. Johnson (1905).

comfort of the audience', but in the 1850s the Chamberlain took steps to improve these, too. He asked the police to report on 'means of egress' in all London theatres. Five were found unsafe. He required from every proprietor a certificate about the building's structural safety and its supply of exits; he circularized all managers with a recommendation for better ventilation; from 1854 onwards he added to every licence a condition that its validity depended upon observation of his rules on ventilation, facility of egress and other precautions; and in 1855 came the first annual inspection of all London theatres —made by the Examiner of Plays, assisted by a surveyor. As a result, over the years, he claimed that new water supplies were installed, with fire-fighting equipment; staircases were strengthened; pewter gaspiping was replaced by iron piping; new exits were provided; wire guards were placed on footlights; doors opening inwards were banned; lavatories were extended and improved. Later the practical work of inspection and survey was largely undertaken by the L.C.C. In 1909 a Home Office official, testifying at a committee of inquiry, explained that 'for some years' there had been an 'arrangement' between the Lord Chamberlain, the L.C.C. and the theatre proprietors that no theatre or music-hall in London should have its licence renewed unless it complied with the L.C.C.'s demands for structural improvements.

The *number* of theatres in London continued to be controlled by the Lord Chamberlain. After the 1843 Act he could and did check theatrical expansion by vetoing applications for licences—especially from musichall proprietors—unless he was satisfied that the building was safe; was supported by local residents; was approved by the police and the local authorities; and would 'satisfy a legitimate want and not create a permanent nuisance'. For many years he also enforced the closure of theatres within his jurisdiction for royal and religious reasons: on the death of a member of the royal family (sometimes for as long as seven weeks): on the anniversary of the execution of Charles I; during Passion Week (until 1861); on Wednesdays and Fridays in Lent; and, of course, on Christmas Day. Some of these prohibitions, not surprisingly, created a good deal of rumbling discontent, and they were dropped as the century wore on.

He still retained, of course, the ultimate deterrent of being able to take away the licence of any manager who flouted him by staging an unlicensed play, or behaving in any other improper fashion. But there are few instances of the Chamberlain actually *doing* this. One recorded occasion where he pursued something of a personal vendetta was in a matter not of scripts but of skirts. In 1874 the Chamberlain, then the Marquis of Hertford, took umbrage at the shortness of the frocks in a can-can danced at the St James's (in Offenbach's *Vert-Vert*). The director, Richard Mansell, accordingly put the girls in long black satin skirts, of a length prescribed by the Marquis, with pink fleshing tights and petticoats, and recorded in the programme that the alterations were designed by the Lord Chamberlain. (They were one and a half inches below the usual length.) His Lordship was not amused. He withdrew the licence, and threatened, in a letter to Mansell, 'I shall leave such instructions with my successors as will prevent you ever holding a licence in your own name again.'[1] He apparently kept his word. The nearest Mansell got to the West End was at Notting Hill, in the Coronet, some thirty years later. It is the only recorded instance of a Chamberlain deliberately breaking a manager, rather than an author.

* * *

Although the Chamberlain's Office was generally accepted in Victorian times, there were of course incidents, when, like all censors, the Stable Yard ones showed that apparently ineradicable tendency to 'strain at gnats and cavil at straws', as Bulwer described it, especially in the niceties of titles. To the Examiner of Plays, it made all the difference what you *called* your work. Rossini's opera *Mose in Egitto* was prohibited on religious grounds, until it was rechristened *Pietro l'Eremita*, and Verdi's *Nabucco* was relabelled *Nino*, for a similar reason. It was not always the censor's own piety which led him into such humbug, but his estimate of public bigotry. Thus W. Bodham Donne wrote to Fanny Kemble:

> Madame Ristori is to play Jiuditta in a few evenings; but to please the thick-skulled British public I have been obliged to find her a new name for the Tragedy, and new titles for the characters, and all because the book of Judith happens to be bound up with the Bible, being all the while as much inspired as *Tom Jones*. When shall we be a wiser people?

The public, in general, was certainly prudish and narrow-minded, but was it really so 'thick-skulled'? Censors usually exaggerate the man in the street's susceptibility to words. It was this same Examiner who banned *La Dame aux Camélias* but licensed *La Traviata*, explaining that 'if

---

[1] *Jimmy Glover His Book*, by James M. Glover (1911).

there is a musical version of a piece it makes a difference, for the story is then subsidiary to the music and singing'; yet said that he treated French plays 'as you would the French Embassy, as part of France . . . Now if I accept a French play at all I never interfere with it. I say "Do it as it is done in Paris." After all, a French play's audience is a very limited one in this country.' The official view of the Chamberlain's Office, as expressed by the Comptroller in 1866, was that 'the modern French drama is almost entirely immoral', or, as the Examiner put it later, that its plays 'unluckily turn for the most part on breaches of the Seventh Commandment'. As the French critic, Augustin Filon, wrote in the 1890s:

> The most absorbing task of the censorship is that of barring the way against French immorality. Its vigilance is eluded, however, by a kind of conventional terminology. Where our authors have had the effrontery to write the word 'cocotte' in black and white, they replace it by the word 'actress'. Where we have unblushingly written 'adultery', they have inserted 'flirtatious'. The censor gives his sanction and pockets his fees, and on the performance of the piece, the byplay of the actors and actresses completes the translation, re-establishing, if not reinforcing, the original sense.[1]

Mr Bodham Donne is memorable for many other dicta. It was he who prohibited *Jack Sheppard* after it had been licensed and in performance, because of its 'incitement to crime', yet later licensed an adaptation of a French version of the same piece; who banned a farce because 'insanity was a much too painful affliction to be treated humorously' (what chance —as William Archer asked—would Malvolio have had with such a censor?); who explained that 'a ballet is rarely understood fully by more than about four people', and that *he* had never been able to make out what *any* ballet meant; who boasted that 'I never allow any association with Scripture or theology to be introduced into a play': who decreed that all the comic 'business' in pantomime—so obviously fraught with possibilities of profanity, sedition and obscenity—should be written down and submitted to him with the text; who informed a parliamentary committee authoritatively in 1866 that '*double entendre* is a species of wit that is very nearly extinct'.

This same Mr Donne explained that he deleted from the English drama 'anything in the shape of an oath, anything which turns religion into ridicule, and any political joke'. His thoroughness in pursuit of the

[1] *The English Stage* (1897).

66

latter rare game is illustrated by his deletion from a popular song of the line 'May Gladstone keep his temper'. Certainly, it was with political and religious offences that the Victorian censors, like their Restoration predecessors, were mainly concerned. Thus, a year after the 1843 Act was passed, Shirley Brooks wrote a stage version of Disraeli's novel, *Coningsby*, which was refused a licence. The astonished author was granted an interview with the Chamberlain himself (still a rare condescension), at St James's Palace, and there the Earl of Uxbridge courteously explained why Brooks's play could not be shown to the public. 'You see, you are writing a kind of quasi-political piece,' said the Earl, 'and here you are exhibiting a sort of contrast between the manufacturing people and the lower classes. Don't you think, now, that that would be a pity?' It was a rhetorical question: *Coningsby*'s author had to acquiesce in its suppression. After that, he told the 1866 Committee, 'I learnt my lesson and made my satire out of milder materials'.

Again, an attempt to present the House of Commons on the Haymarket stage in 1846, with the actor-manager, J. P. Buckstone, playing Lord John Russell, was at once vetoed. Yet Charles Mathews *père* was allowed to impersonate Daniel O'Connell on the stage—because he belonged to the enemy, perhaps, or at any rate, as William Archer suggests, because O'Connell's influence in the Chamberlain's Office was naturally small. In 1848 the Lord Chamberlain stopped the performance at the same theatre after two nights of a piece called *Lola Montes*, which he had already licensed. Perhaps the Foreign Office had objected to its over-explicit public treatment of the King of Bavaria's mistress, but it was a token objection only, for after a few days the piece continued its run under a different title as *Pas de Fascination*, and an allusion to the Bavarian monarch was redirected to a Russian count.

Protection of the dignity of distinguished foreigners sometimes went to absurd lengths. In 1834 an adaptation of a Scribe comedy, *The Minister and the Mercer*, was at first banned, because the chief character was thought to be a thin disguise for Talleyrand, then French Ambassador. When the author and manager, Alfred Bunn, offered to make any necessary amendments, the ban was lifted; but the Comptroller of the Lord Chamberlain's Office visited the theatre to inquire into the costume which the actor in the role would wear, and a drawing of it was sent to the King. The wig worn on the stage, however, was an exact copy of Talleyrand's own; and, what is more, the actors—of their own accord—restored some of the vetoed lines. The King heard about this, sent the Vice-Chamberlain to the Prime Minister and the Foreign Secretary, and they both went to the theatre. They were, Bunn records, 'said to be extremely irate'. But exactly opposite their box sat Prince Talleyrand himself, and he laughed so heartily at the piece, 'without once exhibiting any signs of annoyance at the appearance of his supposed prototype', that all was forgiven—after Bunn promised to see that the vetoed lines remained unspoken.[1]

Another kind of diplomatic offence—and tactical evasion—is recorded of a burlesque in 1873, at the Strand, *Kissi-Kissi*, in which, as H. G. Hibbert says—

> Henry Corri . . . presented a faithful likeness of the Shah (of Persia), with the curious adornment of a necklace of pawn tickets. There was an immediate remonstrance, to which the management opposed the explanation that Mr Corri really couldn't help himself. He was naturally so dark, and habitually wore a moustache. What he did not habitually wear was a pair of gold-rimmed spectacles, a turban and so forth. Corri is known, in fact, to have made a careful and intimate study of the Shah.
>
> The management promised to tone down the picture, but went no further than to introduce to the stage a bucket labelled 'whitewash for Corri'.
>
> Apparently the Lord Chamberlain's office was content to have given *Kissi-Kissi* a bold advertisement . . .[2]

In 1893 the Turkish Ambassador complained to the Lord Chamberlain because 'the Sultan' was mentioned in the third act of a burlesque at the Gaiety, *Don Juan*, which thereby, as William Archer put it, 'imperilled our ancient amity with the Ottoman Empire'. Archer took the occasion to point a moral:

> 'The Sultan' promptly became 'the Pasha' and the storm blew over; but one cannot help observing that when the censorship fails to avert such incidents, it thereby nullifies the most plausible argument of its supporters. All the censorship did, in this instance, was to make the Queen and the nation officially responsible, as it were, for an error of tact which, in the absence of any such office, would have lain at the door of the individual management.[3]

[1] *The Stage*, by Alfred Bunn (1840).
[2] *Fifty Years of a Londoner's Life*, by H. G. Hibbert (1916).
[3] *The Theatrical World for 1893* (1894).

68

The censorship, in fact, so Archer argued, had 'deadened all sense of responsibility on the part of the public' and the managements.

While expert in splitting hairs or following red herrings, the Chamberlain's Office was often slow to detect the real thing when, once in a blue moon, it came into Stable Yard. Thus, in 1873, a burlesque *The Happy Land*, of which Gilbert was part-author, was staged at the Court Theatre. It included a scene in which three actors were made up to represent Gladstone and two other politicians. The Chamberlain's men had passed the political dialogue, without noticing anything suspicious, but after it reached the stage he ordered the actors to discard their make-up, while allowing them to continue with their play, which ran for two hundred performances. (According to William Archer, the 'objectionable masks were retained when the burlesque went the round of the provinces'.) This play contained only twenty-four pages when first submitted to the censor, but forty pages were acted.

Again, although the censor showed a remarkable tolerance towards a number of adaptations from the French, whose humour was by contemporary standards emphatically 'blue', he leapt into action whenever the dignity of a bishop seemed in danger. When a playwright presented a bishop as the twin-brother of a waiter, the Lord Chamberlain's sense of the social proprieties was outraged. This could not be allowed. So the author asked if he could turn the bishop into a professor; the Chamberlain agreed; and the character appeared, but only on the playbills, under his new label for he still *dressed* as a bishop. The censor did not intervene.

Gentle fun was poked at him by Gilbert and Sullivan in *Utopia Limited*, where Lord Dramaleigh—one of the 'heaven-enlightened band' who bring the riches of English wisdom to Utopia—purges the stage

> *. . . beyond a question*
> *Of risky situation and indelicate suggestion*
> *No piece is tolerated if it's costumed indiscreetly*
> CHORUS:
> *In short, this happy country has been Anglicized completely.*

Later we hear that 'the Lord Chamberlain, who has his own views as to the best means of elevating the national drama, has declined to license any play that is not in blank verse and three hundred years old—as in England'. The real Chamberlain never gave Gilbert and Sullivan themselves the slightest trouble (or so it appears) in their cautious but wideranging treatment of social and political topics. Although in one of his earlier prose works, an adaptation of *Great Expectations*, Gilbert felt

69

the censor's unmistakable touch: in a passage where Magwitch says to Pip, 'Here you are, in chambers fit for a Lord', the Examiner, always alert for profanity, had crossed out 'Lord' and substituted 'Heaven'. Or so Gilbert said. These Victorian idols were as fond of four letter words as some of their contemporary counterparts. They added to the Savoy canon a private, obscene joke-work, *The Sods' Opera*, with such characters as the Brothers Bollox, 'a pair of hangers-on', and Scrotum, 'a wrinkled old retainer'. According to Mr Norman St John Stevas,[1] 'for many years a copy of the opera was kept in the guard room at St James's Palace'—on loan from the Chamberlain's Office, perhaps.

Why did the Chamberlain license all those satirical shafts against politics, the law, the armed forces, the police and the Crown which made some euphoric critics compare the Savoy cycle with Aristophanes (as Foote had once been compared)? If he allowed recognizable caricatures of Wilde and Whistler in *Patience*, even to the point of make-up and costume,[2] then his tolerance was understandable: these were artists, and fair game. But would a less idolized author than Gilbert have been permitted to present on stage a First Lord (in H.M.S. *Pinafore*) who was immediately identified with the contemporary tenant of that office? Would anyone but the Savoy authors have been allowed to put the Chamberlain himself on public stage and, what is more, 'correctly uniformed' (according to Granville Barker)? Surely not. Yet Gilbert testified in 1909, before the committee of inquiry into the censorship, that he had experienced no interference (*The Happy Land* apart); and if there were negotiations between the Savoy partnership and the Chamberlain's men over any passages in the operas, we have no record of them. One reason was, no doubt, that Gilbert and Sullivan so rapidly became national institutions that to attack them would have been to risk a dangerous head-on collision, especially as Gilbert himself was a touchy and truculent man, who would have exploded in a storm of controversy at any attempt to meddle with his work.

No one is more timorous than your despot in dealing with popularity. And Gilbert had quickly become popular; he had a tongue and a temper moreover and the press was open to him. It was all very well

[1] *Obscenity and the Law* (1956).
[2] Urging secrecy about the production of *Iolanthe* before its premiere, D'Oyly Carte wrote in a letter: 'If it gets over to the Lord Chamberlain's Office that the sacred orders of the Garter, Thistle, Patrick and Bath are going on the stage the Office may come down bang and forbid it being done.'

to drop on Shelley, who was dead, or on Ibsen, who was a foreigner. . .
But to meddle with the twin pillar of Savoy opera, then at the height
of its success—that might be very awkward.[1]

As Granville Barker suggests, there must have been many anguished
conferences between the Examiner, the Comptroller and the Chamberlain over some passages in the Savoy operas—most of all, perhaps, in
Utopia Limited. Yet the main reasons for the immunity of Gilbert and
Sullivan were that their satire, far from being Aristophanic, was safe,
gentle, good-humoured and friendly; it came from *within* the system,
not outside it; it joked, but never jeered; it reflected, in nearly every
respect, a fundamental acceptance of Victorian society by Gilbert, a
die-hard Tory who disliked reformers, movements, philanthropists,
politicians and the working classes. What is most important of all, it was
all set to music: the Lord Chamberlain has often been disposed to let
you sing something which you cannot be permitted to say.

The Chamberlain was not always so ineffectual, however. E. F.
Smyth Pigott—who was Examiner from 1874 to 1895—described the
Office's attitude to politics in his testimony before a later committee of
inquiry:

> I have taken the liberty to ask intelligent managers to consider for
> themselves whether, in a country and community so saturated with
> politics as our own, the public would care to have places of amuse-
> ment turned into political arenas; and I have cautioned them against
> allowing the stage to be converted, by dull and impudent buffoons, at
> a loss for real wit and humour, into pillories for public men.

Mr Pigott smugly told the committee how the system worked:

> During my first year or two of official experience. I found it necessary
> to restrain (more particularly in pantomimes) an excessive licence of
> offensive personalities and of scurrilous allusions to members of the
> Royal Family . . . The restraint was so persevering and effectual,
> that . . . nothing of the kind has occurred now for years.

In the great traditions of his Office, moreover, this censor continued to
guard the interests of the Church and the susceptibilities of the faithful.
Sometimes, with familiar zeal, he advised the deletion of profane allu-

[1] *Exit Planché—Enter Gilbert*, by Harley Granville Barker, in *The Eighteen Sixties* (1932).

sions to God, Christ or Heaven, but the dramatist could not be sure that his play would pass, even if its text were immaculately inoffensive. Mr Pigott banned a play called *God and Man*, for instance, because, as he explained to the committee, 'The play was good enough, but the title was objected to. Exhibited all through London, it would have given offence to many people.'

It was Mr Pigott, perhaps, who in censoring a play called *London Life*, came to a scene in which the hero ordered a steak and a beer in an inn, and wrote in the margin: 'During Lent it would be better if the order were for a boiled egg and a glass of water.'

* * *

Outside the theatre, in the Victorian era, there was a similar suppression of free debate of sexual relationships and morality; but there was also 'an ever-widening toleration of the expression of heterodox opinion in religion and politics'—and that was conspicuously absent from the stage. The Lord Chamberlain was there to stop it. He kept the dramatist inside such a restricted terrain that, as Charles Kingsley said in 1873, 'few highly educated men now think it worth while to go to see any play, and that exactly for the same reasons that the Puritans put forward; and still fewer highly educated men think it worth while to write plays; finding that since the grosser excitements of the imagination have become forbidden themes, there is really very little to write about'.[1]

Yet although the theatre was effectively warned off the forbidden territories of religion, politics and sex, and although the censors occasionally made fools of themselves as all censors must, the Lord Chamberlain's censorship of the stage was generally believed to be all right. Parliamentary Committees in 1853, 1866 and 1892 all reported that it was working satisfactorily and should be continued. Indeed, the 1866 Committee recommended that the system should be extended 'as far as practicable to the performances in music-halls and other places of public entertainment'. Viscount Sydney, then Lord Chamberlain, told the 1866 Committee that censorship was not a hardship to authors, because they 'know pretty well what will be allowed: the only pieces that we have any difficulty with are pieces translated from the French'. Tom Taylor, the Rattigan of his day, then agreed that 'the interference is null'; and Charles Reade said 'I do not fear the present licenser', although he added: 'but I know, in fact, that it [the system] has been abused, and

---

[1] *Plays and Puritans.*

therefore it may be again'. This objection to the Chamberlain's powers still stands today.

Reade, with a score of other authors—including Dion Boucicault, Edmund Yates and F. C. Burnand—had petitioned in the previous year for the abolition of the censorship. There were objectors to the Lord Chamberlain's Office throughout the century, and to the whole idea of theatrical censorship: they included theatre managers.

Yet, as late as 1892, Clement Scott could report with reasonable accuracy that there was 'not the least' objection among playwrights to the Lord Chamberlain, and Irving, who expressed himself as 'absolutely' content with the current system, agreed, in effect, with the then Lord Chamberlain, that 'there must be some *authority* to prevent certain things being acted, because tastes differ'.

The Examiner of Plays deliberately set out, according to Mr Pigott, 'to eschew even the faintest semblance of a frivolous or vexatious interference with managers . . . to avoid all unnecessary friction'. In giving evidence before the 1853 Commission, Norman Macdonald—Superintendent of the Lord Chamberlain's department ('all matters connected with the licensing pass through my hands')—explained that: 'There are no specified rules, but the understanding is perfectly clear that unless the matter is excessively and extravagantly offensive, that the licence should not be withheld.' Champions of the system pointed to the statistics supplied by the Office, which showed that only half a dozen plays at most were banned in a year. Mr Macdonald reported in 1853 that the proportion of rejections in the past three years had been one out of 230, in 1850; five out of 228, in 1851; and three out of 225 in 1852 (two of these because of 'very offensive allusions to the Roman Catholics'—*La Dame aux Camélias* and *La Tour de Nesle*). From 1852 to 1912, on the figures given in various reports, 19,304 'stage plays' were submitted for censorship and only 103 were refused a licence.

Was Walpole right after all, then? In 1866 the censor invited the committee of inquiry to admire the wisdom of Sir Robert. He was, Mr Pigott said, really a true friend of the theatre:

> Although the somewhat trivial incident that brought about the change was of a political, and even a party character, and was used as a weapon against the Walpole administration by the opposition of the day, the change itself really constituted no infringement of the existing liberties of the stage. It was nothing more than the recognition by the state of the importance of the stage, for good or evil, as a

social influence, and of the public policy and expediency of restraining a degree of licence that might become pernicious to public manners, and subversive to public morality.

If it were not for the Lord Chamberlain and himself, explained the ineffable Mr Pigott:

> the entertainments of theatres and music halls alike would too frequently consist of more or less indecent dances, more or less obscene songs, and of occasional farces and opera bouffes, plentifully garnished with scurrilous doggerel, sparing neither Church nor State, neither religious bodies nor political institutions, neither sex nor age . . .

In fact, asked Mr Pigott, would the committee allow him to protest against the very *word* 'censor'? 'It has an invidious sound, and may be used in an invidious sense, and to many minds it represents the Star Chamber, and the Inquisition, and all manner of ancient institutions.' How unfair that was to himself and the Lord Chamberlain! For, said Mr Pigott unctuously, 'he does not pretend to be an arbiter of taste, or, as he is jestingly described, a *censor morum*':

> what is sometimes rather invidiously called a 'censorship' is nothing in effect but the friendly and perfectly disinterested action of an advisor who has the permanent interests of the stage at heart.

It was to protect those 'permanent interests of the stage' that this 'advisor' prevented English audiences from seeing the Oberammergau Passion Play and Ibsen's *Ghosts*. 'I have studied Ibsen's plays pretty carefully,' said this umpire of dramatic literature in 1892, 'and all the characters in Ibsen's plays appear to me morally deranged. All the heroines are dissatisfied spinsters who look on marriage as a monopoly, or dissatisfied married women in a chronic state of rebellion against not only the condition which nature has imposed on their sex, but against all the duties and objections of mothers and wives; and as for the men, they are all rascals or imbeciles.' There was obviously no room for *that* sort of thing on the English stage, and the censor was there to keep it at bay.

It was all quite simple, really. The Comptroller of the Lord Chamberlain's Department explained it to the 1866 Committee.

> Under 6 and 7 Vict. before a play is performed it is sent to an officer of the Lord Chamberlain's department, called the Examiner of Plays; he looks through that play, and if he sees nothing objec-

74

tionable in it, he sends, for the Lord Chamberlain's signature, a form of licence for that play; if he sees anything which is to his mind objectionable, he sends it to me, and it is then brought to the notice of the Lord Chamberlain, who gives his direction on it.

Then he refuses his licence to that play?

He refuses his licence to that play.

But he does not withdraw his licence from that theatre?

No; that play is merely banished, and there is an end of it.

That was all: it was 'merely banished'. And that was an end to it.

Yet when E. F. Smyth Pigott died in 1895, Shaw could write a long and savage obituary of him in the *Saturday Review*, in which he criticized not only the dead Examiner, and Clement Scott's defence of him, but also the censorship itself:

The late Mr Pigott is declared on all hands to have been the best reader of plays we have ever had; and yet he was a walking compendium of vulgar insular prejudice, who, after wallowing all his life in the cheapest theatrical sentiment (he was a confirmed playgoer), had at last brought himself to a pitch of incompetence which, outside the circle of those unfortunate persons who have had to try and reason with him personally, can only be measured by reading his evidence before the Commission of 1892, and the various letters of his which are just now finding their way into print. He had French immorality on the brain; he had American indecency on the brain; he had the womanly woman on the brain; he had the divorce court on the brain; he had 'not before a mixed audience' on the brain; his official career in relation to the higher drama was one long folly and panic, in which the only thing definitely discernible in a welter of intellectual confusion was his conception of the English people rushing towards an abyss of national degradation in morals and manners, and only held back on the edge of the precipice by the grasp of his strong hand . . .

It is a frightful thing to see the greatest thinkers, poets, and authors of modern Europe—men like Ibsen, Wagner, Tolstoi, and the leaders of our own literature—delivered helpless into the vulgar hands of such a noodle as this amiable old gentleman—this despised and incapable old official—most notoriously was. And just such a man as he was his successor is likely to be too, because a capable man means a known man; and a known man means one whose faults have become as public as his qualities. The appointment of Mr Archer, for instance, would awaken Mr Scott to the infamy of the Censorship as effectually

75

as the appointment of Mr Scott himself would fortify Mr Archer's case against the institution. Yet the Lord Chamberlain cannot possibly find a better man than either one or other of these gentlemen. He will therefore have to appoint a nobody whose qualifications, being unknown, can be imagined by foolish people to be infinite.[1]

Shaw's prophecy was more than usually accurate, but the 'nobody' who succeeded Mr Pigott, George Redford, proved to be even more of a noodle. 'The essence of my office and its advantage to the art and profession of the stage,' Mr Pigott had said, 'is that it is preventive and above all secret.' Mr Redford—a bank manager whose main qualification for the post appeared to be his friendship with Mr Pigott—did his best to be secret; but Shaw and the rest were too much for him, in the end.

[1] *Our Theatres in the Nineties*, Vol. 1 (1938).

6

The laws of decency and order must be administered by someone, and it is better far to check before than to correct after. The preliminary stroke of the kindly blue pencil in a tentative play or sketch is better than the spreading of objectionable matter. Hundreds of ears may be poisoned before the remedy is found . . . CLEMENT SCOTT: 1892

I said [to the Chamberlain's men], 'The play is not immoral,' and they said, 'Yes, it is.' I said, 'A play is only immoral or moral so far as its tendency is moral or immoral'; and I was told that it would be unacceptable—the subject was adultery—but if it could be made more comic, it would pass.—SIR HERBERT TREE: 1909

★ ★ ★

IN THE 1890s Shaw gave up the idea of organizing a petition against theatrical censorship to the Prime Minister from authors and managers (or so he said later) because 'nine out of ten of these victims of oppression, far from daring to offend their despot, would promptly extol him as the most salutary of English institutions, and spread themselves with unctuous flattery on the perfectly irrelevant question of his estimable personal character', just as the Lord Chamberlain's supporters have continued to do for the past sixty years.

The Chamberlain had survived so long with such relative immunity from criticism, not only because he was a managerial convenience, but because of the Puritanism of a large sector of the English public and the general sterility of the English drama. The theatre was dominated by farce, burlesque, opera bouffe and adaptations from the French; most of its artists were treated as third-class citizens; and the stage was generally still despised and neglected by the bulk of the upper and middle classes and the intelligentsia. Most serious writers kept away from the 'unholy trade', as Henry James called it. But the establishment of the long-run system during the 1870s, the recruitment of a big middle-class audience with new standards of behaviour and taste, the transformation of playhouse comfort and conditions of performance, the widening recognition of the stage by the Church, the universities, and the press—all helped

77

to give writers a broader view of the theatre as a possible instrument of self-expression, social progress and even personal gain. Organized opposition to the Lord Chamberlain began seriously only after it demonstrably became both respectable and profitable to write plays, and when it became clear that the more serious new drama was the kind that the Lord Chamberlain was most likely to mutilate or to suppress. For the first time for generations it appeared that the stage was really capable of becoming a social, moral, political and intellectual force, a powerhouse of new ideas and emotions, challenging accepted conventions and institutions. As the Examiner of Plays ruefully explained in 1909, 'there is a tendency rather to enlarge the view of the stage and there is absolutely no limit to the number of subjects that may be dealt with'.

In 1886 William Archer, indicting the censorship, said that although until then it had been 'vexatious rather than noxious' and had not, in his view, 'seriously impeded the development of English drama . . . The conditions of the times were not favourable . . . Had there been sufficient vitality and power of growth in the organism, it would long ago have burst the bonds imposed upon it'—from now on its anomalous and anachronistic power would become steadily more irksome and dangerous. 'There are indications . . . that the rising flood of modern thought will one day sweep the English drama out of the eddy in which it has so long been whirling, to carry it forward on the broad current of the age. It will then need quite other pilotage than that of a Court Censor, whose dominant desire must necessarily be to get it safely anchored in the placid pool of prejudice and convention.'[1]

At the time that Archer wrote his essay, Ibsen was still unknown to the English playgoing public. Although a version of *Pillars of Society* was staged here in 1880, it was not until the 1889 production of *A Doll's House* that the great Norwegian dramatist made an impression in England. Yet Archer's prediction proved remarkably timely. The 'flood' was rising even more rapidly than he guessed. The very next year, 1887, saw the foundation of the Théâtre Libre in Paris, as the home of the new naturalistic drama; this event kindled the establishment of the Freie Bühne in Berlin in 1889 and the Independent Theatre in London in 1891—all three play-producing societies fired by Zola, Tolstoy and, above all, Ibsen, who was acclaimed as the great realist of the drama and who showed what the modern drama could do. Inevitably, this brought

[1] In an essay for the *Westminster Review*, 'The Censorship of the Stage', later published in *About the Theatre* (1886).

his champions into a head-on collision with the man who had to decide what the modern drama could *not* do—the Lord Chamberlain.

Between 1895 and 1909, out of some eight thousand plays submitted to the Chamberlain only thirty were banned. But these included works by some of the leading writers of the age. Another thirteen or fourteen were banned temporarily, because the authors refused to 'modify' their work as the censor suggested, but licences were later granted. Many more plays were altered in pettifogging detail, at the censor's request, for apparently ludicrous reasons. Nobody knows how many were left unwritten because, as the Lord Chamberlain said in 1866, authors 'know pretty well what will be allowed'. And there is no figure for the plays which *were* written but never submitted to the Chamberlain, because he suggested, in anticipation, that it would be a waste of time. Yet it should not be forgotten that the censor did not pursue any systematic, ruthless interference with the theatre. He passed dozens of plays that he *might* have vetoed, judging by the standards he applied to those he *did* ban. It was in fact the unpredictable, inconsistent, arbitrary character of the censorship which did so much to inflame its enemies.

Five years after Archer's essay, moreover, it at last became practicable to print plays without running the risk of American piracy and the theatre caught up with literature in the legal protection of authors' work. The American Copyright Act was passed in 1891 and soon afterwards both Arthur Pinero and Henry Arthur Jones, the leading dramatists of the day, began to issue collected editions—a sign of the new power and status of their profession. Some plays became widely known before production, and the banning of their performances by the censor promoted their sale in print. In this way the Lord Chamberlain helped Shaw to become a household word. The very appearance of the new plays for reading was a sign of change in the dramatist's status and an ill omen for the censor. As John Palmer said, 'The old acting edition was not intended to be read. . . . It conspicuously asserted that the contemporary English drama was unworthy to be printed', and 'the root assumption of the Lord Chamberlain's jurisdiction is that anything fit to print was unfit for a play'.

One curious practice, loaded with the moral ambiguities still characteristic of the Lord Chamberlain's Office, developed at this time. Since the Dramatic Copyright Act of 1883, it was believed (though not proved in law) that the dramatist lost his rights in a play if it was published before it was staged. If a public production had not been arranged before publication, the author contrived what was known as a 'copyright performance', so that he could print his plays as soon as they were written. Through a manager he obtained a licence from the Lord Chamberlain and gave one reading—often with his friends as the cast—without costumes or scenery. One bill was printed and displayed outside the theatre or hall during the performance so that it was technically public and anyone passing could see it by paying at the door. One paying customer—no more was needed—was admitted for a guinea. He was usually another friend of the author, who privately refunded him the price of the ticket and kept both the box office return of the guinea and the bill as evidence of performance. But what if the Chamberlain refused a licence? Then, in a strange pact of mutual humbug, the author submitted the play mutilated in the way required by the Chamberlain, and the Chamberlain solemnly licensed it, although both knew perfectly well that the text he was approving would be given only one performance, to one person, and would never be staged again. Shaw's *Mrs Warren's Profession* for instance, was 'licensed' over thirty years before it was given a public performance, but the text then licensed for one 'copyright performance' at the Victoria Hall in Bayswater omitted the entire second act and transformed Mrs Warren's profession from brothel-keeper into 'female Fagin', as Shaw put it. This hypocrisy went on until the Copyright Act of 1911.

As talented new actors, writers, critics and designers were drawn into the theatre, and as new play-producing organizations and managements sprang up, so the anti-censorship forces increased in the twenty years after Archer's 1886 essay. When the Chamberlain refused to license a passage, or the play as a whole, the authors made a fuss. They enlisted the support of journalists, politicians and novelists. They organized 'private' performances, and published the texts with satirical and protesting prefaces. Sometimes the literary and dramatic virtue of these texts seems exaggerated to our eyes, but propagandist zeal apart, their authors loomed up on the late Victorian and Edwardian scene as genuine martyrs and this martyrdom lent them a temporary splendour. The debate was fundamentally about the *principle* of censorship. The fact that not all the victims were masterpieces was, and is, irrelevant. Yet the censor often defended his bans by pointing out that this or that play was not a commercial success, or had received a bad press.

Open opposition began in 1886 over the right to present on the public stage a seventy-year-old play by one of England's greatest poets. Shelley's poetic melodrama *The Cenci*, written in 1819, had never been staged, although Genevieve Ward had long wanted to play the central figure of Beatrice, the sixteenth-century Italian whose evil father conceives an incestuous passion for her and who plots his murder with her brother and stepmother. Shelley himself underrated the explosiveness of the plot he chose. Sending it to Peacock from Italy in 1820, he explained that he had 'touched very delicately' on the 'chief circumstance'.

> My principal doubt as to whether it would succeed as an acting play hangs entirely on the question as to whether any such a thing as incest in this shape however treated would be admitted on the stage—I think however it will form no objection, considering first that the facts are matters of history, and secondly the peculiar delicacy with which I have treated it.[1]

He wanted Miss O'Neill and Kean to play it and intended it to be staged pseudonymously. If it succeeded, he said, he would 'use the celebrity it might acquire' for his own purposes. But the manager of Covent Garden thought it so indecent that he refused to submit it for a licence or to contemplate a production, and nobody else would consider it. 'I confess I cannot approve of the squeamishness which excludes the exhibition of such *subjects* from the scene', said Shelley. Because of this sexually scandalous topic, no matter how unsensationally and indeed undramatically it was treated, *The Cenci* was considered unfit for the stage by the censor and by such critics as Clement Scott of the *Daily Telegraph* ('hideous', he called it. Shaw called it 'an abomination', but he was speaking of its theatrical deficiencies—to the Shelley Society). In January 1886, the Shelley Society formed, with the production of *The Cenci* as one of its main objects; and in May it decided to circumvent the Lord Chamberlain by announcing a 'private' matinee performance, to which 'members' were invited, at the Grand Theatre, Islington. Browning, Meredith and James Russell Lowell were among those who joined the society for the occasion. The critics were impressed only by the action and the fashionable audience. *The Times* observed that by this production the society had 'effectively demolished its pretensions as a play'. The Lord Chamberlain was not pleased. When, later in the year, the owner of the Islington theatre had to apply for the renewal of his annual licence he was said to have been left in no doubt that any recurrence of this impertinence would mean that his theatre would be closed. A clause was later inserted in the Grand's lease stipulating that no performance of unlicensed plays should be given there.

---

[1] *The Letters of Percy Bysshe Shelley*, edited by F. L. Jones (1964).

This apparent threat was manifest or, at any rate, widely believed. In Shaw's words, 'no manager dared lend or let his theatre' for a later performance of *The Cenci*.

The terror was so complete that a manager who, not realizing his risk, had discussed quite favourably the possibility of placing his house at the disposal of the (Shelley) Society was compelled to write to the press vehemently denying that he had ever contemplated such an enormity, although his letters were in the hands of the very person he was publicly contradicting.

Six years later the manager of the Avenue, 'having nothing to lose', he said, as he was shortly giving up the lease, offered it to the Shelley Society for another 'private' showing. But it was not until 1922 that *The Cenci* was licensed for public performance.

The 1886 ban raised a theatrical storm, even though it was still only one in a matinee teacup. 'To veto *The Cenci* is to degrade English literature and insult the English public,' Archer wrote in 1886 and he predicted that the ban would 'one day prove to be a large nail in the coffin of the censorship'. This was not quite accurate, but it was listed as one of the censor's main crimes in the campaign twenty years later to abolish the Lord Chamberlain's powers over the drama. Moreover, in spite of the Chamberlain's obvious displeasure, the method of performance showed a way of putting censored plays on the stage. It was copied by the Independent Theatre, which not only pioneered the production of Ibsen—for members and their guests—but also introduced Shaw to the stage, and so, incidentally, raised up one of the most powerful enemies of the Lord Chamberlain. The Shelley Society method was followed by several other play-producing societies—notably the Stage Society, which was the first to give 'club' performances on Sundays (and indeed, the first to stage plays on a Sunday for two hundred years). In time, this led to permanent 'club' theatres, in which performances were given only to members. Even though this was widely recognized as an open defiance of the Chamberlain, it was one in which he acquiesced.

It took a Dutchman, J. T. Grein, to launch the challenge to the censor, and an Irishman, George Bernard Shaw, to back it up with plays. Both were dramatic critics. Grein, then twenty-nine, resolved to inaugurate his Independent Theatre Society with *Ghosts* (as the Freie Bühne had done) although he knew that it would be vetoed by the Lord Chamberlain. He was, it seems, a friend of the Examiner, Mr Pigott, who had said to him in horror: 'Never come to me with *Ghosts*. It is a waste of time to ask for a licence.' Grein did not: he expected trouble; and he met it right from the beginning, for he found it difficult to get a theatre for the purpose. At last, he was offered the Royalty for a night, in March 1891, by a proprietress who braved the anti-Ibsen opposition. Leading the reactionary pack, the *Daily Telegraph* demanded that the Lord Chamberlain should intervene and stop such disgraceful behaviour, but the worried owner was assured by the Chamberlain's Office—puzzlingly co-operative in spite of their attitude to *The Cenci*—that the performance, in their eyes, did not exist, as long as it remained legally a private one, attended only by members of the society and their guests. The precedent was confirmed.

By the time Ibsen's *Ghosts* was staged in this way at the Royalty, he had written *Peer Gynt*, *Pillars of Society*, *A Doll's House*, *Enemy of the People*, *The Wild Duck*, *Rosmersholm*, *Hedda Gabler* and other plays. Yet he was still treated by many English critics as a provincial pornographer. True, Ibsen's own compatriots had ignored *Ghosts* at first. It took thirteen years before a second edition was published in Norway and the first performance in its original language was given in Chicago in 1882, by a Danish-Norwegian company. It was banned for a while in Germany, but within three or four years it was established in Scandinavia. In England the reaction against it was unusually hysterical, violent and persistent. The Examiner's view of Ibsen in 1892 (see page 74) may seem stupid and ignorant, but it was shared by some members of the public and by a number of critics, notably by their doyen, the blimpish but influential Clement Scott, who compared Ibsen to a raven 'with an insatiable appetite for decayed flesh' and the play to 'an open drain; a loathsome sore unbandaged; a dirty act done publicly'. It was the censor who had the last word on *Ghosts*. Mr Pigott disapproved of Ibsen, and so one of Ibsen's best plays was banned for years from the English public stage. His successor, Mr Redford, thought no better of it. He declared as late as 1909 that *Ghosts* would *never* be staged. But five years later, another of the Chamberlain's men, a former drama critic of the *Observer*, was especially invited to a private performance of *Ghosts* and was so impressed that he encouraged J. T. Grein to submit it again and got the play through in four weeks, over thirty years after it was written.

No other Ibsen play was vetoed by the Chamberlain. But if the great Norwegian had not been armoured with an international reputation and defended by such aggressive and eloquent partisans *Ghosts* would surely not have been the only victim. And it seems likely that Ibsen's career would have come to a full stop if he had been an English writer, obliged to work under a censorship as inhibiting and restrictive as ours.

Several other distinguished foreign writers living at the turn of the century suffered at the hands of the Lord Chamberlain, who sometimes banned plays which had already been widely staged abroad. Tolstoy's *The Power of Darkness* seemed to the censor merely a sordid recitation of crime and immorality. He was blind to the play's moral purpose until it was explained to him after a 'private' performance by the Stage Society in 1904. He then granted a licence, under pressure. But no such quick reprieve was given to Maeterlinck's *Monna Vanna*: a play which in its time had an international vogue, although it has long since sunk into the limbo where most of the fashionable hits and long-runners quickly find oblivion.

In 1902 Lugné-Poe and his Théâtre de l'Oeuvre were unexpectedly obliged to give three London matinees of *Monna Vanna* as private performances, because the censor condemned the play's 'immorality of plot' (even though it was in French, and thus out of the servants' reach) and he upheld his judgement that it was 'not proper for the stage' before the parliamentary inquiry of 1909. His objection was rooted in a stage direction: to save the lives of her fellow-citizens defeated in war, the heroine, Monna Vanna, acquiesces in the demand of the victorious general that she should go to his tent at night, 'nude under her mantle'. But the general, Prinzivalle, was her boyhood sweetheart. He grants mercy to the city without exacting any price from her. He goes back with the unscathed Monna Vanna to avoid being killed by his own countrymen and, later, wins the heroine from her husband whose possessive love is less noble in her eyes than Prinzivalle's. It was that nakedness under the mantle that appalled the censor. Even though, as he agreed in 1909, we were *all* naked under our clothes, we did not all have improper sexual conduct in mind. One of the aspects of the case which exacerbated the feelings of the censor's enemies was that he had licensed a demonstrably bad play, *The Devil*, which included a very similar episode. Mr Redford made matters even worse at the 1909 inquiry when he explained that whereas *Monna Vanna* was a 'literary work', *The Devil* was 'a flamboyant, lurid piece of stage business'— which apparently made it all right. As in the case of Shelley, a special society was formed to stage the play (in June 1902). The result was that it was probably seen, as Henry Arthur Jones said, 'by four times the number of people who would have seen it if the censor had licensed it'. A protest was made in *The Times*, signed by Hardy, Meredith, Swinburne and many others, and more ammunition against the censorship was provided for the growing campaign. *Monna Vanna* was licensed twelve years later, just after *Ghosts* passed the Lord Chamberlain.

Another 'immoral play' came before the censor's ever-watchful eye in 1903, when he put two world figures in their place by forbidding Duse to present D'Annunzio's *La Città Morta*. This attempt at modern Greek tragedy was staged throughout the world without moral outrage, although it was attacked on aesthetic grounds. But to our Examiner of Plays it was unthinkable that a character should conceive an incestuous passion for his sister, even if he decides to kill her rather than indulge it, even if he *is* speaking in a foreign language.

The censorship's obsession with the protection of the Bible—the Examiner would not even *read* any adaptation from the Scriptures—prompted the veto of several outstanding plays from abroad. One was Sudermann's *Johannes*, a version of John the Baptist's story which Forbes-Robertson proposed to stage. Another was Rostand's *La Samaritaine* (1897), a Biblical poem in tableaux rather than a play, in which Sarah Bernhardt made one of her greatest successes as Photine, the woman of Samaria, converted by the teaching of Jesus. The great Jewish actress showed a religious fervour which, critics said, 'touched on the sublime', and she revived the play every Easter for many years at her Paris theatre, the Sarah Bernhardt. Yet it could not be seen in England, whatever the eminence of the author, the greatness of the actress and the piety of the theme because it presented Christ on the public stage. The performance in German of Hauptmann's *Hannele* was only permitted if 'the Stranger' in no way resembled any picture of Christ, and before it could be staged in English, the manager had to agree that the Stranger would be clean-shaven. Beards looked blasphemous to St James's Palace.

Eugene Brieux suffered most from the pre-1914 censorship of the English stage, no doubt because he seemed, in Shaw's words, 'a ruthless revealer of hidden truth and a mighty destroyer of idols'. Few people would agree today with Shaw's eulogy in 1909 that Brieux was then 'the most important dramatist west of Russia', and 'incomparably the greatest writer France has produced since Molière'. Even then, this was a minority verdict. But Brieux—a graduate of the Théâtre Libre—enjoyed a stormy international reputation. He helped to defeat the official censorship of plays in France, which was abolished in 1905 and his kind of moralizing, crusading, dramatic journalism needed instant communication. Plays of this kind can't keep. They are even more perishable than the best of the 'theatre of comfort' of their time.

For varying periods the Lord Chamberlain suppressed four outstanding plays of the fourteen which Brieux wrote to teach society a lesson. Had he not won an international reputation and been elected to the Académie française, it might have taken even longer to win a hearing for these works. The quickest to gain a reprieve was *Les Hannetons*. In 1907 the Chamberlain objected to its 'bold and outspoken indecencies', which turned out, in sober fact, to be a line spoken to a man by his mistress: 'The first time we met, I told you I'd had a lover: that was a lie.' The Stage Society refused to amend the offending phrase, but when a manager submitted another translation to the Chamberlain, he agreed to a revision—'The first time we met, I told you I'd not been straight: that was a lie'—and the play was staged.

It took longer to get licences for the other Brieux plays introduced to England in 1906–7 and banned by the censor. *Les Trois Filles de Madame Dupont*, an attack on marriage-broking morality among the middle classes, was vetoed because it broke the taboo on the subject of birth control. Brieux indicted the way in which society sanctioned the husband's right to deny children to his wife, while using her as a mistress and a housekeeper. The play was finally passed for public consumption in 1917, twenty years after its first production in Paris; but *Maternité*—which was banned in 1906, 1918 and 1924—was not finally licensed until 1932, nearly thirty years after it was written, and then only on condition that the management omitted a struggle between the husband and wife and that the audience could not see the bed off-stage to which he carried her, while she brought down the curtain with her protesting cries of 'The cave man! The cave man!'

Maternité was first translated by Mrs Shaw. Her enthusiasm for it fired her fellow-members of the Stage Society's executive committee; but when in 1907 it was sent to the Chamberlain, it rapidly came back with a note: 'Inform whoever is responsible for the play that it will *never* be licensed in England.' The Examiner of Plays was clearly fond of pronouncing these sentences of doom. In his eyes, the sin of *Maternité* was that it approached the topic of birth control—or 'Malthusianism', as it was delicately called—from the other side in arguing the right of

86

wives to *refuse* to have children whom they cannot afford to bring up, or who may be the victims of hereditary disease.

The most famous of Brieux's plays was *Damaged Goods* (1902)—*Les Avariés*—because of its attempt to broach the topic of venereal disease. The point of the play was that it was precisely the conspiracy of silence which helped to spread the disease through ignorance, not immorality. The conspiracy was still so strong, however, that it was not until 1911 that it was possible even to *print* the play, in *Three Plays by Eugene Brieux*. Earlier, Mrs Shaw admitted, 'we none of us had . . . quite sufficient courage' to stage it, and publishers jibbed at issuing it in book form. On this occasion the Lord Chamberlain reflected accurately enough the feeling of the public, although this did not mean, any more than it does today, that the play should therefore have been banned. Within a few years, as venereal disease crippled thousands of soldiers in the Great War, many of the objectors may well have wished that it had been more widely shown in time. Not until 1914 was it staged, through the efforts of two crusading Americans, Mr and Mrs George Baxter. Some leading papers then refused to send their critics. The play opened, at the author's request, with a warning from the manager that it was about syphilis:

> It contains no scenes to provoke scandal or arouse disgust, nor is there in it any obscene word, and it may be witnessed by anyone, unless we must believe that folly and ignorance are necessary conditions of female virtue.

Male virtue, too, was in question. Soon after, when war broke out, *Damaged Goods* was toured among the troops, as a kind of educational first aid.

It was not only contemporary Continentals who incurred the Chamberlain's displeasure: Sophocles did not fit in with his conception of what was right and proper for the English stage, and *Oedipus Rex* was vetoed for many years. On two occasions Sir John Martin-Harvey tried to get a version of this masterpiece past the censor. First, fired by a reproduction of a bust of the great French tragedian Mounet-Sully in the role, he commissioned W. L. Courtney, one of the leading drama critics of his time, to write a free version of the story, including the events which Sophocles keeps off-stage. When submitted to the Lord Chamberlain in 1911, it was banned. That was that. The veto was accepted. Some years later when Max Reinhardt made a name in London, Martin-Harvey heard that his production of Hugo von

Hofmannsthal's *Oedipus* had been a hit in Berlin. A star 'illusionist' and animal-trainer of the time, 'the Great Lafayette', saw it and was so impressed that he offered to finance a London production with Martin-Harvey in the leading role. Then a new translation by Gilbert Murray was published, Courtney's version was shelved with his own warm agreement, and a press campaign began to shake the Chamberlain out of his absurdly untenable position.

'Extreme pressure was brought to bear upon him,' says Martin-Harvey in his autobiography, 'and finally, after endless parleys and the appointments of some mysterious "advisory committee", the ban was lifted and Murray's translation was freed.'[1] It is worth noting that a year later, in spite of the licence, the brother of the Examiner of Plays vetoed the play's performance in the theatre he owned in Cardiff, so Martin-Harvey staged it there in a local hall.

Although the Chamberlain was no respecter of foreign dramatists, however venerated, his exaggerated regard for the representatives of foreign powers, however obscure, has provided some of the prime examples in the censorship *sottisier*. The case of the Lola Montes play, mentioned in an earlier chapter, is surpassed in absurdity by his ban on *The Mikado* in 1907, over twenty years after its first production, because he thought it might give offence to our Japanese allies, whose Crown Prince was then visiting England and whose warships in the Medway were playing selections from the operetta (a Japanese favourite). According to Gilbert, 'I was not communicated with by the Lord Chamberlain, there was no preliminary correspondence—there was some afterwards—he simply took my property and laid an embargo upon it.' This was an autocratic action by Lord Althorp, then Lord Chamberlain, who acted above the Examiner's head; and in spite of the outcry he did not take off the ban until the following year. He was unmoved by the appeals of Mrs D'Oyly Carte, who, said Gilbert, was 'at the Lord Chamberlain's weeping for two hours on end'.

Again, a provincial melodrama *The Secrets of the Harem* had been touring for several years when its licence was suddenly withdrawn without explanation at a moment's notice. The management lost several thousand pounds and a whole company was put out of work. The reason for this ukase was that the representative of a foreign potentate objected to the play. In other words, an official of the Turkish Embassy thought it was in poor taste. Not until several questions were asked in Parliament

[1] *The Autobiography of Sir John Martin-Harvey* (1933).

did the Chamberlain both explain and relent, but only on the understanding that the word 'Harem' in the title should be omitted to protect
the susceptibilities of the Turks. From then onwards, it was billed as
Secrets -- -- --- -- ----. 'It need hardly be said that in its revised
form the title was fifty times more suggestive and offensive than in the
original, and the blank spaces of the poster became an attractive goal
for the obscenities of passing schoolboys.'[1]

Sir Henry Irving was the victim in another instance of the censor's
exaggerated concern for the feelings of our Middle East allies. Irving
had wanted for some years to play the role of Mahomet. He believed
that in Hall Caine he had found the right author. Caine produced a
scenario. Then the fact leaked out. 'None of us had the slightest idea that
there *could* be any objection in a professedly Christian nation to a play
on the subject,' said Irving's manager, Bram Stoker. Nevertheless they
received a letter from the Chamberlain's Office, asking for the play to be
dropped because 'protest had been made by a large number of our
Mahometan fellow subjects. The Mahometan faith holds it sacrilege to
represent in any form the image of the Prophet'. In giving evidence to
the 1892 Select Committee, Irving, who supported the censorship in
general, said these reasons 'certainly never had occurred to me'. 'We
can only wonder,' commented Fowell and Palmer, 'why pork was not
prohibited to the English Army for a similar reason . . .' Shaw, too,
wanted to dramatize Mahomet's life, but knowledge of the Chamberlain's attitude deterred him.

What made this censorial care for friendly powers so especially absurd
was that there was nothing but the audience to stop music-hall singers
and comedians from being very offensive to as many foreign states as
they pleased, as long as they kept within the bounds of decency; and
even in the theatre lines which, when licensed, seemed certifiably
fireproof could in changing political circumstances set the house ablaze
for a moment, without disturbing the public peace or the balance of
power in Europe.

Not only in the matter of morality, but in politics, religion and the
general realm of ideas, the Chamberlain's Office continued to be
inspired by the example of Mr Podsnap.

A certain institution in Mr Podsnap's mind which he called 'the
young person' may be considered to have been embodied in Miss
Podsnap, his daughter. It was an inconvenient and exacting institution,

[1] Fowell and Palmer.

89

as requiring everything in the universe to be filed down and fitted to it. The question about everything was, would it bring a blush into the cheeks of the young person? And the inconvenience of the young person was that, according to Mr Podsnap, she seemed always liable to burst into blushes when there was no need at all. There appeared to be no line of demarcation between the young person's excessive innocence and another person's guiltiest knowledge.

7

The Act of 1843 is a permanent Coercion Act for the theatre, a permanent suspension of the Habeas Corpus Act as far as plays are concerned, a permanent proclamation of martial law with a single official substituted for a court martial.—BERNARD SHAW

If it come to prohibiting, there is not aught more likely to be prohibited than truth itself: whose first appearance to our eyes bleared and dimmed with prejudice and custom, is more unsyghtly and plausible than many errors.—JOHN MILTON

* * *

SHAW was the outstanding British writer to suffer from the Lord Chamberlain, and to take arms against him. As a drama critic on the *Saturday Review*, he had maintained a steady fire against the censorship; as a playwright he leapt into personal conflict with it. Although he had to jettison ideas for plays, like the one on Mahomet, because they would have been unacceptable to the Chamberlain, only three of the fifty-three plays he wrote were refused a licence. Yet these three had, in their time, a notable influence on the censorship. Each of them broke a different taboo, in the perilous areas of sex, religion, and the representation of 'personalities'. I will deal with two of them at the end of this chapter. It was with his third play *Mrs Warren's Profession* in 1894 that Shaw first clashed, as a dramatist, with the Lord Chamberlain.

Even if it had been licensed, Shaw admitted, it would not at that time have been staged by any British manager. As Eric Bentley says, 'it is hard to see how Shaw could more boldly have affronted Victorian values'[1] than with this attack upon the roots of middle-class morality. The censor was horrified not only by the exposure of prostitution and by Shaw's diagnosis that society was to blame for it, but also by the implication of the possibility of incest in the revelation that the heroine, Vivie, is the half-sister of her boy-friend Frank and in the momentary but explicit flirtation of Mrs Warren with Frank, whom she knows to be her half-son,

[1] *Bernard Shaw* (1950).

as it were. Shaw realized from the start that he would not get a licence. At first he thought of arranging a performance in Ireland, but then he decided to take the usual course and persuaded a manager to submit the play to the Chamberlain's Office. When the Examiner replied, predictably, that he was unable to recommend it for a licence Shaw asked, 'Could this case be dealt with by the blue pencil?', suggesting—with tongue in cheek—a 'drastic expurgation' which would eliminate the second act and all reference to the exact nature of Mrs Warren's profession, in order to secure a licence for a 'copyright performance'. With restraint Mr Redford replied: 'Most certainly it is not for me to attempt any "drastic expurgation" with the blue pencil, as you appear to suggest. It is for you to submit, or cause to be submitted, a licensable play, and if you do this I will endeavour to forget that I ever read the original.'

Shaw made his own revised version for the copyright performance, which was duly licensed. But it was not till 1902 that two performances of the full text were given in London (by the Stage Society), and then only after over a dozen theatres, two music-halls, three hotels and two art galleries had refused to harbour the play on the premises, some of them withdrawing at the last moment. The Independent Theatre itself would not handle it. J. T. Grein and William Archer, Shaw's allies in the camp of the new drama, were shocked by the play. 'He could not touch pitch without wallowing in it', said Archer; and Grein described the performance as 'unnecessary and painful'.

It was an exceedingly uncomfortable afternoon. For there was a majority of women to listen to that which could only be understood by a minority of men . . . Even men need not know all the ugliness that lies below the surface of everyday life. To some male minds too much knowledge of the seamy side is poisonous, for it leads to pessimism, that pioneer of insanity and suicide.

Not until 1925 was *Mrs Warren's Profession* given a public performance in London, thirty-three years after it was written.

Shortly before it was banned the Lord Chamberlain initiated the ludicrous chain of events which might be described as the Salomé Serial. Oscar Wilde wrote *Salomé* in 1891, in French. According to one story, he wrote it with an eye on the Comédie française; according to another, for performance in Paris at Paul Fort's Théâtre d'Art, the temple of the poetic play set up in opposition to the naturalist drama of the Théâtre Libre. But the temple closed before the play could open.

It seems more likely that he wrote it without any thought of the stage, but Sarah Bernhardt heard about it, asked Wilde to read it to her and prepared a production in London at the Palace Theatre. Nobody had applied in advance for a licence, although, as Hesketh Pearson suggests, Wilde must surely have known that there was a danger that it would be refused since it offended against the ruling that characters from the Scriptures must not be presented on the stage. Rehearsals had been in progress for three weeks when the censor's veto was announced. Sarah was furious with Wilde and the Chamberlain. Wilde was so incensed with everyone that he announced that he was going to become a Frenchman, 'since it is impossible to have a work of art performed in England'. The month after the ban Wilde wrote to William Rothenstein:

> The licenser of plays is nominally the Lord Chamberlain, but really a commonplace official—in the present case a Mr Pigott, who panders to the vulgarity and hypocrisy of the English people, by licensing every low farce and vulgar melodrama. He even allows the stage to be used for the purpose of the caricaturing of the personalities of artists, and at the same moment when he prohibited *Salomé,* he licensed a burlesque of *Lady Windermere's Fan,* in which an actor dressed up like me and imitated my voice and manner ! ! ![1]

This was a musical travesty at the Comedy, called *The Poet and the Puppets* with Hawtrey as Wilde, written by J. M. Glover and Charles Brookfield, who was to figure prominently in Wilde's life and in the history of the censorship a few years later. What Wilde did *not* tell Rothenstein was that when he heard of the proposal to burlesque him, he appealed to the 'commonplace official' and insisted that Brookfield and Glover must read the play to him. This they did, 'while cigars burned, the poet puffed, and punctuated each page as it was read with such phrases as: "Delightful!" "Charming, my old friends!" "It's exquisite!" etc., etc.'[2] It included verses like this:

> *They may bubble with jest at the way that I'm dressed*
> *They may scoff at the length of my hair,*
> *They may say that I'm vain, overbearing, inane,*
> *And object to the flowers that I wear.*
> *They may laugh till they're ill, but the fact remains still*

[1] *The Letters of Oscar Wilde,* edited by Rupert Hart-Davis (1962).
[2] *Jimmy Glover His Book,* by James M. Glover (1911).

A fact I've proclaimed since a child.
That's taken, my dears, nearly two thousand years
To make Oscar O'Flaherty—Wilde.

At Wilde's insistence, the last line was changed to:

To make Neighbour O'Flaherty's child.

It was curious, to say the least, that—as William Archer wrote:

A serious work of art, accepted, studied and rehearsed by the greatest actress of our time, is peremptorily suppressed, at this very moment when the personality of its author is being held up to ridicule, night after night, with the full sanction and approval of Statutory Infallibility.

Wilde was also caricatured in other plays of the period: by Beerbohm Tree in *Where's the Cat?*, *The Colonel* and *The Charlatan*. The character of Bunthorne in *Patience*, too, was recognized as an indirect presentation of Wilde's personality. Later, Wilde wrote:

The curious thing is this: all the arts are free in England, except the actor's art; it is held by the censor that the stage degrades and that actors desecrate fine subjects, so the Censor prohibits not the publication of *Salomé* but its production. Yet not one single actor has protested against this insult to the stage . . . This shows how few actors are artists. All the *dramatic* critics, except Archer of the *World*, agree with the Censor that there should be a censorship over actors and acting. This shows how bad our stage must be . . .[1]

Because of the notoriety which Wilde acquired soon afterwards, it was assumed by the general public (if they thought about it at all) that *Salomé* had been banned because of its obscenity. This seemed all the more likely because the censor's hitherto slender religious tolerance soon afterwards extended to the presentation of Christ as a butler in one play and a lodger in another—*The Passing of the Third Floor Back*. As one critic said, he seemed to work on the principle that you could call your leading character Christ outside the theatre, but not inside. This tolerance also permitted adaptations of the Salomé story in two operas within a few years. The first was Massenet's *Herodiade*, which was retitled *Salomé* for its Covent Garden performance (in French) in

[1] *The Letters of Oscar Wilde* (1962).

1904, but out of respect for the censor's scriptural obsession the action was moved to Ethiopia and several names were tactfully changed, notably those of Herod and Herodias, who emerged as Moreame and Hésotoade. In this more decorous version of the tale Salomé begs for 'Jean's' life against the demands of her mother, the Romans and the King. When her plea fails, she asks to be killed with him, and when his execution is announced she rushes forward to stab her mother but kills herself instead. The other was Strauss's *Salomé*, which used the banned Wilde play as the basis of its libretto. Its Covent Garden production in 1910 was permitted only after a personal appeal to the Prime Minister by Sir Thomas Beecham who put it on, and careful bowdlerizing of the story so that John the Baptist—whose presence on the stage was the main affront to the Chamberlain's sense of propriety—was called, simply, The Prophet; and other 'safeguards', as the censor called them, were contrived—notably, the elimination of The Prophet's head on a platter (served to music). In the event, as Sir Thomas Beecham described it in his autobiography, *A Mingled Chime*, the Covent Garden cast slipped unconsciously back into the original, inflammatory text— *and nobody noticed*. On the contrary, the Chamberlain himself congratulated Beecham for the way in which he had met all the censor's demands. But *Salomé* sans music remained on the black list.

Salomé was acclaimed as a masterpiece before the 1914 war throughout Europe, ever since its Paris premiere in 1896 (when Wilde was in prison) and the profits it made helped largely to rescue his estate from bankruptcy; but in England it was known only in print. It was published in Paris in 1893 with inapt illustrations by Aubrey Beardsley, which helped to keep the play embalmed in a legend of mysterious pornography. *Salomé*'s reputation for decadence, sacrilege, and general corruption was not improved by the curious events in 1918 when J. T. Grein planned a private production of the play in aid of war charities with the famous dancer Maud Allan in the leading role. During preparations for the production a newsletter *The Vigilante*—run by a somewhat shady M.P. and publicist, Noel Pemberton Billing—featured a paragraph linking it with 'several thousands of the first 47,000'. This referred to Pemberton Billing's 'discovery' of a secret dossier compiled by the Germans of over 47,000 prominent men and women whose moral, sexual and financial weaknesses would, he said, expose them to the pressure of German agents, who could blackmail them into treason. Only potential traitors, it was implied, would want to see a decadent play by Wilde. This legendary document was known as the Black Book.

When Grein sued for libel, Pemberton Billing was acquitted after a stormy trial and *Salomé* was, in effect, condemned as both indecent and unpatriotic. Grein, who had done so much for the English theatre, was 'crippled financially', as his wife records.[1] He was 'dropped overboard' by the Ministry of Information. And when he offered his resignation as drama critic of the *Sunday Times* it was immediately and disgracefully accepted.

Clearly, it was the thread of incest running through the play that made the Chamberlain continue to refuse a licence until 1931, long after the old rigid ruling about dramatizing Scriptural subjects had been relaxed. Herod, the Tetrarch, heavily fancied his step-daughter. After all, it was for him, against her mother's repeated wishes, that Salomé did the Dance of the Seven Veils; and her sudden murder at Herod's command may have appeared in St James's Palace not quite so much the retribution of the Almighty as the spite of a jealous, would-be incestuous stepfather.

Scriptural trespassing was again given as the reason for the censor's ban in 1902 on *Bethlehem*, a nativity play by another distinguished man of letters, Laurence Housman, who suffered more than any dramatist from the Lord Chamberlain's Office during his long and varied writing life, because he had the misfortune to write plays about the Holy Family *and* the Royal Family, to whose joint defence the Lords Chamberlain were, and still are, deeply committed. There was no detail in *Bethlehem* to which the censor objected. It was the *subject*. Mr Redford explained that he had 'no power ... to make any exception to the rule that Scriptural plays, or plays founded on or adapted from the Scriptures, are ineligible for licence in Great Britain'. That was that. Or was it? After all, a year earlier a play had been licensed in which the Almighty Himself not only appeared on the stage but *spoke*. There had been no riots, no demonstrations, no 'breach of good manners, decorum or the public peace', let alone a stroke of lightning—when *Everyman* was produced. Admittedly, it was written before the institution of the censorship, but why, sceptics asked, should an Act of Parliament inhibit an Act of God? Moreover, soon after the banning of *Bethlehem* another nativity play, Florence Buckton's *Eager Heart*, was licensed by St James's Palace without question. When Mr Redford was asked to explain this apparent contradiction, before the investigating committee of 1909, he said that *Eager Heart* was a 'very simple little imitation of a

---

[1] *J. T. Grein*, by Michael Orme (1936).

miracle play', and that it 'was done at Christmas'. To him these appeared conclusive reasons. To other people the censorship was more than ever a puzzlement. Even more so when the puzzle was explained.

Ten years after the ban, Housman tried again, through Gertrude Kingston, who built the Little Theatre in London. When she applied for a licence she was rebutted with the traditional explanation that the Holy Family was forbidden to be presented on stage. But, as she pointed out, It had appeared in *Eager Heart*. The censor at first denied this, says Housman in his autobiography:

> but the text of the play convicted him; inattentively he had given a passport to the Holy Family, because it had come upon the scene in peasant-disguise. He then fell back for defence upon the fact that in *Eager Heart* the Holy Family did not speak. To that I nailed him: if I so arranged matters that in *Bethlehem* our Lady should remain speechless, would he grant a licence? He could do no other than say yes. And so, for the next five years, with an 'Earth-Angel' standing by as interpreter, the not-to-be-spoken words were spoken; public performance was permitted, and once (I think it was at Peterborough) a bishop came before the curtain and spoke the prologue.
>
> Then another fortunate thing happened. Rutland Boughton took one of the old mystery plays, set it to music, and without question it was publicly performed. Apparently the old medieval play had, like *Everyman* (in which the Deity Himself appears), common law rights which the censor could not over-ride. But in Boughton's *Bethlehem*, our Lady not only spoke, but—being accused by Joseph of improper conduct—answered him back handsomely. Again I approached the censor, and having set the facts before him had the satisfaction of making him at last climb down from an untenable position.[1]

The next big case against the censorship was not on religious but on sexual-political grounds. In 1907 Harley Granville Barker's *Waste* was banned, because the author refused to make the changes requested by the Examiner. These requirements were not specific. When asked to elucidate them, Mr Redford said that it was 'not necessary . . . to indicate particular lines', but that Barker 'must be prepared to moderate and modify the extremely outspoken reference to the sexual relations' between the hero and a married woman, and that he should also 'eliminate entirely all reference to a criminal operation' (the woman

---

[1] *The Unexpected Years* (1937).

becomes pregnant, has an abortion which results in her death, and the hero commits suicide). On the question of the abortion, as Barker told the 1909 Committee, 'I had myself produced at the Court Theatre a few months before under the Lord Chamberlain's licence a play the plot of which partly turned upon a criminal operation, which was quite openly referred to on the stage. What was I to do? What is any playwright to do in parallel circumstances?' (This was Elizabeth Robins's *Votes for Women*.) On the main question, Barker testified, 'I replied that I considered in such a play sober plain-speaking to be the only honest course, that innuendo would be indecent, and that while I naturally could not admit that I had written anything unfit to be spoken in the theatre and it was difficult to delegate my responsibility in such delicate matters to him, still if he would name the particular phrases which he objected to I would consider their alteration'. Mr Redford 'paid no attention'. He told the author what he required and that was an end of it. One of Barker's best plays—one of the best plays of the time—was kept off the stage. It was not until 1920 that it was passed, in a completely rewritten version. Barker was deeply injured by the ban, partly, as Mr C. B. Purdom suggests, because he was so deeply involved in the play, identifying himself with its central figure, especially in the later, revised text. Trebell was 'manifestly a self-portrait of the dramatist at a moment when he, himself, perhaps was prophetically conscious of personal waste'.[1] The ban helped to kill the Vedrenne–Barker management, which did so much for the English drama in its brief span of adventurous life.

Clearly, it was not only the abortion which upset the censor: it was the profession of the hero, Henry Trebell. He is a radical politician, who wants to disestablish the Church and organize a new national education programme. On him turns the fate of his party at an imminent general election and personal considerations are subjected to political necessity. Trebell shoots himself not so much because his mistress has died, but because his party has thrown him over. How could the Lord Chamberlain permit such seditious reflections upon the ethical purity of the political machine? At the same time, how could he openly admit his real motives? In a time-honoured way, he made use of moral indignation to camouflage his political aims. 'Nothing was said about this aspect, but it must have been the decisive one . . . In terms of sexual conventionality the play commits no more offence than a

---

[1] *Harley Granville Barker*, by C. B. Purdom (1955).

Victorian melodrama,' wrote Penelope Gilliatt in 1966, after visiting the revival of the original text at Guildford.[1] 'The woman and the baby die and the man kills himself. As far as preserving sexual propriety goes, the carnage is more than adequate.' What struck her, even at that distance in time, was the 'ferociously intelligent account of the dynamics of achieving power in English politics'. It is interesting to note the contemporary (but by no means representative) view in 1907 of *The Times*, which stressed the political rather than the sexual improprieties:

The play is a work of extraordinary power dealing with some of the most fundamental facts of human life with an unflinching truthfulness, and at the same time blending these facts with certainly the most vivid, and probably the most authentic presentation we have yet had on the English stage of great social and political questions, that come home to all Englishmen's homes and bosoms. But this is not the end of the matter. For our part we have no hesitation in approving the censor's decision. The subject matter of *Waste*, together with the sincere realism with which it is treated, makes it in our judgement wholly unfit for performance, under ordinary conditions, before a miscellaneous public of various ages, moods and standards of intelligence. Questions of art are one thing and questions of public policy and public expediency are another thing.

At the plea of Vedrenne, who was manager, the Office specified the necessary cuts, now that the danger had been removed, in order to stage a copyright performance. At eleven one January morning the play was read at the Savoy by a dazzling cast which included Bernard Shaw and his wife, Laurence Housman, Granville Barker, William Archer, H. G. Wells, St John Hankin, and Gilbert Murray.

Another eminent victim in that year of 1907 was Edward Garnett, whose *The Breaking Point* was vetoed because it dealt with an unmarried girl's fear of pregnancy: torn between her father and her married lover, she kills herself. Frederick Harrison, the Haymarket manager, knew that—as he wrote to Garnett—'there is no money in *The Breaking Point*, because the general public sets its face stubbornly against sad plays. And yours is more than sad. It is tragic.' Yet Harrison wanted to stage it: 'I should be proud to introduce your dramatic work to the public, or to that section of the public which is alive to what the theatre might be.' The censor, however, had other ideas. He wrote

[1] *The Observer*, 13 March 1966.

privately to Harrison, suggesting that the play should be withdrawn before it was submitted for a licence, in order to avoid friction and, perhaps, publicity. But his action had quite the opposite effect. Garnett insisted on sending his play up to the Chamberlain's Office. A fierce renewal of the anti-censor agitation broke out when it was banned, and Garnett added fuel to the fire by publishing with the book of the play an account of the negotiations, including a letter to the censor, asking him why *The Breaking Point* was vetoed. Mr Redford had replied, in characteristic form:

> I trust you will absolve me from any discourtesy if I point out that my official relations are only concerned with the managers of theatres. It is always painful for me to decline to recommend a licence, and in this case I hoped to avoid any possible appearance of censure on anyone by suggesting privately to Mr Harrison the desirability of withdrawing this piece. I cannot suppose that he has any doubt as to the reason.

The picture of an official censor hoping to 'avoid any possible appearance of censure on anyone' is an apt illustration of the gentlemanly double-think which is still one of the prime traditions of the Lord Chamberlain's Office. In a different key, Garnett replied:

> Is it possible you really imagine that any intelligent person feels the slightest stigma in your disapproval, or would be at the smallest pains to conceal from the world the fact of his having incurred it?[1]

In a better, more obedient world, that was exactly what had once happened, and Mr Redford 'really imagined' that things were what they used to be. This affair of *The Breaking Point* which he had tried so maladroitly to smother, combined with the banning of *Waste*, gave a final impetus to the staccato campaign against the Lord Chamberlain. (Yet *The Breaking Point* stayed banned long after other plays of this period were reprieved: as late as 1925 a licence was still refused.)

Later in 1907 as many as seventy-one authors appealed to the Prime Minister, who agreed to receive a deputation, and they sent a letter to *The Times* (27 October 1907), protesting against 'An office autocratic in procedure, opposed to the spirit of the Constitution, contrary to common justice and to common sense.' What particularly helped to set the ball rolling, however, was not the task force of seventy-one but just

---

[1] *The Breaking Point*, by Edward Garnett (1907).

one author who happened to have reached the House of Commons a year earlier: Robert Harcourt. He also happened to be a member, by birth, of the Liberal Party elite. His father ('Lulu') had been one of its leaders in the time of Gladstone. Mr Asquith, in Shaw's words, recognized 'his hereditary right to a parliamentary canter of some sort', and under Harcourt's pressure he appointed a Joint Select Committee of both Houses to make an inquiry.

That year the campaign against the censorship came to a head with the banning of two plays by Shaw, neither of them calculated as a deliberate challenge to the Lord Chamberlain, whose objections were, rationally speaking, unpredictable. First there was the case of *The Shewing Up of Blanco Posnet*, the one-act 'sermon in crude melodrama', as he called it, which Shaw wrote at Sir Herbert Tree's request, for the Haymarket. Set in the Wild West, its theme could be described as a horse-thief's discovery of God ('He made me because He had a job for me . . . I played the rotten game; but the great game was played on me; and now I'm for the great game every time. Amen'). But in the censor's view this was not the right kind of language to use about the Almighty. In an attempt to avoid the play's official submission to him the Examiner sent it back to Tree with a private letter advising its withdrawal. When this ploy misfired he agreed to license it, on condition that a number of 'blasphemous' passages were withdrawn. To most of these cuts Shaw agreed (Tree wanted him to alter the play, too); but he finally decided that he could make no further compromise and the play was banned. The passages which Shaw refused to cut were two references to God which most people outside the Lord Chamberlain's Office would take as the utterances not of a blasphemous but of a religious man: 'He hasn't finished with you yet. He always has a trick up His sleeve', and 'He's a sly one. He's a mean one. He lies low for you. He plays cat and mouse with you. He lets you run loose until you think you're shot of Him; and then, when you least expect it, He's got you.'

When Lady Gregory decided to present it at the Abbey in Dublin, an attempt was made to revive the Lord Lieutenant's power of censorship, which had not been exercised for one hundred and fifty years, but this was defeated and *Blanco Posnet* was staged successfully in peace. No riots broke out, only arguments. Lady Gregory then arranged a private performance in London through the Stage Society and the play was submitted again to the Lord Chamberlain. But it was not until 1916 that he licensed it, and then only on the condition that all the passages which appeared to implicate God in Posnet's personal life must be omitted. Shaw wrote then:

All the coarseness, the profligacy, the prostitution the violence, the drinking-bar humour into which the light shines in the play are licensed, but the light itself is extinguished. I need hardly say that I have not availed myself of this licence, and do not intend to.

In 1921, however, *Blanco Posnet* was publicly performed, in full.

While *Blanco Posnet* stirred up a religious and moral debate, the other Shavian work banned in 1909—*Press Cuttings*—sparked off a small political storm. Shaw subtitled this one-acter 'a topical sketch compiled from the editorial and correspondence columns of the daily papers during the Women's War in 1909', and it includes a number of squibs about conscription, the honours racket, the arms race and, of course, the suffragettes, whose militancy supplies the main, farcical action. What the censor objected to was the two central figures, the Prime Minister, Mr Balsquith, and the War Minister, General Mitchener. Their names were clearly a compound of Balfour and Asquith, Milner and Kitchener; and although they themselves bore no resemblance as individuals to any of those great men the censor was not taking any risks, especially as a little extravagant satirical fun was poked at the Government and the Conservative Party. The ban, which aroused strong protests, seemed all the more surprising because the Chamberlain had passed two recent plays in which contemporary political personalities had been clearly and widely identified: one of Barrie's few flops, *Josephine*, and a piece about Joseph Chamberlain, called *The Orchid*. Shaw himself was astonished, because the censor had accepted without demur his ridicule of Liberal politicians in *John Bull's Other Island*, a play which by the Chamberlain's own standards was ultimately far more subversive than *Press Cuttings*. He concluded that it was a question of party ties:

The objection is clearly to my politics, and not to my personalities. The fact is that I have to ascertain what the censor's politics are before I know whether the play will pass.

When he wrote *Back to Methuselah* in 1922, with a couple of leading politicians in the cast, he called them Lubin and Burge. Although they were far closer to their originals—Asquith and Lloyd George—than the 'Balsquith' compound of 1909, no offence was taken by the Chamberlain, perhaps because the names were more discreetly chosen, but more

probably because the men at Stable Yard had more common sense·
Yet perhaps that ban on *Press Cuttings* was not, after all, prompted so
much by political bias as by loyalty to the throne: for Archibald
Henderson, Shaw's official biographer, suggests that the censor may
have seen in Mitchener a portrait of the old (and notoriously inept)
Duke of Cambridge, Victoria's uncle, and one of the most unsuitable
Commanders-in-Chief that the British Army has endured in recent
times.

8

With dramas of a certain class, it is only after performance, and by reference to their effect upon the audience, that a final opinion as to their propriety can be reached.—Report of the Joint Select Committee on Censorship; 1909.

* * *

THE LAST committee of inquiry into the censorship of the English stage opened on 29 July 1909 and reported three months later in about half-a-million words, on 2 November. It was a Joint Select Committee of the Lords and Commons under the chairmanship of Herbert (later Viscount) Samuel, a brilliant Liberal lawyer, and its members included —apart from Robert Harcourt, under whose pressure it had been set up—Lords Plymouth, Gorell, Willoughby de Broke, and Ribblesdale, together with Commoners Hugh Law, Colonel Lockwood, and A. E. W. Mason. Two of these members were authors.

The omens for the Chamberlain were good. At the outset the committee ruled out all examination of particular plays, 'much as if', Shaw said, 'a committee on temperance were to rule that drunkenness was not a proper subject of conversation among gentlemen'. This meant that there was no possibility of publicly demonstrating in detail the bizarre processes whereby works of literature were vetoed, while plays were passed which were so unsavoury, so Shaw asserted, that he could not expose them in the press—'because no editor of a paper or magazine intended for general family reading could admit into his columns the baldest narration of the stories which the censor had not only tolerated but expressly certified as fitting for presentation on the stage'. Open discussion of such plays was prohibited, and the committee ordered the room to be cleared. It took the same action when Shaw—following the precedent of the 1892 committee and with the Select Committee's original agreement—attempted to read a written, personal statement, of which he had already distributed copies to the members. (Next day Shaw wrote about it to *The Times*, which published both the letter and a summary of his statement.) The committee did not insist, moreover, on the attendance of the chief censor himself. Among the forty-nine witnesses were both the Examiner of Plays and the Comptroller of the Lord Chamberlain's department, but the Chamberlain stayed away. 'It was regarded as strange,' said Fowell and Palmer, 'that a Parliamentary inquiry into the working of a State department should not have been honoured with the presence and evidence of the head of that department in person.'[1]

Great names testified in person: Granville Barker, Shaw, Barrie, Gilbert Murray, Galsworthy, Forbes-Robertson, Gilbert, Pinero, Chesterton, Laurence Housman, Tree, Alexander, Bancroft. Henry James testified, by proxy:

I *do* consider that the situation of the Englishman of letters ambitious of writing for the stage has less dignity—thanks to the censor's arbitrary rights upon his work—than that of any other man of letters in Europe, and that this fact may well be, or rather *must* be, deterrent to men of any intellectual independence and self-respect. I think this circumstance represents, accordingly, an impoverishment of our theatre; that it tends to deprive it of intellectual life, of the *importance* to which a free choice of subjects and illustration directly ministers, and to confine it to the trivial and the puerile. It is difficult to express the depth of dismay and disgust with which an author of books in this country finds it impressed upon him, in passing into the province of the theatre with the view of labouring there, that he has to reckon anxiously with an obscure and irresponsible Mr So-and-So, who may by law peremptorily demand of him that he shall make his work square at vital points with Mr So-and-So's personal and, intellectually and critically speaking, wholly unauthoritative preferences, prejudices, and ignorances, and that the less original, the less important, and the less interesting it is, and the more vulgar and superficial and futile, the more it is likely to so to square. He thus encounters an arrogation of critical authority and the critical veto, with the power to enforce its decisions, that is without a parallel in any other civilized country, and which has in this one the effect of relegating the theatre to the position of a mean, minor art, and of condemning it to ignoble dependencies, poverties, and pusillanimities. We rub our eyes, we writers accustomed to freedom in all other walks, to think that this cause has still to be argued in England.

[1] *Censorship in England* (1913).

Joseph Conrad wrote:

> You know my feelings as to the censorship of plays. I have always looked upon it with indignation. It *is* an outrage upon the dignity and honesty of the calling. But whether a dramatic author is ever deterred from producing good work by the existence of the censorship, I cannot say. I am certain that he may be shamefully hindered, and that such a situation is intolerable—a disgrace to the tone, to the character of this country's civilization.

Arnold Bennett weighed in by letter:

> Most decidedly the existence of the censorship makes it impossible for me even to think of writing plays on the same plane of realism and *thoroughness* as my novels. It is not a question of subject, it is a question of treatment. Immediately you begin to get *near* the things that really matter in a play, you begin to think about the censor, and it is all over with your play. That is my experience, and that is why I would not attempt to write a play, for the censor, at full emotional power. The censor's special timidity about sexual matters is an illusion. He is equally timid about all matters, and in the very nature of his office he must be. I have to give reasons for my dislike of a dramatic censorship. I regard it as monstrous and grotesque and profoundly insulting, and to condescend to reason against a thing so obviously vicious humiliates me.

James Barrie, who had never been bothered by the Chamberlain, appeared to witness against the censorship:

> I feel strongly that it makes our drama a more puerile thing in the life of the nation than it ought to be, and is a stigma on all who write plays. I think we are at the root of the matter if we accept the following as true, that the important objections to abolition are not founded on what is best for the drama, but on the practical difficulties, real or imaginary, of running theatres without such an official to simplify matters for the managers. Safeguard the managers in some sort of way, or remove their fears, and I think there remains no argument of great strength in favour of the retention of a censor. If a censor, however efficient, is a real help to any one, it is, I think, to the managers only—not to the public.
>
> The better the drama—that is, the more sincere, the more alive— the better for the public, and the drama must make most progress

106

when it is untrammelled, and the work of authors anxious to say, whether sportively or seriously, what is in them to say, and allowed to do it. Most of us do so now, according to our lights, and some with success, because their views of life happen to be of the kind for the present accepted as the right views. Others—not perhaps more able, but perhaps quite as able, and equally sincere—are less fortunately placed. Their minds, not necessarily more original, are more unconventional; they think many of the accepted views are wrong, and they work out their ideas on the subject in plays. But to the official mind (this is what I feel strongly), whatever is not the accepted conventional view is a thing suspect. Officialdom is created to carry out the accepted view; and so those authors are regarded as dark characters.

Granville Barker was one of the most eloquent and practical witnesses against the system. He was asked if he considered that the effect of the censorship is not to be measured merely by the number of plays rejected, but also by the indirect effect in preventing the writing of plays ?

Yes, I hold that opinion very strongly indeed. You see a dramatic author passes through a time when he writes in uncertainty with regard to whether his play will be accepted by a manager or not. If he has passed through that period of uncertainty, it is very hard that he should enter upon another period when it is extremely uncertain whether his play will be accepted by the censor or not. The result is, if he does not wish to enter on that second period of uncertainty, that he has one of two courses open to him: he must either write purely conventional plays, which he practically knows the Lord Chamberlain will not object to, or he must take to some other form of literary work, such as book-writing—the writing of fiction—where he is not hampered by any such dictation.

It has constantly happened to me as theatre manager that a dramatist has come to me and said: 'I have an idea of writing a play on such and such a subject'; and I have very often felt it my duty to tell him that if he treated the subject in such and such a way he ran a very grave risk of the play being destroyed, or of the property in the play being destroyed by the action of the Lord Chamberlain. I have done that, I should think at least half a dozen times within the course of the last four or five years . . .

A dramatist, in sending in his play for a licence, or in having his play sent in for a licence, is running a great risk of having his property destroyed, and therefore the one thing that he does not want to do is to make the censor think about his play, and he naturally is inclined to send in a play which contains only such subjects, and such a treatment of subjects, as have grown so familiar to the Licenser of Plays that he no longer thinks about them at all. For instance, I think it may be said without offence to the authorities that the censor no longer stops to think about a certain treatment of the subject of adultery on the stage.

If that treatment comes within certain dramatized limits—I mean limits practised by dramatists—he passes it practically without question. But the moment that any original point of view, or unusual point of view, on any subject is put before the censor he naturally stops to think about it, and the process of his thinking very often interferes with the licensing of the play. That is my particular point. The result of that has been to narrow the field which drama covers in England, and I regard the extreme narrowness of the field in English drama as being distinctly influenced and brought about by the operation of the censorship.

Other weighty voices, however, spoke on the other side. The Home Office and the Speaker solemnly expressed their general satisfaction with the status quo. Not surprisingly, the evidence of the writers conflicted with that of the managers and the Chamberlain's Office. There were some extraordinary insights into the behaviour and attitudes of the censor's department, which displayed in cross-examination a singular bewilderment and inconsistency about its working role and its principles of action. The Examiner said that plays written before 1737 were exempt, but added later that a Restoration play, if indecent, would have to be referred to the Chamberlain. He revealed that he had acted unofficially for years as assistant to the previous Examiner, who happened to be a personal friend; that this was, apparently, the main qualification for his appointment, as his previous occupation was that of a bank manager; that he applied no principles to his job but simply followed precedent, 'kept up a standard', and 'brought to bear an official point of view'; that he believed it was 'no part of my duty to give any reason for vetoing a play', and that he had once submitted to himself one of his own plays— and had passed it, 'in the ordinary way', as he explained. 'Of course there is nothing to which anyone could take exception. It was the most ordinary straightforward piece that ever was,' said Mr Redford.

The evidence also disclosed that an Advisory Board had been set up 'to strengthen the position of the censor'—so the Comptroller said—though it was not clear how this was achieved by giving another chance to the plays which the Chamberlain and the Examiner could not quite decide to ban. There were six members of this board—two actor-managers, Sir John Hare and Sir Squire Bancroft, one literary don, Sir Walter Raleigh, two lawyers, Sir Edward Carson and S. O. Buckmaster; and Sir Douglas Dawson, the Lord Chamberlain's Comptroller. It was formed, said Sir Douglas, 'more with a view of giving confidence to the public than from any feeling that the system did not work well'. The Chamberlain was not bound to ask its advice or to act on it.

Attitudes to the censorship of the stage turn ultimately, now as then, upon the fundamental question: is there something so especially dangerous about the theatre, that it needs to be regulated by a special law? To this the 1909 Committee returned an unhesitating 'Yes' (see page 207).

They did not really believe that the managers or the public or the authors could be trusted without the Lord Chamberlain to look after them, although they were willing (as we shall see later) to propose an alternative.

The support of the managers for the Chamberlain came on mixed grounds. Summing them up, in an alarming picture of the managerial mind, the committee reported that some of these managers believed that abolition of the censorship would encourage 'objectionable' plays, which would discredit the theatre as a whole. Others were unwilling 'to assume the responsibility of judging what is proper for performance and what is not': they needed 'a tribunal of authority' to tell them what was improper. Others championed the censor as 'a machinery for bringing to bear on an author a pressure to induce him to modify his play, which they themselves would be unable to exert'. But all the managers believed that if he was removed from power, the possibility of local prosecutions would make their position 'intolerable' because of the resulting uncertainty about pre-planning and provincial touring.

The committee was strongly influenced by this managerial backing for the censorship; and by the support of most actors. The Actors Association—unlike its present-day successor, Actors' Equity—backed censorship because it believed that if the right of veto was transferred to local authorities the actor's economic security would be jeopardized. But the association asked for a court of appeal of three wise men, as Gilbert had suggested, if a veto on a play was questioned. Yet the Joint Select recognized that there were serious objections to the current system, because, for instance, 'its effect can hardly fail to be to coerce into conformity with the conventional standards of the day, dramatists who may be seeking to amend them'; and that the censor's influence could not be measured only by the number of his vetos. Moreover, it handsomely agreed that the theatre could not be made comprehensively fit for Young Persons—so that 'parents can rely upon it to ensure that in no theatre will anything be produced unsuitable for youth to see. This is not so under the existing censorship; and ought not to be so . . .' The committee recognized, too, that the demand for the abolition of the censorship or, at least, for the possibility of appeal from its decisions was not the partisan propaganda of a literary pressure group (as so many of the censor's champions alleged) but came, 'with rare exceptions', from 'all the dramatists of the day . . . of all schools', supported by 'many men of letters'.

Yet the fact was that the retention of the censorship was desired by 'a large body of public opinion, of which the Speaker of the House of Commons . . . may be regarded as representative, on the ground that its abolition would involve serious risk of a gradual demoralization of the stage'. Here is the voice of that representative, responding to the chairman. 'It has been suggested to us,' said Herbert Samuel to Mr Speaker, 'that the censorship causes serious injury to the growth of a fine drama in England by stopping the liberty of playwrights to deal with certain problems of life which are of grave importance to every one. Do you consider this is so?'

'I should think it was very doubtful,' Mr Speaker replied. 'I should think that any healthy-minded author with a wholesome plot would have no difficulty in writing a good drama, if he is capable of writing a good drama at all. He is not obliged to go to these very unhealthy and disgusting subjects, as many of them do, and seem to revel in them. I think a good many plays have been very demoralizing in their tendency.'

How then could the 'licensing authority' be retained, as Mr Speaker and the committee wanted, without incurring what it described as 'the danger that official controls over plays before their production may hinder the growth of great and serious national drama and of the grave injury that such hindrance would do to the development of thought and art . . .'? The answer was that the censor must not have power to impose a veto on the production of plays. *On the other hand,* said the committee, plunging deeper into vacillation, an unlicensed stage might promote 'centres for the spread of demoralization' throughout the nation: 'The freedom designed for the "drama of ideas" may be made an oppor-

110

tunity for a drama of indecencies and personalities.' How would the national symbol, Mr Speaker, like that?

So, after long deliberation, the members of the Joint Select came to one main recommendation: that although the Lord Chamberlain should remain in authority, it should be *optional* to submit a play for licensing, and legal to stage an unlicensed play, whether it had been submitted or not to the Lord Chamberlain. Either the Attorney-General or the public prosecutor could act against offenders. If the Director of Public Prosecutions considered that an unlicensed play was 'open to objection on the ground of indecency', he should take action against the manager and the author. If the court found against the play, it could—as it thought fit—ban it for any period up to ten years, and fine the manager or the author, and endorse the theatre's licence. Once a play was banned for the full ten year period it must be licensed by the Lord Chamberlain before it could be performed again. For graver offences than indecency the ball was passed to the Attorney-General, who could apply to the Privy Council if he thought an unlicensed play 'improper for performance' on any of the seven groups specified by the committee. A Standing Committee of the Privy Council would be nominated, comprising—naturally—'men of distinction, of impartiality, and of large experience of the world', both lawyers and laymen. The Attorney-General could ask for an order prohibiting the play's performance for a period of up to ten years, and also, 'if he thinks fit', for an endorsement of the theatre's licence. While the case was under consideration, all further performances were prohibited; but in the case of licensed plays against which proceedings were taken, there was *no* suspension of performance, the manager and the author were *not* liable to any penalty, and the theatre licence was *not* liable to endorsement. 'It may be anticipated,' bumbled the Report, 'that the more elastic system we propose will develop, as our institutions usually do, along the lines that experience indicates. To seek a licence for a play will remain the rule, or it will become the exception, according as licences are found in the future to be necessary, or to be superfluous, in the public interest, and for the protection of producers.'

The committee also recommended that the censor should be brought within parliamentary range, as far as the 'general administration of the functions entrusted to him by statute' was concerned; that the ban on Scriptural characters (as applied by Mr Redford) should be dropped; that the period for the examination of plays should be extended from seven to fourteen days; that both music-halls and theatres should have a single class of licence, 'giving them freedom to produce whatever enter-

111

tainment may best conform to the tastes of the public which they serve';
that it should not be regarded as a valid reason for withdrawing a
theatre's licence if a licensed play has been staged there to which objection has been taken, or if an unlicensed play has been staged and
prosecuted without an endorsement of the licence, and that the licensing
of fourteen London theatres should formally be transferred from the
Lord Chamberlain to the London County Council, which already made
regular inspections of the buildings.

For the Lord Chamberlain, it recommended, in effect, that the
Examiner should be taken down a peg and that the reason for banning
plays should be codified. The Chamberlain should, it proposed, license
any play *unless* he considered that it could be reasonably held:

(*a*) to be indecent
(*b*) to contain offensive personalities
(*c*) to represent on the stage in an invidious manner a living person or
 any person recently dead
(*d*) to do violence to the sentiment of religious reverence
(*e*) to be calculated to conduce to crime or vice
(*f*) to be calculated to impair friendly relations with any foreign power
(*g*) to be calculated to cause a breach of the peace.

Moreover, the Office 'should make it clear that it is the Lord Chamberlain and not the Examiner of Plays who is responsible for granting or
withholding a licence' (a rebuke for the Redford regime). Every author
should have the 'right' to receive a copy of the Chamberlain's decision
on his play, and the Chamberlain should be on 'somewhat stricter guard
than hitherto' against 'the indecencies that sometimes tend to appear in
plays of a frivolous type'.

The 1909 report, said Shaw that year in his preface to *The Shewing Up
of Blanco Posnet*, was a 'capital illustration' of 'the art of contriving
methods of reform which will leave matters exactly as they are'. It tried
to please both the authors and the managers by both abolishing the
censorship and keeping it at the same time. In effect, its proposals meant
that a pre-production licence had so many advantages that few managers
would not apply for it, and that a post-production censorship would be
put in the hands of a secret body, a Committee of the Privy Council,
with virtually unlimited discretion and a strong political bias.

John Palmer, who wrote *The Censor and the Theatres* in the following
year, described the Report as 'one of the most chaotic and puzzling
volumes that has ever been offered to the public. Witnesses agree neither

as to their arguments nor as to the facts upon which their arguments are based. Arguments in absolute contradiction are put forward by witnesses on the same side, supported by facts which are flatly opposed . . . It is characteristic of the censorship question that it hopelessly corrupts the logic of all but the strongest heads.' How many questions it left unanswered! Was any representation of a political personality forbidden, or only his *offensive* representation ? Was all religious drama vetoed; or were there to be exemptions, like *Eager Heart*, because it 'was such a slight little thing, which was done at Christmas time', or like the opera *Samson and Delilah*, apparently allowed because it was 'the most popular opera of the season' ? Were plays read with regard to their literary and artistic merit ? Were pre-1737 plays exempt from all regulation—or not ? Should the Examiner visit theatres to see if the censor's directives were being observed? Could a play which had once been vetoed be reconsidered later ?

Among the Report's curiosities is its recommendation that *licensed* plays may be prosecuted, but are not liable to penalties: how *could* the State punish a manager for producing a play which it had already certified as lawful ? 'The difficulty is not a mere matter of chance or minor detail. It is inherent in the very nature of censorship before production, which, against every principle of English law, declares the prisoner to be innocent or guilty before he has committed the crime of which he is accused.' Realization of this anomaly brought Lord Gorell—who originally supported the pre-production censorship—to oppose it, but not until the very last meeting of the committee, when he proposed the abolition of 'prior licence' and reliance on control *after* performance. Then it was too late.

'By no conceivable amount of reform,' Palmer wrote, 'can censorship be made into anything but censorship. No control of the theatre outside the law can ever be anything but uncertain, arbitrary and repressive.'[1] That judgement is still relevant today.

[1] *The Censor and the Theatres*, by John Palmer (1910).

9

What is a censor of plays? He is an official of infinite wisdom, infallible judgement, and encyclopaedic erudition for whom time does not exist. That is a fiction that can never come to life.—BERNARD SHAW

Gad, sir, reforms are all right as long as they don't change anything.—COLONEL BLIMP

* * *

AFTER the report of the Joint Select Committee was published in November 1909 the debate over censorship flared up all over again. Upon its half-million words, hundreds of thousands more were piled. A book was written about it. Questions were asked in Parliament. But the Government temporized and did nothing. There were, understandably, more pressing matters on its mind, and the Joint Select Committee had been revealed as deeply confused. It gave no decisive verdict against the current system and, not surprisingly, the ameliorations it proposed did not appear urgent except to all those dramatists who opposed the Chamberlain because he was, to them, not only an anomaly but a pest and even a menace. The committee's recommendations joined all the other reports filed away in the Whitehall limbo, often invoked but never implemented.

The anti-censorship lobby might well have dwindled away, faced by the steady stonewalling of the Government, had it not been for the curious fact that during the next few years the Lord Chamberlain's Office not only continued practices condemned in the Report but also perpetrated some of its silliest blunders, in a series of muddled, meddlesome vetos which brought it into even blacker disrepute among those who were not already satisfied that it was an irreplaceable institution of British life. It was as if the censor and his men felt, after a pause to see how the Government would move, if at all, that the Report had given them not only a clean sheet but an open warrant. After 1911, in particular, they seemed to lose their heads.

At the end of the year two new censors were appointed. First of all, in November, Charles Brookfield became Joint Examiner of Plays, with George Redford. A month later Redford resigned and a sixty-six year old drama critic, Ernest Bendall, shared Brookfield's throne. About Bendall there was no dispute. The doyen of the London critics, a bland, unshowy but sober judge of drama, he had worked as a civil servant for thirty years, and for much of that time he had served as the *Observer's* critic. But Brookfield's appointment was a different matter.

Charles Brookfield, then fifty-four, had been on the stage himself for some years. In his autobiography he quoted from a premature obituary of himself, published on a false report of his death, that 'he was invaluable in small parts. But after all it is at his club that he will be most missed!'[1] With a Westminster and Cambridge background, he had many friends in 'Society'. He was described by eminent contemporaries as 'the sharpest-tongued cynic of his time' and as 'the wittiest man in the world', and Ellen Terry paid tribute to him in her memoirs as 'the prince of story-tellers'—'he was so brilliantly funny off the stage that he was always a little disappointing *on* it'.[2] He had written some forty plays, so that his literary qualifications were, at least, no less than those of his predecessors.

To Brookfield the new job was a joke ('How he used to laugh to me over this appointment,' said his friend H. Chance Newton).[3] But the news aroused a fury of protest in the theatre world, all the stormier because in that very month of joining the Lord Chamberlain's staff he had published—with singularly infelicitous timing—an article in the *National Review* criticizing the barrenness of the modern English drama and singling out for attack the theatre of Shaw, Granville Barker, Galsworthy and the other avant-gardists of social realism (as it then appeared) —or, as Brookfield put it, the theatre of 'misguided dramatic aspirants' who 'brayed' their views on social problems 'of their own projection'. With what seemed like deliberate provocation, Brookfield claimed— light-heartedly enough—that the Ibsenite drama might well be more damaging to a Young Person than the wholesomely frivolous burlesques and farces from the French which the Lord Chamberlain rightly passed. The new dramatists' only equipment for the drama, he said, was a 'morbid imagination—an ingenuity for conceiving horrors in the way of unusual sins, abnormal unions, inherited taints. And this is the kind of young man who inveighs against the discretionary powers of the Lord Chamberlain.' Looking back for a Golden Age, he found it between 1865 and 1885 (before Ibsen came to town); and to bring it back he sug-

[1] *Random Reminiscences*, by Charles Brookfield (1902).
[2] *The Story of My Life*, by Ellen Terry (1908).
[3] *Cues and Curtain Calls* (1927).

gested the establishment in Bristol of 'an old-fashioned country stock company', subsidized by a 'stage-stricken millionaire', with actor-managers but no 'modernists' on the board, and all the country's very best players on the payroll.

There was another reason in some quarters for opposition to Brookfield's appointment as an umpire of moral tone. Oscar Wilde does not appear to have treated him badly. He bore Brookfield no resentment for his burlesque of him in 1892 and indeed gave him a small part in *An Ideal Husband* together with Hawtrey, who had appeared as Wilde in *The Poet and the Puppets*. Yet Brookfield seems to have conceived for Wilde a deep hatred, partly perhaps out of jealousy, for he had never achieved the success which had been expected for him as an actor or as an author. If it had not been for Brookfield's help at the time of Wilde's action against Queensberry, according to Hesketh Pearson, 'the defence would have been in a bad way'.

> 'Brooks', as he was affectionately called by his friends, enlisted under Queensberry's flag, not for money but for pure love of the thing, and not only put a detective in touch with a female who stated that her profession had suffered from Wilde's activities, and who knew the haunts of his accomplices, but suborned a commissionaire at the Haymarket Theatre to give the addresses of Wilde's blackmailing associates.[1]

When Queensberry was found not guilty, Brookfield and Hawtrey gave a dinner for the Marquis to celebrate his victory—and Wilde's defeat.

What made Brookfield so especially odious to the theatrical *avant-garde*, however, was the fact that some years earlier he had written a light comedy, *Dear Old Charlie* (adapted from a French farce, *Célimare le bien aimé*), which was widely attacked because it seemed more suggestive than plays vetoed for 'indecency' by the censor ('it really was "the limit" in cerulean, not to say ultramarine tints,' said Chance Newton), and because it took a dig against Mr Bleater and his play *Sewage*, an unmistakeable allusion to Mr Granville Barker and *Waste*. John Galsworthy had treated *Dear Old Charlie* ironically, as an example of a model Chamberlain play that *ought* to be licensed, in his *Justification of the Censorship of Plays*, published in 1909 shortly before the committee began its sittings. 'We do not for a moment say that it should not have been licensed,' said the *Morning Post*, 'we do say that it makes it more than

---

[1] *Oscar Wilde*, by Hesketh Pearson (1946).

ever difficult to imagine why such a play as *Monna Vanna* should have been prohibited.' The piece was revived after Brookfield's apotheosis as censor and was greeted by *The Times*, among others, with the observation that 'There really could be two opinions about the cynical, shameless immorality that underlines the play.' On occasion the opponents of censorship could be every bit as priggish as its champions; but in this matter their apprehensions were soon to be justified.

In the month of Brookfield's appointment the Lord Chamberlain's Office committed some of its most curious absurdities to date. An Oriental spectacular, *Kismet*—the basis of an American musical forty years later—had been running successfully at the Garrick Theatre since April, without a word of public protest; but it included a brief 'harem' scene in which a girl appeared in the moonlight, slipped off her robes, and plunged into a bathing-pool ('the Sapphire Bath'). She wore pink fleshings underneath. After 245 performances the Chamberlain's Office suddenly registered shock. It issued an order in November that the girl must wear more clothes. As Fowell and Palmer say, this was 'so unmitigated a piece of asininity that only two solutions seemed open. One was that the censor was deliberately trying to kill his office by smothering it under ridicule, and the other was that he was not acting as a free agent.' On the whole, the second explanation seemed the more likely one—that he was influenced by backstairs snoopers and prudes like the clerics who, at that time, were lobbying for higher standards of purity in the dress of London chorus-girls. This action reinforced the campaign for ending the Chamberlain's powers. In December 1911 it was already proposed that Mr Brookfield's appointment should be cancelled.

About that time, Laurence Housman again came under the censor's guillotine. His play about the trial of Queen Caroline, *Pains and Penalties*, was banned, after the Chamberlain had tried, unsuccessfully, to persuade the manager to withdraw it without submitting it for a licence. Housman tells the story in his autobiography:

> It then became my task to extract a reason for the refusal, and to find out whether the cutting-out of anything that seemed undesirable to the official mind would save my dramatic property from ruin. It took me some time; and for several weeks I was given no reason that could be made public. Letters marked 'private' were no satisfaction of my claim that the refusal of a licence for a public performance should be publicly explained.

Yet before a word of the play was printed, defenders of censorship supported the Lord Chamberlain's decision with blind zeal, and industriously set themselves to assert that their beloved defender of the dramatic proprieties must be right. The author had dared to pass unfavourable comments on the character of King George IV; and hostile reference upon the stage to the great-grand-uncle of our reigning Sovereign was declared incompatible with respect for the institution of monarchy.

But at last the Lord Chamberlain was persuaded to give his reason publicly—perhaps it would be more correct to say 'his public reason'; and then, hey presto! the defence of our monarchy, in the person of so bad a representative as this happily-distant relative of a later name-sake, was sent to the limbo of untenable foolishness, and a brand-new reason was fitted out for public consumption. The Lord Chamberlain, it then appeared, had refused to license my play, not for the supposed reasons at all—on those I had been ' misinformed'—but because it dealt with 'a sad historical episode of comparatively recent date in the life of an unhappy lady.' The 'unhappy lady', as I at once pointed out, had been dead for ninety years; and during the whole of that period her memory had rested under a cloud, which it was the main purpose of my play to remove. Driven to give a public reason for his action, the Lord Chamberlain decided that such an attempt to rehabilitate her character was not to be allowed. . . .[1]

The Caroline Society was then formed 'to preserve the memory of Queen Caroline . . . from the oblivion designed for it by the Lord Chamberlain': in fact, to give a 'private' performance of *Pains and Penalties* at the Savoy in November 1911. Afterwards, the audience was addressed by Granville Barker and passed both a vote of censure on the Lord Chamberlain and a resolution attacking the appointment of Charles Brookfield. Clearly, the ban was due to the Chamberlain's solicitude for his royal employers whose 'comparatively recent' relations must not be presented on the stage, especially when they might appear to put the monarchy in an unfavourable light.

In the same month the Chamberlain, faced with the thornier problem of a play in French, faltered and attempted to call in his newly fledged Advisory Committee. Two members were out of town: one with the Khedive in Egypt; another with the King in India. Meanwhile the play, *La Vierge Folle*, by a distinguished contemporary dramatist, Henri Bataille, had to wait. Finally, the machinery of censorship creaked for-

[1] *The Unexpected Years* (1937).

ward to the conclusion that it was, after all, safe to stage it at Notting Hill and thus it ended a season of French plays instead of opening it. Far from expediting the consideration of plays since the 1909 Report, the censor seemed to have slowed it up. At this period several productions were delayed for several weeks at considerable expense of time and trouble for the management.

Just how little the censor had reformed was shown in January 1912 when he denied a licence to *The Next Religion* because the author, Israel Zangwill, a leading novelist of the time, refused to make the alterations requested by the Chamberlain. These offensive phrases included 'That shrine of superstition in Westminster'; 'The real Good Friday would be that which brought the cure for cancer'; 'I've got my eye on a workman-like little place in a commanding position with a ten year lease; it was in the Baptist line before.' The bad word in the last sentence was 'Baptist'. But the Chamberlain was prepared to accept 'Nonconformist'. And he helpfully suggested 'Our Lord comfort you' as an alternative to 'Christ comfort you', a phrase which he really could not tolerate on the public stage. His feverish attachment to the Crown was illustrated once again in the same month when, 'after taking the advice of his Advisory Board', he banned a one-act play, called *The Coronation*. This was about an idealized king in an imaginary country who has a change of heart about the social system on the way to his coronation. No reason was given for the ban but it appeared that 'the offence consists in the mere representation of a king', even though the play's imaginary monarch was so excellent a person that he could hardly be mistaken for any existing ruler. A private performance was given to the people who had already bought tickets, who were nominated members of the Coronation Society for the event.

There was trouble in the following month over a more illustrious author. Eden Phillpotts had been persuaded by Granville Barker to write his first play, a stage version of his successful novel *The Secret Woman*. No objections were anticipated, but while it was already in rehearsal at the Kingsway the Chamberlain refused to license it unless certain 'improper' lines were deleted. Both Granville Barker and the author refused to accept these cuts. Phillpotts wrote forty years later that the offending sentences—he said there were two, but there were rather more than that—'mattered nothing to the play and involved no sacrifice of art; but compliance with his direction did involve sacrifice of principle and I declined to erase the sentences', although he recognized that he was 'in truth but a scapegoat or a makeshift for a cause and no martyr in any case'.[1] The odd thing was that the censor refused to make public the passages he thought unfit for consumption by an English audience, but agreed to show them *privately* to any interested Members of Parliament. They included this explanation of the facts of life, spoken by a husband to his wife:

> You won't understand. An angel from heaven wouldn't understand. It would take a devil from hell to do that—according to what you believe. The way of a man's body. . . . My flesh and blood's a bit too much for you and always was. And a bit too much for me sometimes.

Barker felt that he had to 'take a firm stand against any interference', and organized a letter to *The Times*, signed by twenty-four authors, including Barrie, Conrad, Conan Doyle, Galsworthy, W. H. Hudson, Henry James, George Moore, Gilbert Murray, Masefield, Pinero, Shaw and Wells. They pointed out that Phillpotts had never been accused, as a novelist, of acting indecently. Yet this was the charge against him as soon as he turned to the theatre:

> Many of us have never written plays, though most of us would like to do so. There is not perhaps another field so fine in the England of today for a man or woman of letters, but all the other literary fields are free. This one alone has a blind bull in it.
>
> We who sign this letter may be otherwise engaged; some of us may be old and done, and no longer matter. Our chance has gone by. But there are men and women who are coming—are they also to be warned off? Can we strike no blow for the young?

The letter by twenty-four authors was followed a fortnight later in *The Times* by a letter from one peer which had, in many ways, more influence. It was from Lord Ribblesdale, in whom the Phillpotts ban had produced a change of heart. As a member of the 1909 Committee, he said, he had come 'with some misgiving to the half-hearted conclusion that no sufficiently strong case had been made out' for the abolition of the censorship; but having seen *The Secret Woman*, 'I feel most uneasy about the notions I then entertained. We all know that the old censorship moved in a mysterious way—it is the nature and essence of that kind of engine to do so—but what is going to happen now that it has been reconstructed? I confess I do not like the look of things . . .'

A couple of weeks later there was still another incident. The Chamber-

---

[1] *From the Angle of 88* (1951).

lain licensed Lawrence Cowen's *Quits !*, which turned out to have almost exactly the same plot as Lawrence Cowen's *Tricked !* which the Chamberlain had banned three months earlier, together with another play by the same dramatist, *The Pity of It*. Here are the comparative synopses, as given by Fowell and Palmer:[1]

Tricked !

In this play, the scene of which is laid in a garrison town in Russia, the wife of a student sentenced to death for an assault on a military officer, in order to save her husband's life yields herself to the general in command of the troops, who has, in such event, guaranteed the condemned man's reprieve. Her sacrifice is in vain, for her husband is shot, and she strangles her betrayer the following morning.

Quits !

In this play, the scene of which is laid in London, an actress, the wife of a struggling actor, who is committed to prison for debt on the eve of his appearance in a new play which is to give him the chance of his life, yields herself to a dramatist-manager, from whom she obtains the money—some £37—in time to fulfil his engagement. She stabs her betrayer dead the following morning.

Some months later, the litigious Mr Cowen had the audacity to bring an action against the Chamberlain of the day. He appears, somewhat surprisingly, to be the only English dramatist who has ever done this, but he was challenging not the censor's right to pronounce judgement on his plays but his right to keep the manuscript afterwards. When Cowen first pressed the Chamberlain for the return of his play *The Pity of It*, he promised that the originals would be returned after copies had been made. But when the Chamberlain heard that the dramatist had actually applied to Bow Street for a summons against him, he wrote to Cowen at once to say that his previous offer was cancelled and that he would now await the verdict of the magistrate. Shortly after this a new Lord Chamberlain—Lord Sandhurst—succeeded and *he* maintained that he was entitled to keep the scripts of all plays sent to him. There was nothing in the Theatres Act, as his counsel pointed out, that made it obligatory to return them to their authors or managers. On the other hand, as Cowen's lawyer also pointed out, there was nothing in the Act that

---

[1] *Censorship in England* (1913).

entitled him to *keep* the scripts. But the case went against the dramatist. The Lord Chamberlain, it was decided, was only doing his duty.

It was not surprising that by June over sixty dramatists, together with many other men and women of the theatre, M.P.s, journalists, dons, artists and musicians, had signed a petition to the King, protesting that the censorship as administered inflicted 'grave injury' on the art of the drama, placed obstacles in the way of its 'further development', and made dramatists 'either avoid the treatment of many of the vital problems of human life or approach them with a timidity which gravely injures their work', so that the theatre fails to be what it 'could and should be'— 'one of the greatest educational forces of the time'. Not only had nothing been done by the Government since the Joint Select Committee's Report, said the petition, but the Chamberlain's department had 'rendered its office more burdensome and grievous than it was before', notably by exercising its powers of prohibition 'far more oppressively than before'. The author-signatories included Barrie, Bennett, Conrad, Galsworthy, Garnett, Edmund Gosse, Henry James, Laurence Housman, Maurice Hewlett, Henry Arthur Jones, John Masefield, H. W. Massingham, George Moore, Gilbert Murray, Henry Newbolt, Eden Phillpotts, Pinero, Quiller Couch, Arthur Symons, Wells and Yeats, while among the non-theatrical signers were Granville Bantock, A. G. Gardiner, Patrick Geddes, Sir Oliver Lodge, Lord Lytton, Sir Alfred Mond, T. P. O'Connor, Lord Redesdale, Charles Shannon, G. M. Trevelyan and Sir Henry Wood.

But the climate seemed to favour *more* censorship, not less. And there was renewed support from actors and managers who forestalled this protest by petitioning the King in support of the Lord Chamberlain. They included most of the leading names of the day, young and old— Lena Ashwell, Mrs Patrick Campbell, Robert Loraine, Robert Courtneidge, Gerald du Maurier, George Edwardes, Edmund Gwenn, Sir John Hare, Sir Charles Hawtrey, Mrs Kendal, Mrs Langtry, Cyril Maude, Julia Neilson, Sir Herbert Tree. Moreover, in July 1912 a British Board of Film Censors was set up, as an independent body with the backing of the trade: and the first President was none other than Mr George Redford, until recently Examiner of Plays, who now began a new career with four examiners to help him, and a personal announcement that he hoped to keep the country's cinemas 'clean and free of any stigma, even of vulgarity'. Before he began his appointment, Mr Redford suggested that a number of topics should be banned: he stipulated that these should include:

No cremations.

No final, tear-impelling scenes at funerals.

No scenes representing murder, sudden death, or suicide.

No mixed bathing.

No 'compromising situations'.

No cock fights, no dog fights, and nothing where unnecessary cruelty is brought in, either to man or beast.

All Biblical scenes to be watched very carefully.

No Sovereigns, Judges, Ministers or such high officials of the land to be treated in an unbecoming or undignified or ridiculous manner, and no living individual was to be lampooned.

In its first year the British Board of Film Censors under Mr Redford's leadership banned twenty-two films, on the following grounds:

Indelicate or suggestive sexual situations.

Indecent dancing.

Holding up a Minister of Religion to ridicule.

Cruelty to animals.

Indelicate accessories in the staging.

Judicial executions.

Excessive drunkenness.

Subjects depicting procurations, abduction and seduction.

Native customs in foreign lands abhorrent to British ideas.

Impropriety in conduct and dress.

Materialism of Christ and the Almighty.

Alterations were requested in another 166 films for such additional reasons as:

Scenes suggestive of immorality.

Situations accentuating delicate marital relations.

Scenes tending to disparage public characters and institutions.

Medical operations.

The irreverent treatment of sacred or solemn subjects.[1]

The spirit of the Lord Chamberlain was abroad, and the codes of St James's Palace were being applied to the new mass medium of the cinema.

The Lord Chamberlain, too, gained more power in his other role as licenser of the London theatres, which reinforced his authority as dramatic censor. In January 1912—at the time of Brookfield's succession

[1] *The History of the British Film*, vol. 1, by Rachael Low (1949).

and the sudden flurry of petty censorship—he began to issue licences for the performance of plays to music-halls inside his jurisdiction. This resolved a long-standing dispute over the anomaly that a music-hall could present 'sketches' without applying to the Chamberlain for a licence for both the sketch and the right to present plays.

Later that year, one of the most famous of European producers came into the censor's danger area. Max Reinhardt, who had already staged *The Miracle*, *Sumurun* and *Oedipus Rex* in London, planned to present *A Venetian Night* at the Palace in November. Elaborate and widely publicized preparations were made including the erection of a revolving stage, then something of a novelty, and final rehearsals were in progress when on the day of the first night the manager received a letter from the Lord Chamberlain's Office vetoing the whole production. No objection was taken to the presentation or performance. It was the 'theme' which could not be exhibited to the British public. This dangerous plot was that a girl who is married to a man she does not love gives a rendezvous in her bedroom to her lover on her wedding night. Later they are interrupted by the husband, who kills the lover. As the manager pointed out, the triangular situation of husband, lover and wife was not unknown in the licensed drama throughout the ages and was the basis of several plays then running in the West End. The Lord Chamberlain had specifically absolved the treatment and production of offence, so why was the plot so wrong in *A Venetian Night* and not elsewhere? Smaller fry might have had to swallow the inconsistency, as dozens of authors and managers have had to do before and since, but Reinhardt and his colleagues, secure in their knowledge of his European reputation, the play's innocuousness and the big capital investment at stake, raised a storm and created a precedent. They insisted that the Chamberlain himself should see a rehearsal; and although the visit was delayed because he was shooting in the country, he came to the theatre later in the week and with 'some small modifications' passed the play.

It was a rebuff for the Examiners, especially as they appeared to be testing their powers in an area hitherto outside their range—the music-hall stage (the Palace held a music-hall licence). For years this had been self-regulating, and intervention by the L.C.C. had been needed only on rare occasions. Self-censorship worked well without any referee of good taste and decorum from the Royal Household.

* * *

If the Lord Chamberlain's Office had continued to act as it did from

1911 to 1913 there seems little doubt that the Government would have *had* to take action to reform it in order to meet the rising anger of the playwrights and to recognize the change of heart among moderates who had previously supported the censorship. Indeed it might have been abolished fifty years ago.

Two facts saved the censor: the early death of Charles Brookfield in 1913 and the outbreak of the first world war. From 1914 to 1918 the serious drama vanished almost completely from the English stage. The London theatre was given up to light entertainment, much of it at a level even lower than that of the kind normally favoured by the Examiner of Plays, none of it presenting the least moral, social or political problem to St James's Palace, where G. S. Street and Ernest Bendall were in joint occupation of the Examining chair. Under the pressure of wartime needs the censors, indeed, proved themselves to be rather more enlightened than their predecessors, as they showed by their licensing of *Ghosts* and *Damaged Goods*. But the more the censorship changed, the more it stayed the same. There is, for the contemporary reader, an especial irony in John Palmer's forecast in 1913—in *The Future of the Theatre*— that the censorship 'will be abolished in 1917 as a natural corollary, of the endowment of the National Theare'. Increasingly, it seemed apparent that the only way was the one mockingly advised by Shaw— 'You must begin by abolishing the monarchy'—and *that* was beyond a joke.

10

A magistrate has laws to administer; a censor has nothing but his own opinion. A judge leaves the question of guilt to the jury; the censor is jury and judge as well as lawyer . . . The law may be only the intolerance of the community; but it is a defined and limited intolerance.—BERNARD SHAW

More liberty begets desire of more;
The hunger still increases with the store.

DRYDEN

* * *

EVEN in the Lord Chamberlain's Office, the 1914–1918 war made a difference. Its enemies seemed to have declared an armistice and its own rigours were relaxed. A sign of the times was the capitulation of the Stage Society, whose annual report for 1916–1917 announced that 'With the production of *Ghosts*, *Damaged Goods* and *The Three Daughters of M. Dupont* our fight against the censorship appears to have attained its purpose.' With the advent of the 1920s some of the changes in the world outside were reflected on the stage, with the censor's acquiescence. Situations and dialogue were passed—generally without comment by the press—on which Pigott, Redford and Brookfield would have imposed, without a moment's hesitation, a disgusted veto. A few plays like *The Vortex* and *The Fanatics* provoked cries of moral outrage, but without any placatory action by the censor. Most of the plays banned during the Redford regime were passed for public consumption during the 1920s. In some cases the censor moved with significant slowness. It was not until 1931 that *Salomé* was sanctioned and Brieux's *Maternité* had to wait till 1932. For some authors it was too late. But three of the battle-pieces in the pre-1914 campaigns—*Mrs Warren's Profession*, *The Cenci* and *Waste*—were licensed within three years of Lord Cromer's succession in 1922.

Some minor taboos entrenched a few years earlier were broken. You could, for instance, use the name of God, even suggesting that some people might not entirely approve of Him, as Somerset Maugham did in

The Unknown (1920), when a vicar declares that the war was due to 'the loving kindness of God, who wishes to purify the nation by suffering: to err is human, to forgive divine'. 'And who is going to forgive God ?' replied a woman whose two sons had been killed. For this *cri célèbre* the actress was given a special ovation at the end of the act, and the play became the talk of the town. In passing this rhetorical question, the censor appeared to recognize the growing force of disillusionment with official Christianity created by the war.

There was one main difference between pre-war and post-war censorship: leading dramatists such as Maugham, Lonsdale, Rattigan, Emlyn Williams, Priestley, Coward and even O'Casey experienced only minor interference from St James's Palace and rarely took the field against the Chamberlain. None of their plays was severely mutilated, only one or two were banned, and most were left untouched by the censor's hand. There was no single revolutionary influence comparable with Ibsen's in the earlier period and no one English dramatist was as dominant a rebel as Shaw had been. On the whole they played the game inside the censor's rules, without undue resentment.

The vitality of the drama—and of the commercial theatre which carried it—diminished in the 1920s. The dominant system gave little incentive to serious drama while ignoring Shakespeare and the classics. With occasional irruptions of native and foreign talent, the mainstream stage contracted into a narrow-based theatre of comfort which made few challenges to the middle-class audience and not many more to their protector, the Lord Chamberlain. The drama's relative insulation and sterility cannot be blamed entirely on the censor. Apart from the inadequacy of theatrical organization, there was, and still is, a time-lag between Britain and the rest of Europe. In the theatre, as in other areas, it seemed as if the country were caught in some air-pocket of history, sealed off for a couple of decades from the social, intellectual and political changes which were gathering momentum across the Channel. We apparently did not want to *know* about many facts of twentieth-century life: and the theatre helped us to ignore them.

The Chamberlain's Office itself made some small adjustments of the machinery of censorship, as a result of the 1909 Committee's Report. In January 1926 it officially announced some minor revisions of the regulations in a statement apparently designed as an up-to-date clarification of the Chamberlain's role. From then on producers and authors could submit manuscripts to him, but only when definite dates of production had been fixed with a theatre; and the licences were still issued to the manager, not to the author. The announcement expressly specified that manuscripts should be typewritten and would be kept by the Office, emphasizing that any proposed alteration or addition, or any change in the title, must be submitted for approval before production, that pantomimes and revues (including topical additions) must be read and licensed before they were staged. Several months later a new ruling was made about Sunday performances. It stipulated that a theatre licensed by the Chamberlain could allow Sunday performances only by a *bona fide* society established for the private performance of stage plays; that tickets should be available exclusively from the society's office or address; that no tickets should be issued except to a member of at least seven days standing; that no actors should be paid, 'directly or indirectly, beyond a honorarium for expenses'; and that no intoxicants should be sold or supplied.

The main change in Stable Yard, however, was not detailed in any official announcement but was none the less detectable early in the 1920s in the role of the Examiner of Plays. Instead of merely delivering his yea or nay on a text, the Examiner was now required to submit a report ('including some synopsis') to the Lord Chamberlain. The Chamberlain, in doubtful cases, consulted his Advisory Board, and the final decision sometimes went against the Examiner. His heyday was over, and he vanished from sight under the Chamberlain's ceremonial mantle. When Brookfield's successor (G. S. Street) was appointed he attempted to explain the Examiner's true function in a letter to *The Times*; 'but', he complained in 1925, 'the human mind admits fresh facts with reluctance. My letter was regarded by some people as a disingenuous evasion of responsibility, and to this day, eleven years later, I find myself still explaining the matter in private over and over again.' After the death of Brookfield—or so it appears to the outsider—it was the Chamberlain who took the blame and the brickbats. He kept his Examiners firmly under his thumb, together with the English drama and the Royal Household.

This was all the easier to achieve because from 1924 onwards his own job was given a new security and continuity of power. Before Britain's first Labour Government came to power in that year, George V quickly and quietly took the initiative in introducing a change in his Household which may be seen in retrospect to have had a lasting effect upon the theatrical censorship. In the words of Lady Cromer, wife of the Lord Chamberlain of the day, the King 'obtained the acquiescence of the Conservative, Liberal and Labour leaders to the principle that the posts of the Great Officers in the Royal Household and certain other Court appointments should be considered as non-political. This . . . obviated the necessity for frequent changes in the personnel of the King's immediate entourage, as had hitherto been the constitutional practice.'[1] The King no doubt apprehended that under Labour rule his entourage might well have been infiltrated by nominees who went to the wrong school or had been in the wrong regiment. The new deal saved embarrassment all round. Henceforward, the job of Lord Chamberlain (and other officials) was 'at the King's pleasure', subject always to the Prime Minister's approval; and this meant that the man in possession remained under the Government of Ramsay MacDonald, Stanley Baldwin and Neville Chamberlain, whereas his predecessors had moved out of St James's with every change in Downing Street. From 1924 onwards, moreover, the job carried greater responsibilities. In a Palace reorganization, it absorbed the office of State Chamberlain, and—as Lady Cromer testified—'the day when much of the work was of a nominal character was of the past'. Now, once chosen, a Lord Chamberlain who kept his sanity, health and loyalty to the Crown stayed in power till he resigned or died.

From 1922 to 1938 the Lord Chamberlain was Lord Cromer, P.C., G.C.B., G.C.I.E., G.C.V.O. A member of the famous Baring family and son of the eminent proconsul, he was forty-four when he took over at St James's Palace—after a somewhat obscure career in the Diplomatic and Foreign services. He had acted as private secretary to two Permanent Under-Secretaries, served briefly as A.D.C. to the Viceroy of India, and was chief of staff to the Duke of Connaught and the Prince of Wales on their 'India Missions'. When he was appointed Lord Chamberlain he at once attempted to surrender his power of censorship over the stage, because he felt—as his wife wrote later—'that in the course of recent events it was increasingly difficult for one individual to control the tide of modern thought, even were it advisable to do so'. Accordingly, he wrote to the Home Secretary, Sir William Joynson Hicks ('Jix', later Lord Brentford), a militantly unliberal Puritan, proposing that the theatrical censorship should be transferred to an official body or agency such as the Home Office. When 'Jix' dismissed this bolshy suggestion, Cromer did not apparently pursue it further. He shouldered his theatrical burden and sustained it for sixteen years without provoking any of the large-scale, violent campaigns which

[1] *Such Were Those Years*, by Ruby Cromer (1939).

129

had been waged against the Office before the war. Indeed, theatre managers paid him glowing tribute. After he had been in office for three years, C. B. Cochran said that 'a very different state of things' now prevailed in the Lord Chamberlain's Office. 'I attribute the present dramatic revival in no small measure to Lord Cromer's desire to see a theatre in this country which can be an intellectual force and not merely a place of entertainment.'[1] And when he retired, in 1938, the West End managers presented him with an address testifying to their 'abiding gratitude for the courtesy and patience in which you have never failed, and for the sagacity you have so constantly exhibited'—an impressive testimony, even when you allow for modern managers' 'abiding gratitude' to *all* the Lords Chamberlain, who do so much for them at so cheap a rate, in providing insurance policies for the drama.

For most of the period, the Examiner was G. S. Street, a former civil servant who had published several books and an edition of Congreve before his appointment, and, like Bendall, had been a dramatic critic. He worked in partnership with Bendall from 1914 to 1920, and then on Bendall's retirement became the main Examiner. When he was appointed, he noted in 1925, he had 'an open mind' about the necessity of the Chamberlain's censorship but 'I soon was convinced that this was indispensable . . . in the interests of the theatre.'[2] Why? Because the Puritans outnumbered the libertarians and defenders of theatrical art. According to Street, the people 'with whom the art of the dramatist counts for less than their immunity from being startled or shocked' form a group which is 'very powerful and insistent and capable of extremely articulate pressure. . . . Every extension of the subject matter allowed the dramatist, or of his freedom in representing character or speech, would have been attacked with such violent protest that . . . few managers would have cared to face it'. Yet, although the censorship acted in the best interests of the theatre, Street complained, it was still 'so widely and deeply misunderstood and misjudged':

> A great deal of its work is necessarily unknown to its critics. They know what it allows; they do not know what it prohibits, save in the case of plays with some reputation, and of these there have been few instances in late years.

The Public Morality Council—originally known as the London Council for the Promotion of Morality—was one of the main voices in

[1] *Daily Mail*, 30 July 1925.
[2] *Fortnightly Review*, 1 September 1925.

this 'very powerful and insistent' group, mentioned by Street, which did its bigoted best to get the censor to prohibit more. In 1926, for instance, it not only memorialized the Lord Chamberlain 'regarding offensive language in plays and improper reference to the Deity', but it also lobbied the Prime Minister about 'the atmosphere and general tone of certain plays'. The Council was proud to announce in one report that, but for their 'activities', 'certain plays of very doubtful character would have been submitted to the Lord Chamberlain; that, particularly in the early days, many alterations have been secured . . .' At a conference in 1933, a bishop exulted that 'again and again alterations had been made to meet the criticism of the council'. Every year reports were made on plays and shows in the West End and in many provincial towns. In 1929, for instance, out of 125 productions visited by the Public Moralists, twenty-six went on a black list, and were, no doubt, the subject of remonstratory letters not only to the Lord Chamberlain but to other pillars of society such as the Archbishop of Canterbury, whose help was later recruited in the attempt to keep the stage clean and decent. Sometimes prosecutions resulted: in 1932 the Lord Chamberlain instigated legal action against five productions of which two had been the council's targets, and in 1934 as many as seventeen proceedings, all of them successful, were taken by the Director of Public Prosecutions. But most of these offences concerned nudity and near-nudity in revues, and all were committed outside London. It was in its attacks on the exhibition of bodies rather than ideas that the Public Morality Council appears to have scored most of its victories.

In this matter of exposure, theatrical practice changed rapidly in ten years. In 1902 *Monna Vanna* was banned, as we have already seen, because the heroine was *said* to be naked under her cloak. In 1906, after a special campaign by moral vigilantes 'living statuary'—that is to say, the *poses plastiques* and *tableaux vivants* which had been a feature of London night life for some fifty years—were banned in London by the L.C.C. In 1916 the Lord Chamberlain (Lord Sandhurst) objected to the nudity of a *poster* outside a theatre. It advertised a Cochran revue, *Half Past Eight*, at the Comedy, and reproduced a caricature from the *Bystander* depicting a certain amount of leg-show, or, as Lord Sandhurst complained, the artist 'seemed deliberately to have created an effect of feminine garments being blown up'. The poster was removed at the Chamberlain's instructions. Two years later some sections of the press —and the professional moralists—were so shocked by the plunging pseudo-sixteenth century neck-lines and at least one skin-tight dress in

131

another Cochran show, *As You Were*, that Lord Sandhurst ordered the costumes to be made more decent. One star dancer's dress was so transformed by the Chamberlain's improvements—'from being exquisitely tactful it became an atrocity'—that she resigned her role in the revue and returned, indignantly, to Paris. Of this vigilant—and 'thoroughly Victorian'—censor, Cochran told the story that

> When he went through a book, six months after the show had been passed, the first line he fastened on was 'The girls don't seem to *fall* for me as they used to do'.
> 'Now,' he said, 'there can be but one meaning to that line. We all know the term, "a fallen woman".'[1]

By 1930, however, near-nude dancing in stage revues was frequently seen, and even complete nudity was permitted, under special regulations thought up by the Lord Chamberlain. The main requirement was that the girl should remain completely paralysed while in view of the audience. To move was illegal.

Producers had to submit photographs of the poses or the decor in which they were set to Stable Yard. The Chamberlain had to be satisfied that they had 'sufficient artistic merit, as against being merely an excuse to exhibit nude figures upon the stage', or that 'they must be accurate representations of actual works of art, paintings, or sculptures'. In addition, the lighting had to be 'suitably subdued'. But this kind of exposure proved hard to control, especially with the advent of striptease from the U.S.A. in the late 1930s, and the Lord Chamberlain summoned special conferences on stage nudity in 1937 and again in 1941. This was followed by an increase in the number of prosecutions and the heaviness of the fines—without apparent effect. The impulse to defy the law seems to have been much stronger among strippers and their sponsors than among dramatists and their managers, but then the girls catered for an appetite more widespread than the taste for 'straight' theatre.

★　★　★

Was it true, then, that—as the Stage Society declared in 1917—there were no battles left to fight ? Had the censorship, under Lord Cromer's liberal direction, become a harmless and even protective institution concerned only with the best interests of the majority theatre which,

[1] *The Secrets of a Showman* (1925).

132

after all, cannot move too far ahead of its audience? The Chamberlain's Office had obviously changed with the times. Did it change fast enough? Emphatically, demonstrably, not. In Britain at that time the area of dissent and heresy may have been proportionately small: the national climate may have favoured conformity;[1] but the censorship of the stage —as of the cinema—aided and abetted with unnecessary solicitude the British preference for keeping heads down, deep in the sand, and for maintaining the theatre under sedation. How could any Lord Chamberlain—however liberal, however diplomatic, however popular among the managers—give free play to the drama as an intellectual force (as Cochran said of Cromer) or as any other kind of force, when he would not permit open criticism of the Crown, the Government, or heads of states abroad, or the general social order; when he might stop a dramatist from presenting on the stage a public figure who had died during the last century, because some surviving relatives might object;[2] when he vetoed openly favourable presentation of Communist or Left-wing revolutionary regimes, and openly critical plays about Fascist governments; when he prohibited not only the representation of Christ on the public stage, but even the use of His name and criticism of the churches operating under His auspices; when—to take the area on which, until recently, discussion always focused—he generally kept the discussion of sexual behaviour and morality within the genteel conventions considered fit for a rather sheltered middle-class schoolgirl.

One of the more celebrated instances of Lord Cromer's enlightened despotism in practice was his treatment of John van Druten's *Young Woodley*, a sentimental play about the calf-love of a public schoolboy for the wife of his housemaster. This contains no visible hint of sexual impropriety: the *Daily Telegraph*—no champion of pornography—

[1] Symptomatically, a leading critic such as James Agate was surprisingly passive in his attitude to censorship. Reviewing Schnitzler's *Reigen* (staged in 1933 at the Arts Theatre Club in French), he praised it as 'terrifically first-class', but added—without irony—'but, of course, the play must be banned for all except specialized audiences'.

[2] Two curious insttances of his special protection—in plays about Rossetti, and about the Thompson–Bywaters murder—are described below. In a more recent case, I have heard, importunate relatives appeared at a provincial theatre during the tour of a play in which a distant family connection was dramatized; and they suggested that they would be satisfied with a small sum to discourage them from lodging an objection with the Lord Chamberlain. The sweetener of £200 with which the management is said to have parted was cheap at the price: a ban by the censor, at that stage, would have landed all concerned in deep, hot water.

described it as 'perhaps the most exquisite study in existence of a boy's awakening to love, the young Romeo of our times'. It was, perhaps, the underlying *social* impropriety of disturbing the public school status quo which upset the Old Etonian censor. But whatever the reasons for his ban may have been, he maintained it obstinately for over a year. The play had to be staged first in the U.S.A., where it was an immediate hit, Basil Dean, who wanted to produce it in London, discussed it with Lord Cromer for eighteen months. After a 'private' performance by the Stage Society, the play was given generally glowing notices by the press, who —though not all quite as doting as the *Telegraph*—all evinced blank amazement at its prohibition. But although the Chamberlain read the play three times, he remained unmoved. Not until he *saw* it in performance at the Arts Theatre Club, and after one last cross-examination of Mr Dean, did he at last relent. 'He had been struck with the sincerity of our playing,' Mr Dean told a reporter, 'and the delicate way the theme had been treated'—but the 'delicacy' was there in the text, to start with. 'He insisted that the same treatment should be given to any provincial touring production, and that the play might go on the road only if it was well cast with sincere artists.' In fact, as Herbert Farjeon said, any company was 'free to act *Young Woodley* in the indelicate and unrestrained way (whatever that may have been) originally envisaged by the Lord Chamberlain in his mind's eye'. Happily for the English stage, the sincerity test for actors is not one which the Lord Chamberlain has yet found it possible to enforce, although he has, from time to time, returned wistfully to its feasibility. The play was a box-office hit at the Savoy— with cuts. Mr Dean summed up this curious episode at the time of the censor's change of heart by announcing: 'Such an act restores public confidence in the idea of a play censorship', a deduction which deserves its place in the records of Chamberlain humbug.

Another harmless, sentimental play which offended Lord Cromer, and which he firmly refused to license (in 1925), was one of the dramatic works of Marie Stopes, the pioneer of the birth control movement. The offence of *Vectia* was that it ventilated the facts that some husbands cannot give their wives children—or marital satisfaction, because they are undersexed or even impotent; and that many women were kept in such sexual ignorance, as a consequence of their social subjection, that they accepted their deprivation as a mystery of Nature. The play's tone and plot seemed so irreproachable that all concerned were astonished when the Chamberlain pronounced his sentence of death, while it was in rehearsal. Miss Stopes wrote, indignantly:

It seemed to all of us obvious that a play in which there is no adultery, no prostitute, no illegitimate child, no erotic intensity, no sex vice of any sort, and of which the theme is the desire of a sweet girl wife to have a baby and by her husband and to carry on the race, was (and is) essentially in line with the objects desired by officialdom and held as our social ideal. Hence we expected it to be welcomed warmly. The poooibility of ito being dioapproved never crossed any of our minds ... It was banned at a time when plays and revues of prodigious filth were being staged with the approval of the Lord Chamberlain's department.[1]

According to her own account, she said to the manager: 'Give me a day and I will give you a play.' She called in a shorthand reporter from the Central Criminal Court, and in six hours dictated to him a new play about the birth control movement, *Our Ostriches*, which had been 'fermenting' in her mind for some time. It passed the Chamberlain untouched, and ran for three months. There are, as Dorothy Knowles[2] pointed out, some discrepancies in Marie Stopes's story. *Vectia* is a revised version of a play refused a licence in 1923, and *Our Ostriches* was first licensed in the same year, *not* a few weeks after the ban on *Vectia*. But Miss Stopes hit the target when she complained that only in a 'man-controlled', man-censored society would such a mild exposure of the sexual injustices and servitudes of marriage and the sexual impotence of husbands be labelled as morally objectionable, while hundreds of plays flattering and even exalting male promiscuity were passed without demur. She saw the Lord Chamberlain several times, and offered to make alterations; but 'he said that he did not object to a single sentence in the play and very kindly added: "You have done it beautifully, there is not a word or a thing to which I can take exception, but I cannot allow the *theme*" '.

According to the Examiner in 1925, the Chamberlain prohibited only plays 'the performance of which would have been a real scandal'. This is a selective list of some plays banned between the wars: Aristophanes's *Lysistrata*, Strindberg's *Miss Julie*, Pirandello's *Six Characters in Search of an Author*, O'Neill's *Desire Under the Elms*, Schnitzler's *Reigen* (or *La Ronde*), Simon Gantillon's *Maya*, Leonhard Frank's *Karl and Anna*, Lillian Hellman's *The Children's Hour*, George Moore's *The Passing of the Essenes*, Toller's *Hinkemann* and *Hoppla, We Live*,

[1] *A Banned Play and a Preface on the Censorship*, by Marie Stopes (1926).
[2] *The Censor, the Drama, and the Film* (1934).

Bruckner's *The Criminals* and *Malady of Youth*, Wedekind's *Earth Spirit* and *Spring Awakening*, Emil Ludwig's *Versailles*, Alfred Savoir's *The Lion Tamer* and *Lui*, Lenormand's *Man and his Phantoms* and *The Eater of Dreams*, Marc Connelly's *Green Pastures*. Two of these are known to be *still* banned (*The Passing of the Essenes* and *Green Pastures*); two more (*The Children's Hour* and *Maya*) were not licensed until the 1950s; *Spring Awakening* was not licensed (with heavy cuts) till 1964. As Mr Street eloquently said in 1925, 'always to succeed is not in human labours'; but this register of failure corrects the Panglossian picture of Lord Cromer's regime in St James's Palace.

Why were plays banned? First of all, of course, on familiar religious grounds: because they represented God or Christ on the stage, which ruled out *Green Pastures* with its blackface Jehovah and *The Passing of the Essenes* (based by George Moore on his novel, *The Brook Kerith*); or because they questioned the Christian faith (of which the censor's royal employer is Defender), and this meant no public performance of a play like *Lui*, which threw doubt on the existence of God, and suggested that it is Man who does all the miracles, in God's name. Or because they depicted the Royal Family, like *The Queen's Minister*, a piece of 1922 about Queen Victoria and Melbourne: which contained 'nothing that was not already to be found in the Queen's journal, in the *The Creevey Papers*, or Lytton Strachey's *Queen Victoria*'.[1] Sir Basil Bartlett's play about *The Jersey Lily* could only be given a club performance in 1940; its heroine, Lily Langtry, may have been his wife's grandmother, but she was also the mistress of the King's grandfather. Even earlier passages in the history of the English Royal Family proved to be perilous stuff for the stage, as Laurence Housman discovered when he tried, once again, to get a licence for his play about Queen Caroline, *Pains and Penalties*, in the belief that the censorship had shown itself to be more liberal through the licensing of *The Cenci* and *Mrs Warren's Profession*.

I wrote to the Lord Chamberlain, and suggested that as more sense had now been shown in the matter of these two plays, it should be exercised on mine also. In reply I received a letter from Sir Douglas Dawson, the State-Chamberlain, asking me to go and see him. I did so. I found him very polite, and very flattering: he had re-read the play and had found it 'very amusing'; 'I laughed and laughed', he assured me. 'Very nice of you', I said: 'but I wrote it as a tragedy.'

[1] *The Censor, the Drama, and the Films*, by Dorothy Knowles (1934).

But comedy or tragedy was not the point. What mattered was that the Lord Chamberlain (it was no longer Lord Spencer) authorized him to say that, if I would leave out one word and one sentence, a licence would be granted to any manager who applied for it.

The sentence I was to leave out was this: 'Heirs male of the last generation have not been a conspicuous success.' The reference was, of course, to the sons of King George III. In the Lord Chamberlain's office there was apparently a fear that it might be applied—more recently. It seemed to me a fantastic notion: but I consented. The word I was to leave out was 'adultery'. It came in a sentence which Queen Caroline had actually spoken: 'If I ever did commit adultery, it was when I married the husband of Mrs FitzHerbert.' It was a magnificent answer to her tormentors; it put the case in a nutshell; but—it contained the forbidden word. 'But, my dear sir,' I protested 'the word adultery is said in church every Sunday, in the ears of men, women, and children. What does it matter?' 'Nothing at all,' he said: 'in church it means nothing, but on stage it means everything.'

There, of course, he was quite right: the stage being so much more alive in meaning what it says, than the Church. Still, it was comic.

'Well,' I said, 'I can do this: I can make Caroline say "If I ever did commit . . ." and then Lord Brougham can interrupt with an exclamation of horror, representing the mind of the Lord Chamberlain's office up-to-date, so that the word never gets spoken.' But this, I found, did not satisfy him. 'No,' he said, 'I'm afraid that directly you say the word 'commit' everybody will know what the next word is going to be.'

And so (that my play might have the possibility of life restored to it) I agreed that the word adultery should be left out, and that the sentence should run: 'If ever I did *that thing*, it was when I married the husband of Mrs FitzHerbert.' . . .[1]

Another play by Mr Housman was banned until 1942, when Victoria's last surviving son, the Duke of Connaught, died. The Duke had objected to the intimacy of a scene showing how Victoria had the dead Prince Consort's evening dress laid out every night as if he were still alive; and the Chamberlain, of course, carried out the Duke's wishes.

An indication of the comic lengths to which the Chamberlain could go to protect the Royal Family was given by Leon M. Lion in his auto-

[1] *The Unexpected Years* (1937).

biography, *The Surprise of my Life*. He was producing a comedy by Nesta Sawyer which included a snatch of dialogue between 'an ultra-modern young girl and an ultra-serious young man'. She told him she was breaking her date with him because she had been asked to a garden party at Buckingham Palace; he denounced her for being a snob; and she retorted:

> 'Of course, I'm a snob. Everybody is, about something. You're an intellectual snob. You'd much rather hobnob with—er—Pontius Pilate than the Prince of Wales, wouldn't you?'
> 'Naturally,' replied our young intellectual.
> 'Well, I wouldn't,' she answered flatly. 'Give me Buck House and the Prince every time.'[1]

A message came that the play could not be licensed until the reference to the Prince of Wales had been deleted. Would Mr Lion submit for their approval the name he proposed to substitute? Recovering from his surprise, he entered on tactful negotiations which—after several rebuffs—led to an eventual compromise.

The protection of 'personalities' was, and is, one of the Lord Chamberlain's self-appointed tasks; but between this field of invasion of personal privacy and near-libel and the realms of political privilege and royal susceptibilities, the boundaries are somewhat confused. It seems clear, for instance, that the censor banned Alfred Savoir's *The Lion Tamer*, one of the most distinguished French plays of the 1920s, because he believed that the central figure, an English peer following a travelling circus, was a caricature of Lord Lonsdale. As he was called Lord Lonsden, the censor's suspicion is understandable, even though the peer was, it seems, intended as a symbol of idealism in pursuit of abstract justice.

Yet the affair of the *Parnell* and *Gladstone* plays is a good deal less simple. Elsie Schauffler's *Parnell* was first staged in New York, because the British censor had banned it on the familiar ground of trespass: it exposed to view people and events which were not yet remote enough for theatrical treatment. He assured Norman Marshall, indeed, that a play on this topic would *never* be allowed in either of their lifetimes. Mr Marshall presented it as a 'club' production at the Gate, with its star on Broadway, Margaret Rawlings. It was generally acclaimed by the critics, who all attacked the Chamberlain's veto; *The Times* devoted

---

[1] *The Surprise of My Life*, by Leon M. Lion (1948).

three leading articles to a discussion of the case and a demand for the ban to be lifted; and lifted it finally was, but only after further lobbying by the press and weeks of discussion between Norman Marshall, the Chamberlain and representatives of the families of the characters in the play.

Influenced by the success of *Parnell*, Norman Marshall commissioned Hugh Ross Williamson to write a play about Gladstone, to whom—Williamson believed—*Parnell* had been unfair. The play was a success at the Gate. But when Marshall tried to transfer *Mr Gladstone* to the West End the Chamberlain vetoed it because it presented Queen Victoria in two scenes, and did so with some flavour of criticism. Williamson had largely used the Queen's own words, from her published letters;[1] but that did not matter to the censor. Again, the press protested eloquently against the ban. 'It seems to me monstrously unjust,' said St John Ervine in the *Observer*, 'that one author should be forbidden to do what may be done by all other authors without asking for permission . . . She (Queen Victoria) belongs to this nation, and not to any individual in it. What she did and said affected profoundly the lives of vast multitudes of men and women, and it is absurd that any effort to increase our knowledge of her should be frustrated merely because somebody objects in general to her impersonation on the stage.'

Ivor Brown pointed out that it looked uncomfortably like political partisanship:

> what are we to think of a censorship which permits the idealizing of the Queen and the producing of Gladstone and suddenly says 'No!' when something different is said about Queen Victoria, and Gladstone is rescued from a mockery which is undeserved? The treatment of the Gladstone play might suggest that the censorship is simply an asset of the Tory party and exists to keep historical truth off the stage. I do not for a moment allege that the Lord Chamberlain or his assistant are activated by this motive. But it is very foolish of them to give their opponents . . . any opportunity to hold this view.

Yet in spite of such voices, the campaign did not repeat the effect of its predecessor: *Mr Gladstone* stayed banned.

---

[1] 'I put nothing of consequence into the Queen's mouth which she did not either say or write except for one invented sentence when Gladstone quoted Cromwell at her: "We are not interested in the views of that unfortunate regicide." '—Hugh Ross Williamson, in *The Walled Garden* (1956).

Plays were also banned for political and diplomatic reasons. Emil Ludwig's *Versailles* was prohibited because its cast included Lloyd George, Wilson and Clemenceau, and it dramatized the signing of the Peace Treaty of 1919. Hubert Griffith's *Red Sunday* was vetoed in 1929 because its subject, the role of Lenin in the Russian Revolution, was considered 'too recent' and, more to the point, because its dramatis personae included a brother-in-law of the King, the late Czar. Tretyakov's *Roar China*—acclaimed in Berlin in Max Reinhardt's production and in Moscow, where Meyerhold produced it—was banned because it was a Soviet propaganda play directed against white imperialism. The Cambridge Festival Theatre, which presented it in the spirit of 'send-up', 'like the holding up of a wasp by its tail', declared that if the Chamberlain took the play seriously and banned it, 'history would have one of the best jokes so far against his Department'. The censor's vigilant opposition to Communism extended even into the cinema in 1930, when he intervened against a film by a master director—Pudovkin's *Mother*, by forbidding the London Workers' Film Society to show it on Sunday in a theatre which he licensed. He stopped Sewell Stokes from writing a play about Sir Roger Casement: this, he said, could never be licensed.

On the other hand, a number of plays were banned—or heavily amended—because they were less than reverent to Mussolini and Hitler, and would thus offend the heads of friendly powers. These included *What Made the Iron Grow?*, an attack on Nazi anti-semitism; *Lucid Interval*, a satire on the dictator of an unspecified country; and *Follow My Leader*, an anti-Hitler satirical farce set in Moronia and Neurasthenia—of which the part-author was Terence Rattigan. It was his third play, and was not licensed till after the outbreak of war: by then its original bite and point had gone. Some distinguished American writers had troubles in this field, though without incurring the censor's final veto. In 1937 he at first attempted to ban Elmer Rice's *Judgement Day* because it contained a disguised dramatization of the Reichstag Trial; and in 1938 he insisted that Robert Sherwood's *Idiot's Delight* should contain no direct reference to Italy or Mussolini, and that the soldiers of the totalitarian state should not wear Italian uniforms, although the political geography of the play was perfectly apparent to anyone who saw the play, and the original text was on sale in the theatre. Revues were carefully watched for indiscriminate suggestions that Hitler and Mussolini were figures of fun—or worse. As late as 1939, a Herbert Farjeon lyric was banned because it began:

140

> *Even Hitler had a mother*
> *Even Musso had a ma.*

The banning of Toller's *Hinkeman* was no doubt mainly due to the fact that its central figure—a soldier back from the wars—has been neutered by his injuries, and makes no bones about revealing it; but also, perhaps, to such passages as this speech at the end:

> The war came and took them and they hated their chiefs and obeyed orders and killed each other. And it's all forgotten. They'll be taken again and kill each other. Again and again. That's what people are. They might be different if they wanted to. But they don't want to. They mock at life. They scourge it and spit upon it and crucify life.

It was on the time-honoured score of moral turpitude, however, that the Chamberlain usually moved against a play, especially if it contained incest. Even unsuccessful and oblique incest was disallowed. It was the unconscious attempt of a man to sleep with his stepdaughter in a brothel that brought *Six Characters in Search of an Author* under the Lord Chamberlain's veto for a time. A somewhat more distant relationship, but still too close for the censor's liking, was dramatized in Louis Verneuil's *Maica*, which showed a girl selling herself—to support her lover—to a count who proves to be his father.

Homosexuality, which became a crucial problem for the censorship in the 1950s, did not concern Lord Cromer. St John Ervine wrote, in 1933, in *The Theatre in My Time*:

> The most daring English dramatist would not have dreamt of introducing a homosexualist into the cast of a play before 1914 . . . I do not think I am exaggerating when I say that if either *La Prisonnière* or *The Green Bay Tree* had been performed in England before 1914, the vast majority of people would not have known that each of them treats of sexual perversion or that there was such a subject to treat. I doubt if there was one person in a thousand who, before 1914, knew the meaning of the word *Lesbian*. It is notorious that when a novel on the subject was banned in England [Radclyffe Hall's *The Well of Loneliness*, in 1928] and a discussion on its prohibition took place in the House of Commons, the great majority of the members of the Labour Party had not the faintest notion of what the book was about.

Edouard Bourdet's *La Prisonnière* was not, in fact, licensed by Lord Cromer. It was banned because although it was recognized as a play

141

of delicate distinction, by a leading French dramatist, which had been staged throughout Europe and in New York, it presented the unsuccessful struggle of a girl to conform with orthodox sexuality and to suppress her own Lesbian drives by marriage, only to plunge into an affair with another Lesbian wife. Lord Cromer saw the play himself, unofficially, on the first night, but maintained that it was unstagable in public; and when it was revived in 1934, it could still only be given a club performance at the Arts. Yet it was written so discreetly that (according to St John Ervine) it 'might easily leave an audience with no other impression than that two women were unduly fond of each other'. Again, Mordaunt Shairp's *The Green Bay Tree*—a box-office success of 1933—displayed such 'immense discretion' that the audience might imagine that the moral corruption exercised by the central figure over the younger man was one only of cynical materialism and not sexual love. This was, in fact, the nearest thing to a play overtly about homosexuals that any Chamberlain licensed until the 1950s. Several others were attempted. In 1930 he banned a stage adaptation of *The Well of Loneliness* (Marion Norris's *Alone*). But, in face of the censor's stand, the theme was rarely handled. The play about Oscar Wilde in which Robert Morley made his first success was not submitted to the Lord Chamberlain and could not be publicly staged in London.

It was the heterosexual frankness of many Continental and a few American plays which kept them off the English public stage or exposed them to heavy cutting. The Lord Chamberlain, for instance, banned scenes in a brothel (like the uncensorable *Pericles*); or the presentation of characters in bed together (as in *Othello*); or promiscuous sex without punishment. Wedekind, Lenormand, and many more offended against the censor's canons of decency. His nervousness may be judged by his attitude to one of the Aldwych farces, *Cuckoo in the Nest* (1925), in which the fun turned on a couple separated from their spouses and obliged to spend the night together, in absolute chastity, in the same bedroom. When the script was sent in, says Ben Travers, the Lord Chamberlain's Office 'expressed great concern about the bedroom scene . . . so much so that, for the only time in my experience, a special (and very inconvenient) rehearsal was called for inspection by a representative of the Censorship Department'.[1] Thanks to Yvonne Arnaud, who played the lady in this delicate situation, all was well: 'The genial major detached to pass final judgement did so without hesita-

[1] *Vale of Laughter*, by Ben Travers (1957).

142

tion and almost apologetically . . .' But, in this climate, what chance did Strindberg have—or undiluted Aristophanes?

During the war Ben Travers wrote a comedy for Robertson Hare, as 'a country vicar at loggerheads with his parishioners', *She Follows Me About*. In the middle of rehearsals, the Lord Chamberlain informed the management that it could not be licensed unless 'fourteen of my most promising lines were omitted'. Mr Travers describes what happened next in his autobiography.[1]

At that time the Lord Chamberlain's office was in Windsor Castle. Bill Linnit [S. E. Linnit, the manager] and I journeyed thither by appointment and, after being conducted past long ranks of an intimidating guard of honour consisting of unoccupied sets of armour, we were shown into the handsome sunlit suite which contained the two gentlemen who had drawn up the catalogue of my fourteen mortal offences.

The spokesman was a small but virile, emphatic and mobile personage. I was dismayed—though with respect and admiration—to discover that he had studied and memorized every detail of the contested passages, their context and their meanings, both simple and double. His enthusiasm and efficiency were most impressive, but so was his determination.

He thoroughly agreed with the accepted principle that affliction and menace must be visited upon Mr Robertson Hare. His objection was to their being visited upon him as a member of the cloth. 'I will *not*,' he cried and clouted his table, 'I will *not* have Mr Robertson Hare suspected of what he calls hi-tiddly-i-ti- in a clerical collar.'

At one point of the discussion I ventured to charge him with inconsistency. 'Here,' I said, 'I have wrapped up a vulgar expression neatly, in order to avoid any crudity, and you rule it out. What do you want? Do you want me to say straight out "He slapped my bottom"?'

'Yes,' he replied immediately, and his eyes lit up. 'Yes, I pass bottom.' He relapsed and gazed past me in the manner of one indulging a momentary, rhapsodical lapse from his customary modesty, and he added proudly, 'I was the first censor to pass bottom.'

A little later—'I can't understand,' I said, 'why you want *that* word out. What's the matter with it?'

[1] *Vale of Laughter* (1957).

143

'*That* word? Oh, but it can be put to an utterly unspeakable meaning.'

'Really?' I said. 'I'm surprised I've never heard it.' I turned to Bill Linnit. 'Have you?' Bill Linnit shook his head. Even the rather dumb second inquisitor had to admit, on being challenged, that he had never heard it either.

'Well, come on then,' I said. 'What is it? Let's have it. What is the horrifying hidden significance of this poor word?'

The spokesman bit his lip. He half raised himself with his hands on his chair and surveyed the room anxiously, as though fearful that it might harbour some sneaking eavesdropper. Then he sat back, drew a deep breath and eyed me guiltily. His voice dropped to an almost inaudible whisper. 'Cock,' he said.

We patched up our differences somehow and they didn't affect the issue because, in any case, the play received a general castigation from the critics, whom it seemed to catch in a severely sanctimonious mood which kept several of them in the bar for most of the evening. And, although I had run up against a punctilious and slightly ridiculous representative of the Lord Chamberlain, this personal encounter confirmed what I had always thought—that the censorship of plays is valuable and expedient. It safeguards managements and dramatists by lulling the public into an obtuse sense of assurance that any play they go to see has been officially declared to be moral. Abolition of the censorship would expose the play to the mercies of the local legislators and pietistic fanatics of every city in the land. And the censors carry out their task with good sense and equity. Besides, they know the meanings of words that we don't.

According to G. S. Street, the censor not only 'prohibited plays the production of which would have been a real scandal', but he 'removed from innumerable plays, not prohibited, that which would have needlessly outraged any audience'. Many authors and managers were willing to compromise with the censor when he would allow reasonable changes. But sometimes the 'removals' destroyed the play. This happened to a play about Elizabeth and Essex which showed an unwelcome candour about the psychological roots (in childhood rape) of the Virgin Queen's failure to marry, André Josset's *Elizabeth, Le Femme sans Homme*. The Chamberlain licensed this play reluctantly, 'after so heartily blue-pencilling it that it had lost most of its point'. It closed in a few weeks. An adaption of Evelyn Waugh's *Vile Bodies*—for which Ivor Novello was refused a licence—was trimmed of some of its references to sex, given a happy ending and equipped with a wildly incompatible Harlequin to supply a moral. This was another compromise with the censorship, and, not surprisingly, it flopped.

An example of one of these 'needlessly outrageous' passages may be found in Somerset Maugham's *Our Betters* (1923). In the published text, a young American girl discovers—off stage—her married sister and a 'gigolo' making love in some unspecified way in a summer-house, but the Lord Chamberlain ordered the discovery to be made by a *man* who was not related to the apparently adulterous lady. As the manager explained at the time, elucidating a review by Desmond MacCarthy in which he had criticized the dramatist for this point, 'in the interests of morality, stage innocents must really be prevented from receiving imaginary shocks in imaginary summer-houses; else what's the object of having a censor at all?'

It was on the fringe of the commercial theatre during these two decades that much of the most vital and influential work was done. Many writers and artists found their opportunities and developed their talent in this precariously marginal territory—'the other theatre', as Mr Norman Marshall labelled it in his excellent book of that name, which describes how, between the wars:

> The English theatre was saved from stagnation and sterility by the small group of producers, players and playgoers who, supported by many of the dramatic critics, refused to accept the drab monotony imposed upon the theatre by the managers and by the censor, seemingly united in a determination to keep the theatre in a state of arrested development.[1]

About a dozen play-producing societies, mostly short-lived, sprang up during the 1920s and 1930s. Not all were devoted, all the time, to the staging of unlicensed new plays. Two, the Phoenix and the Renaissance, were concerned only with the sixteenth- and seventeenth-century drama, while the Repertory Players turned their back on anything which the West End managers might not fancy. At the other extreme the Venturers were only established because an author, Lord Lathom (the grandson of a Chamberlain) wanted to stage a play which the censor had vetoed (*Wet Paint*). The Venturers produced two more of the founder's plays during a creative five-year span which included work by those

[1] *The Other Theatre*, by Norman Marshall (1947).

145

Continental writers who failed to come up to the ideas of Lord Cromer.

The first time that the 'club' device was extended beyond one or two 'private' performances was in 1925 at the Gate Theatre, a converted loft in Floral Street which soon acquired a reputation for the presentation of banned plays. Peter Godfrey opened it as a club theatre, however, not primarily for this reason, but because the Lord Chamberlain and the L.C.C. refused to license it as a public playhouse, on the grounds of public safety: one 'rickety wooden staircase', as Norman Marshall says, supplied the only entrance and exit combined. After two seasons it opened in a converted skittle alley in Villiers Street. Those who were prepared to risk both physical danger and moral contagion saw a series of plays by leading English, American and Continental writers, which would never have reached a licensed stage at that time, either because they could not gain a licence themselves, or, more frequently, because they would never be selected by the ultra-cautious 'commercial' managers and lessees or by the handful of hard-up and therefore necessarily conservative repertory theatres.

Another centre of revolt against the censorship was the Cambridge Festival Theatre, whose founder and director, Terence Gray, not only staged between 1926 and 1932 a number of outstanding plays banned by the Chamberlain, but kept up a withering fire of comment upon the curious behaviour of St James's Palace in the lively programme-review which he published. Sometimes he took freakish measures in production. When an excised passage was reached, 'Omitted by order of the Lord Chamberlain' was shouted through a megaphone. When the censor deleted a number of references to 'Christ' and 'My God', Gray inserted 'Oh My Lord Chamberlain', instead, as the next in omnipotence to God (the Chamberlain said he was flattered). When a scene was suppressed, on the door of the room in which it *should* have been enacted was hung a notice, 'Closed by order of the Lord Chamberlain'. This was not his only purpose in running the Festival Theatre. He experimented boldly and brilliantly in unrealistic production techniques, notably lighting, and he helped to energize the theatre in general while prodding the Chamberlain out of some of his more frumpish attitudes and reminding a minority public, at least, of those postures in which the censor remained adamant.

A great deal of time and effort was usually required to dislodge the Chamberlain from a prepared position. The old ban on *Salomé*, for instance, was maintained in 1927, when the Cambridge Festival Theatre applied for a licence. It was so well received at one special, free performance that Peter Godfrey decided to stage it at the Gate. This 1929 production was so successful that the censor changed his mind, after nearly forty years, and offered it to its Cambridge sponsors, although as they could not then take advantage of the thaw it was not until 1931 that *Salomé* was publicly performed, at the Lyceum. This little victory—like many others—might have been postponed for many years, had it not been for the persistence and initiative of the fringe theatre.

II

The Modern Poets seem to use smut as the old Ones did Machines, to relieve a fainting Invention.—JEREMY COLLIER

In the last analysis, all censorship is political censorship.—WILLIAM SEAGLE; *Cato: or The Future of Censorship*, 1930

* * *

UNTIL the mid-1950s, opposition to the Lord Chamberlain's or to *any* censorship of the stage rumbled on in the theatre world. Outside that world few crusaders came forward and stayed forward. The censor, under pressure, moved back an inch here, conceded a point there, keeping carefully behind the times, as the times moved elsewhere, and in line with public opinion as he saw it from St James's Palace. Indignation against his crasser vetos swelled up—and receded again. Resolutions were passed: in 1948, at the British Theatre Conference, out of 450 representatives of the theatre only three voted against abolishing the censorship. But nothing happened. Bills were carried: in 1949 Benn Levy's Censorship of Plays (Repeal) Bill introduced by a Conservative M.P. (E. P. Smith) and supported by a Labour M.P. (Michael Foot) was carried, on its second reading, by seventy-six votes to thirty-seven. It proposed the abolition of the censorship, 'so as to exempt the theatre from restrictions upon freedom of expression in excess of those applicable to other forms of literature', and introduced the safeguard that no criminal prosecution could be brought without the agreement of a judge in chambers (a protection against irresponsible prosecution afforded to newspaper proprietors). But the Bill failed to interest the Labour Government (many Labour M.P.s opposed it). Nothing happened. Motions were introduced: in 1962 Dingle Foot submitted one for leave to present a Bill abolishing the censorship; but after a short debate, the motion was rejected by 134 votes to 77. And nothing happened.

Yet by 1966 the Lord Chamberlain's Office had been repeatedly exposed as almost as inefficient, unfair and absurd as ever before. Several managers, for the first time in a century, had actually joined playwrights, actors and critics in supporting its abolition. The Lord Chancellor had proposed this in the House of Lords, and the Prime Minister had said in the Commons that the Office required 'modernization'. The Government had promised an official inquiry. And the Lord Chamberlain himself—breaking the traditional silence of the Office—had agreed that it had certain drawbacks, and had indicated that he was ready to step down, if required so to do.

How, and why, has this happened? Partly because of the repercussions of social, sexual and moral change: notably the break-up of the once-dominant middle-class conventions of taste and behaviour, with their certainties that something is 'not done' and that another thing 'can't be talked about', that you mustn't 'make a scene' or 'show your feelings'. The erosion of taboos in books, newspapers and conversation has reinforced the resistance in the theatre, which has been supported by the new freedoms of television in drama, documentary and 'satire'. These side-effects have taken more quickly because the theatre is more open to the outside world that it has been for many generations, and because—which is partly the cause and partly the result of this breakdown of former barriers—it has recruited in the past decade a new body of younger dramatists, widely different in talent, style and approach, but sharing a common impatience with the old games of compromise with the censorship. Most of them come from the lower middle class and the working class (and three, at least, have been in prison); and to them, more than to their predecessors, the Chamberlain appears as the symbol of a social, political and religious order, the relic of a dead England which won't lie down.

These writers are influenced by other media and other theatres; by television and films (for which a number of them write), and by Artaud, Brecht, Strindberg, Genet and other dramatists unpopular in Stable Yard; and they are unwilling to accept the gentleman's agreement that the liberties enjoyed elsewhere should be denied to them, because they are writing for the stage. Most of them ignore the theatre of comfort. Although some have been picked up by the commercial system, and a few have made a lot of money out of it, they reject its neutering of realism and sweetening of taste, its tendency to avoid offence at all costs, in the belief that this is necessary to get past the Chamberlain and hold a majority audience for a long run. But these dramatists can only afford such relative independence because they have come to rely on the subsidized theatre and the freedoms it can offer. This has resulted in the bizarre spectacle of the State investing in plays with one hand and banning them with the other.

The most decisive single factor in the defeat or, at least, the retreat of the Lord Chamberlain has been the innovation of State aid for the theatre, and the expansion of the Arts Council budget for the theatre within twenty years from £30,000 to nearly £900,000. The most seminal theatrical events have been the establishment of the English Stage Society at the Royal Court, of the Royal Shakespeare Company from Stratford at the Aldwych, and of the National Theatre Company at the Old Vic. Throughout the past seventy years opposition to the censorship has always come from outside the majority theatre of the big managements, the big stars and the big money. It has been sustained by individual crusaders like Grein, Shaw and Terence Gray, who could subsidize his defiance from a private fortune; and by small groups, societies and clubs, like the Stage Society, the Gate and the Arts Theatre Club. But, inevitably, they could seldom, if ever, guarantee either an audience or a living to a dramatist. It is only since a sector of the theatre was freed from the treadmill of the long-run system by grants from public funds both in London and the provinces that there has been a practical possibility of developing a serious challenge to the Lord Chamberlain.

Meanwhile, during the last ten years, the censor has not stayed on the defensive all the time. Every now and then he has taken action to remind the theatre of his powers. In 1951, for instance, he moved against the Unity, the King's Cross home of amateur Left-wing theatre, which describes itself as a 'people's theatre, built to serve as a means of dramatizing their life and struggles, and an aid in making them conscious of their strength and of the need for united action'. Under the Theatres Act of 1843, two charges were brought: one for presenting a revue at a place which was neither a patent theatre nor licensed as a theatre, and the other for putting on a play which the Lord Chamberlain had not licensed. Up till then, it had been assumed that as long as 'club members' only were admitted to performances the censor would turn a blind eye. The customary forty-eight-hour wait for admission, on which the clubs insisted, had no legal warrant, but was thrown in as a sop to the Palace. In fact, the Act makes it clear that it is an offence *anywhere* to act plays 'for hire' without a licence; and the sale of liquor on the premises, or the payment of anyone connected with a production, brings it within the meaning of the Act as a play acted 'for hire'. In moving against the Unity, the Lord Chamberlain was taking full advantage of the Act.

150

Was this prosecution due, as some suspicious critics proposed, to some political prejudice? Perhaps the Communist complexion of the Unity may have had an influence on Stable Yard's decision. But the main reason, it seems clear, was that the 'club' device had been extended to include, by block-booking, a potential membership of millions. Under its rules, any society or company could become a corporate member, thereby entitling all its individual members to buy tickets. As the T.U.C. could add eight million of them, this was stretching the 'private' label a bit far. In the result, one producer was discharged, and another was convicted but won his appeal to the High Court. The Unity continued, warily.

Another Left-wing company, Theatre Workshop, was apparently singled out for prosecution in 1958. At the Lord Chamberlain's instigation the police brought a summons against the manager, producer, author, licensee and one actor concerned with *You Won't Always Be On Top*, at the Theatre Royal, Stratford, for presenting parts which had not been licensed. Not only was there a 'very wide divergence' between the text as passed in St James's Palace and the play inspected by one of the Chamberlain's emissaries to Stratford-atte-Bowe, but these unlicensed sections were declared to be 'vulgar and not in good taste'. It was not the policy of the Lord Chamberlain's Department to allow such things, whatever regular visitors to the Crazy Gang, strip shows or revues might suppose, in their innocence of the mysteries of Stable Yard. One passage which gave particular offence to the censor, according to *The Times*, was 'a scene outside a building bearing the word "Gentlemen" in which a character called "Mick" made a speech in which he appeared to be opening the building. During his speech he altered his voice and the accent was taken as being an imitation of Sir Winston Churchill. He went on to give his version of what Sir Winston Churchill would have said if he had been called upon to open a public lavatory.' The defendants pleaded guilty because, as their counsel (Gerald Gardiner, Q.C., now Lord Chancellor) explained it was against the law to say *anything* on the stage which had not been passed by the Lord Chamberlain. Fines and costs were nominal—a total of less than £17; they were met from a special fund, for which Lord Harewood, among others, appealed; and the main result of it all, apart from reminding all theatres of the illegality of departing a jot from their licensed scripts, was to bring further discredit on the Lord Chamberlain's Office. As the *Guardian* said, there was 'nothing to show that anyone attending the performance would have been any the worse for anything they saw or heard there, or that any part of the unlicensed text was in any way obscene, libellous or seditious. It was suggested that some of it was "vulgar" and "not in good taste". Do the public need a censor to protect them from vulgarity ?'

If the Chamberlain's aim was to warn Joan Littlewood of the error of her ways—which included an impatient belief in improvisation as the basis of the actor's art—it is unlikely to have succeeded. Thereafter, indeed, he apparently gave Theatre Workshop little trouble—in 'Oh, What a Lovely War!', for instance, though at least one manager refused to stage it. But under the Act which he is required to administer, improvisation is illegal; and the ban on it was spotlighted in 1962 when the cast of the American revue *The Premise* were discovered by the Chamberlain's Office to be acting unlicensed material every night and were ordered to stop—after they had been improvising (or at any rate, had *announced* they were doing it) for four months. This intervention produced a most unEnglish reaction from the American company: unaccustomed to the native traditions of playing ball with the censorship, they declared gallantly that they would go on ad libbing, in the interests of theatrical art and against the Lord Chamberlain's orders, 'until they move the troops in'. But the Comedy remained inviolate; the Guards stayed down the road in the barracks; and, somehow or other, the argument dribbled on, without bloodshed, until the revue folded.

* * *

In the religious field, the censorship has tried in the last twenty years to maintain its traditional taboos. For most dramatists these showed most frequently and consistently in the prohibition of 'Christ' and 'Jesus' as expletives. Although these are, as Lord Cobbold agreed in 1965, 'admittedly used in common parlance and are not put forward in any irreverent spirit', they still 'give offence to a great number of people', that is to say, the minority of playgoers who belong to the minority of Christian believers. So out they go: three of each from *Chips with Everything*, four 'Christs' from *The Kitchen*, a 'Jesus' from *Mother Courage*, and so on. The Lord Chamberlain also sometimes bans the use of prayers and hymns when not in a context of proper devotion. He vetoed the singing of 'When I Survey the Wondrous Cross' in Christopher Logue's *The Trial of Cob and Leach*, and even insisted on this prohibition some years later when the scene was staged *for one night only* as part of a special charity performance to raise money for the George Devine Award, before an audience which can scarcely have included half a dozen people ready to raise an eyebrow at this indelicacy.

Among the more remarkable instances of nannyish conduct by the censor was his niggling over Samuel Beckett's *endgame*. On its world *première* as *Fin de Partie* at the Court in 1957 in French, no objections were raised to it. When it was submitted a year later in *English*, he insisted that parts of it were blasphemous. To some changes Beckett consented: over others he was intransigent. After half a dozen months of negotiation and a good deal of expenditure of spirit, time and money, agreement was reached on the main issue. It was the scene where Hamm, Nagg and Clov all pray to God, and then give up (as usual) in despair. Hamm was forbidden to say 'The bastard! He doesn't exist!': instead he had to say 'The swine!' To the author, and the theatre, it was a gross interference with a piece of dramatic literature; and it is difficult to perceive how much more or less offensive it might be to the kind of playgoer the Chamberlain is bent on sheltering. Yet by Stable Yard standards it was a remarkable and perilous indulgence that any actor should be allowed to call God a swine without a thunderbolt through the roof from the Almighty or his terrestrial protector nearer at hand. The language question, however, attracted some attention. 'Does this mean,' asked the *Evening Standard*, 'that the Lord Chamberlain considers all people who understand French beyond hope—unredeemable atheists or agnostics who need not be protected from blasphemy? Or does he believe that knowledge of the French language bestows immunity from corruption?' As readers of earlier chapters will have noted, the Chamberlain's distinction between the corruptibility of French and English was a tradition of the Office, but it was peculiar enough to merit the interest of the Home Secretary, then Mr R. A. Butler. In the House he admitted, with characteristic frankness, that the censorship was 'not without its difficulties, which I am studying'. No results of that study were, I understand, made public.

The uncertainly protective attitude of the censorship was earlier illustrated in his handling of *Valmouth*, Sandy Wilson's musical version of Ronald Firbank's novel. The material passed by the Chamberlain went further, in some ways, than had hitherto been allowed in playful treatment of religious believers—Roman Catholics at that, normally considered as touchier than members of the Church of England. But he enjoined that there should be no 'parody of Catholic ceremonial' and 'no ridicule of religious things', and he required a score of cuts, including phrases like 'the married sister of the Madonna'; 'Adorable Jesus' and 'O My Saviour Dear' in a prayer by a devotee, and a reference in the excommunication of Cardinal Pirelli (taken from another Firbank novel) to his 'sin of christening a dog'. In agreeing with most of the cuts, Mr Wilson pleaded for the restoration of several passages, especially the one about the dog, as it was 'the most famous incident in Cardinal Pirelli's career'. Mr Wilson wrote:

> I do not think the mention of his christening would give offence because (*a*) an English audience would be in sympathy with anything that concerned a dog, and (*b*) in Catholic countries, and also I believe in this country, the blessing of pet animals in a church service is a frequent and quite acceptable occurrence. I would like to point out that the Cardinal does get his just deserts for any infringement of ritual that may be involved by being defrocked and finally stricken dead. So I would most earnestly plead for a reconsideration of this point . . .

It is hard to understand why the Chamberlain should have banned the following passage from *Valmouth*, in which a character reads from a history of the saints:

> One day St Automona di Meris, seeing a young novice yawning, suddenly spat into her mouth, and that without malice or thought of mischief. Some ninety hours afterwards the said young novice brought into the world the Blessed St Elizabeth Bathilde, who, by dint of skipping, changed her sex at the age of forty and became a man.

And it is even more perplexing to comprehend the veto on this conversational exchange between Mrs Thoroughfare, Mrs Hurstpierpont and Cardinal Pirelli:

> *Mrs T:* How do you like our new relics, your Eminence? I think St Automona's tooth looks a treat now that Eulalia has had it set.
> *Mrs H:* It's only a molar of course and rather small at that—
> *Mrs T:* We are used lately to big flashing dentures.
> *Cardinal P:* Size isn't altogether important when one is dealing with the eternities.

The best-known religious prohibition by the censor is on the presentation of God, Christ and presumably the Virgin Mary on the stage: in any play, that is, since the Miracles and Mysteries. As we saw in the opening chapter, the history of the secular drama and of its censorship began with the deliberate suppression of these popular plays. Yet in the last twenty years they have been widely revived—not only in the open air or on consecrated ground, as at York, Chester, Coventry and Win-chester but also on public stages, as at the Mermaid in London; and they have been shown on television and in the cinema, without in any way interfering with the preservation of good manners, decorum, the public peace or the Established Church. Yet the censor still refuses to license Marc Connelly's *Green Pastures*, a thirty-year-old Pulitzer Prize-winning play which has been broadcast many times, filmed and televised, because it puts God on the stage. Perhaps Mr Connelly's offence is that his God isn't white. He is a *Negro*, smoking ten-cent cigars at a fish-fry in Heaven, and this is a disturbing thought for that secluded Anglican bigot who seems, on these occasions, to be the censor's ideal spectator. It is worth recalling that among the scenes recently banned in *The Premise* was one in which this notion was confirmed, showing as it did an anti-nigger Governor of a Southern state arriving in Heaven to find a blackface Almighty.

In English, at least, the presentation of Jesus was also vetoed—until 1966. It seems that the first man in a modern play to appear on the London stage as Christ, as distinct from a Stranger or a Lodger, was Vittorio Gassmann, who in 1948 acted in Gian Paolo Callegari's *The Man Who Murdered Pilate*. At first the Chamberlain said that Gassmann must not appear: his voice could be heard, he said, but He could be represented only by a spotlight. Later, relenting, he agreed that Gassmann could come on the stage, as long as he made no attempt to impersonate Christ. The actor accordingly wore an open-necked shirt with casual trousers and although on a later entrance he donned a crown of thorns, it was made clear that he was only rehearsing a Passion Play. And, in any case, this was all *in Italian*.

The veto has been broken, though the Chamberlain's Office never acknowledges the force of precedent, by *A Man Dies*, a modern passion play which was banned by the censor, although it had been seen by millions on television and was backed by a wide range of Church opinion. As the Religious Drama Society pointed out, in a special memorandum:

If a modern dramatist, Christian or non-Christian, is prohibited from creating his picture of Jesus Christ, the impression is given that the belief in the incarnate Son of God, true God and true Man, is either irrelevant or a fable in need of artificial protection. This impression is reinforced when it is seen that medieval representations are the only ones shown on the stage. And the case for the prohibition of modern treatments is greatly weakened by the appearance of such

155

on television. The Churches have given warm support to many of them; and there is every reason to think that the same would be true of stage presentations, since drama is now widely valued among Christians for the teaching power which it exercises now as in former ages.

After persistent criticism in Parliament and in the press, the ban was lifted in the summer of 1966.

By this time the Lord Chamberlain had taken another step forward, though it seems doubtful if he knew quite how far it was taking him, by licensing Peter Shaffer's *The Royal Hunt of the Sun* and John Osborne's *A Bond Honoured*. The difference between the authors and their work is an obvious one: but the theatrical historian will note with interest the appearance at virtually the same time of two plays with such common ground—fiercely anti-Christian in thought and feeling, both containing Crucifixion tableaus, both staged by State-aided companies, and both passed by the censor—against his four hundred-year long tradition of suppressing religious dissent and heresy. Reviewing Shaffer's play, Bernard Levin wrote: 'If the Lord Chamberlain had sufficient understanding to know what this play is about it would be banned from the stage.' How much more does that observation apply to *A Bond Honoured*. But it was a misunderstanding which the censor shared with several critics.

Royal bans have continued much as before. In a revue, *We Are Amused*, a duet between Disraeli and Queen Victoria was vetoed because, they said in Stable Yard, 'we can't have the old girl portrayed singing and dancing on the stage'. A whole operetta about Victoria and Albert was banned in 1951, although its authors were the highly respected Norman Ginsbury and Eric Maschwitz, because it was said to be guilty of historical inaccuracies, in showing the Queen singing, for instance. Yet, two years later, in a musical whose historical authenticity was, to say the least, open to question, Anna Neagle was permitted to appear as Victoria not only singing 'Drink to me only with thine eyes' but also teaching Albert to waltz. The bizarre explanation of the immunity of this show, *The Glorious Days*, was not, apparently, that it was a patriotic spectacular for Coronation year or that its star had already established acting rights in the Queen's great-great-grandmother by her screen performance of the role, but that Miss Neagle, who began the musical as a gallant ambulance driver in 1944, only *dreamed* that she was Queen Victoria, under the influence of advanced concussion, and that this removed any suggestion of impersonation or *lèse-majesté* from her appearance in royal disguise. Other prohibitions have included sketches about the education of Prince Charles and the amours of Edward VII; the reproduction of a sketch televised to an audience of millions about the sinking of a royal barge; the playing of a record of the National Anthem during a play; the use in a Ruritanian play (by John Osborne) of the Christian names of two members of the Royal Family, attached to the title 'Prince'; a reference to George VI not wanting to be King; and the use of the recorded voice of George V in a documentary. Nothing much has changed here since, just before Queen Victoria's marriage, *Ruy Blas* was banned 'lest playgoers should perceive in it allusions to the matrimonial choice Her Majesty was then about to make'.

Political censorship continued to be applied, spasmodically, to revues during the 1950s and the 1960s. In 1961 a new theatrical freedom appeared to have been won by the authors of *Beyond the Fringe*, which presented unscathed a directly satirical send-up by Peter Cook of Mr Macmillan, then Prime Minister. As he was not mentioned by name in the script, the real purpose of the sketch was apparently overlooked by the censor, who was understandably unwilling to intervene after the opening of the revue, when it became at once a smash hit. Later it was visited not only by Mr Macmillan, but by the Lord Chamberlain, accompanying the Queen. It was not in the theatre, however, but on television that political satire and personalities were exploited before many millions at a time with an edge and boldness which the Lord Chamberlain would never tolerate, but which, significantly, has provoked no disturbances of public order—whatever it has done to the blood-pressure of staider viewers. But the fact that an actor once sent up the Prime Minister on the stage and got away with it did not establish a precedent for the Lord Chamberlain's Office.

Apart from political satire, political plays are still rare in the English theatre. This is partly because there is still no great demand for them and partly because managers have always maintained that the stage should not, in any event, be 'turned into a political arena'. But it is probable that their scarcity is also due to the fact that the Lord Chamberlain is thought to cherish a similar belief and to enforce it, even in the most trivial detail. Ambitious revue-writers have frequently been shown the error of their ways. In 1946, for instance, several verses were banned in 'The Left Honourables', a song about new Labour Ministers in *Between Ourselves*, mainly—it was suggested—because they implied that old-guard Socialist M.P.s were illiterate. After protracted negotiations most of the cuts were restored—with the aitches that the author had dropped. In 1954 the Chamberlain, then Lord Scarbrough, banned a song in a Hammersmith revue, *Light Fantastic*. Called 'Right Hand Man', it purported to be sung by Anthony Eden, then Deputy Prime Minister, complaining about the waiting game which Churchill, then Premier, had apparently played against him. The delay of Eden's accession to power was then a common topic in print and in conversation; but it was considered unfit for the stage by Lord Scarbrough, who had once been Eden's P.P.S.

Open social criticism has generally been discouraged. It is instructive to see what the censor disallowed in a little-theatre partisan political documentary of 1953—Oliver Martin's *Guilty and Proud of it*. This set out to dramatize the Poplar 'battles' in 1921 of George Lansbury, who was jailed with the rest of the Poplar Council for refusing to pay its rate allocation, as a protest against the overburdening of poor London boroughs. The cuts ordered by the Chamberlain included the elimination of an off-stage scream in a jail scene because this 'might suggest ill-treatment'; a reference to the beating up of demonstrators by the police (widely reported at the time); a V.C.'s statement expressing disgust with the authorities' behaviour; and a phrase that British troops had been sent to 'murder' people of different nations and colours, in the colonies. The Chamberlain here saw it as his duty to redress the balance of a picture of official Britain, criticized in a Left-wing play about recent history.

Ten years later his successor was faced with a somewhat similar problem of historical controversy in a different area of experience: Pope Pius's wartime attitude to the Nazis' liquidation of the Jews, criticized in Rolf Hochhuth's *The Representative*. The scrutiny of this play presented Lord Cobbold, he has confessed, with his most difficult task as censor, and he finally agreed to license it only on condition that the management of the Aldwych published in the programme a statement by a Roman Catholic spokesman giving the opposite side of the case presented by the dramatist. This apparent attempt at enforcing 'balance', though it may seem merely pedantic, was among the censorship's cruder interventions in theatrical freedom since the war. What hope has the theatre of ever establishing closer links with the events of the outside world, of interpreting, celebrating or exploding the happenings, the institutions, and the people—past and present—that mould our public and our private lives, if every theatrical 'nay' which may offend some pressure group must be cushioned, at least nominally, by an official 'yea'—even if it is only in print?

That decision by Lord Cobbold, patently conscientious and fair-minded as he is, reflects the nagging mistrust of the stage which has run through the censorship's history, and the persistent assumption that it is both permissible and necessary to interfere not only to ensure the physical safety of the audience, but also to try to protect it from disturbing opinions and events in an author's work. It is not unlikely that if *The Representative* had been by an English writer, unheralded by the flood of publicity and argument which swept Hochhuth's play into London, it might never have seen the stage. But what English author would ever tackle such a theme, knowing the rooted objection of the Chamberlain's Office to the presentation of heads of state, including those recently dead, and to the dramatization of up to date history? It is the dearth of a living drama about the recent past—even more than the lack of political plays—which is directly attributable to the Lord Chamberlain.

It was an American author who dared in 1958 to write *Shadow of Heroes*, a semi-documentary about the Hungarian revolution which had taken place only two years earlier—although here the risk was smaller, as the politicians shown on the stage, such as Mikoyan, Kadar and Rakosi, were nearly all Communists, and they do not qualify for special protection by the Lord Chamberlain. On the other hand good-humoured sketches about Jacqueline Kennedy were prohibited in several revues during the 1960s, even though—on one occasion—President Kennedy gave his assurance that no offence was taken. In this same revue a sketch about Mrs Khrushchev was passed without demur.

If the present system remains intact, it is in this terrain that some of the strongest arguments for its abolition are likely to explode in the next five years, if the recent-history documentary and theatre of fact contemplated by the National and Royal Shakespeare are run against the brick wall of the Chamberlain's vetos. Little trouble is expected by the Royal Shakespeare, for instance, in dramatizing Chairman Mao in its projected historical documentary on 'The Long March', the legendary trek of the Chinese Communists in the 1930s; or in putting Stalin and Trotsky on the Aldwych stage in its plans to mark the fiftieth anniversary of the Russian Revolution; but in the latter project it has already encountered difficulties over the presentation of Kerensky—for Kerensky is not only alive, but on the Western side. The Royal Shakespeare had to drop its version of the trial of Robert Oppenheimer, because of opposition by the Lord Chamberlain, and it had to tread warily in its ambitious production about the Vietnam war, *US*. The National is expected to have similar problems with its 'living newspaper' reconstructon of the Cuba crisis, when Khrushchev backed down before Kennedy's threat of war. Yet, as this book goes to press, a play about Oppenheimer—presented by another management—has been licensed with only a few cuts: a significant concession on the censor's principle of keeping political personalities off the stage.

Another heavily mined area into which dramatists sometimes unwittingly stray is concerned with the presentation of people with some degree of fame or infamy whose relatives object to their impersonation in the theatre. Here are two revealing case-histories.

In 1923 Frank Vosper wrote *People Like Us*, around the events of the Thompson–Bywaters murder case. The Chamberlain then banned it, because to him it seemed too close to life (and death); but twenty-five years later—after it had been broadcast, and after several applications by managements for a licence—the Assistant Comptroller informed A. D. Peters, agent for the play, that 'the Lord Chamberlain has decided that it will no longer be subject to his ban and restrictions which have hitherto been placed upon it'. *People Like Us* was staged by Henry Sherek. After it had begun its London run, another play on the same theme—*A Pin to See the Peepshow*, by H. M. Harwood and Tennyson Jesse—went into rehearsal, under Peter Cotes's direction, at the Manchester Library Theatre. But Percy Thompson, the brother of the man executed over twenty-five years earlier, read about the play in the press and wrote to the Lord Chamberlain to protest against its production. And the Chamberlain banned it. Meanwhile, *People Like Us* was still on view in London. The fact did not escape comment in the press, although reports were somewhat contradictory.

The *Daily Express* quoted 'an official in the Lord Chamberlain's department' as saying:

> It is a rule to withhold a licence from a play dealing with people who lived if a near relative objects. The play *People Like Us* was licensed only after it had been submitted many times. The Lord Chamberlain consented in the end because more than twenty years had elapsed without any relative coming forward. This play had been running for some time when Thompson's brother objected to the play by Mr Harwood and Miss Jesse. There could be little point in interfering with the earlier play.

160

Yet H. M. Harwood explained, in a letter to the *Manchester Guardian*, that he and his wife had consulted the censor, by sending him a copy of their book on which the play was based.

> The censor, having read the book, expressed the opinion that there was nothing in the circumstances dealt with unsuitable for stage production, but that the question of a licence would depend on the treatment.

Harwood also pointed out that there was nothing in the Act of 1843 to warrant such an objection, and that when this was raised with the Lord Chamberlain's Office they replied: 'We have made it a rule not to grant a licence when an objection is raised by a surviving relative.' Again, Harwood pointed out, 'no indication is given as to what degree of consanguinity is necessary in such a case, and what it amounts to is that the Lord Chamberlain makes up his own rules as he goes along'.

Armed with apparent inside information the *Star* said, on the same day, that:

> It is the usual rule to refuse a licence for at least three generations if a near relative objects . . . He does not seek objecting relatives, but waits for them to come to him.

Then Mr H. R. Thompson, it was learned, was trying to stop *People Like Us*. He was quoted as saying:

> I have not read the script of *A Pin to See the Peepshow* or the book, nor have I seen the Vosper play. It makes no difference; I am not interested in the treatment given to the subject. It is the subject itself to which I object. All I ask of anyone is that I shall be given peace.

On 9 September, the *Evening News* reported that according to 'a spokesman of the Lord Chamberlain's Office' the Chamberlain had decided to take no action. But meanwhile his men had sent for Mr Sherek, who tells the story in his autobiography:[1]

> We opened at Wyndhams Theatre and had a very good press. In spite of a heat wave we were doing well, when I received a cable while I was in New York some months later, saying that the Lord Chamberlain was objecting to the licence.
>
> I had a Lord Chamberlain's licence, otherwise I could not have

[1] *Not in Front of the Children* (1959).

put on the piece, and I could not understand this cable, so flew back to London immediately and made an appointment to see Sir Terence Nugent, the Comptroller. When I called on him there were also present the Assistant Comptroller and a quietly dressed elderly man.

As soon as I entered the office in St James's Palace, the Comptroller said with a flourish:

'Henry, this is Mr Thompson, the brother of the murdered man . . . He's objecting to the licence.'

I asked Mr Thompson what his objection was, because his late brother was depicted very sympathetically in the play, was in fact rather the hero of the story.

'It makes me look ridiculous where I live,' he said sullenly.

'Where do you live?' I asked.

'Tooting,' was the reply . . .

There was no moving him.

When he departed, the two officials approached me with menacing gestures exactly as if they were going to cane a boy at school.

'You're going to be a good boy and give up your licence, aren't you?' said one of them, grinding his teeth and looking most aggressive.

'Can you force me to?'

'Not sure, but I think we can. We'll have to look it up. Anyway, in view of that chap Thompson's visit, we've got to stop another play on the same subject which has just started rehearsing at the Library Theatre in Manchester, and it would be madly complicated unless you take your play off—and at once.'

I didn't wait for them to look up whether they could withdraw a licence after it had been granted, but told there and then that I would withdraw the play immediately.

They are both charming men of whom I am very fond and I would not have done anything to embarrass them.

Besides, I was quite sure that they had every right to make me disgorge my licence.

The play was resubmitted in 1954. Sir Norman Gwatkin replied that the Lord Chamberlain had communicated with the dead man's surviving relative, his sister, and 'has used some persuasion to endeavour to secure a modification of the family attitude towards this and similar pieces. His approach has drawn a most moving plea that the ban should not be raised, as a result of which he is of the opinion that it would be detrimental to the mental health of this lady to allow plays on the

162

subject . . . this prohibition is unlikely now to be lifted whilst Mr Thompson's sister is alive.' Replying to another application in April 1958, he said: 'So long as that lady lives, the Lord Chamberlain will feel obliged to continue his policy of not permitting her unhappy memories to be exploited.' (The ban was lifted in 1964.)

Yet, as Samuel French's pointed out:

> If Mr Thompson had neither seen nor read the plays, how could he know what the subject was? . . . Only the press had identified the events which had fired the author's imagination. Mr Thompson was condemning the play on hearsay evidence . . . had it been necessary for Mr Thompson to apply to the Courts, one fancies he would have had a very rough passage.

The play, moreover, could be published, broadcast and televised; the lady was far more likely to attract attention to herself by a continued objection to the play than by allowing it to be performed; but, in any case, the right of veto allowed to Mr Thompson and his sister by the censor could not have been acquired through any court of law. The 1909 Report recommended that it was the Chamberlain's *duty* to license any play unless it, for instance, represented *in an invidious manner* a living person, or one recently dead. But nobody knows what principle the censor applies to such cases today, apart from rule-of-thumb compassion.

In 1945 T. B. Morris wrote a play about Dante Gabriel Rossetti, *We Dig for the Stars*: it was banned by the Lord Chamberlain because of objections by surviving members of the Rossetti family. Below Mr Morris describes the story.[1]

> My play was accepted for West End production by a new management formed by the late C. B. Cochran and Lord Anthony Vivian. They were getting ahead and casting the play when on 1 January 1946 the Lord Chamberlain's Office told me to get in touch with those nearest of Rossetti's living relatives and get their reactions to the play, adding: 'Some ten years ago a play on this subject was the cause of considerable correspondence and distress to some members of this family.' (The Lord Chamberlain has been 'cagey' about relatives' reactions ever since Rudolf Besier's treatment of Edward Moulton-Barrett in *The Barretts of Wimpole Street*, which the existing Chamberlain then passed.)

[1] In a letter to the author.

The letter gave me the last addresses of a Mr G. D. Rossetti, with whom they suggested I should get in touch. He had died some years ago. I then went through the London telephone Rossettis—none of them were right. Then I had a brainwave and 'phoned Mr G. D. Gordon Hake of Bristol, whose father had had associations with Rossetti. He gave me the address of Rossetti's great-nephew, to whom the play was sent. This man sent the play to two aunts, Miss Mary Rossetti and Mrs Helen Rossetti Angeli (daughters of William Michael Rossetti). I had a long wait, but eventually got this, from H. F. Rossetti:

'. . . our position is that we do not like it at all but do not propose to ask you not to proceed with its production on one condition, namely, that you agree that a statement as follows shall appear prominently on every programme of the play:—"ALL THE SCENES AND CONVERSATIONS IN THIS DRAMA ARE THE PRODUCT OF THE AUTHOR'S IMAGINATION."

'It will be apparent from the above that we would much prefer it if this play were not produced, but, provided you will agree with the condition set out above, we will not, as I say, take any action to try and prevent its performance.' This was agreed to. A few days later I had a telegram: 'PLEASE SUSPEND EXHUMATION PLAY WRITING.' Then came a letter from Mrs Angeli very abrupt and rude, using words like 'repulsive' and 'disgusting' about the play, saying that she'd been ill for three months and suggesting that I'd made her worse. She had the grace to apologize for the 'indecision and delay for which I alone am to blame'. This, after she'd held us up for a month!

I wrote again to her nephew, pointing out that my characters were truthfully drawn, etc., and offering to cut out the small part of William Michael Rossetti. The play contained no material fact not mentioned in dozens of biographies and well known to all intelligent people. It was sympathetic to Rossetti's work and personality, though it naturally presented him 'in the round'. I pointed out that there was no reference to Mrs Angeli and the other relations in any of the many books I had then read on Rossetti (by way of acknowledgment for help received or otherwise). But from the wording of the letter and the description 'exhumation play' it was obvious that the real objection was to my inclusion of Fanny Cornforth and having as one of the scenes the night of the exhumation of Lizzie Siddal. My further efforts, and those of the management (who took legal advice) did no good, and I had to borrow money to refund the advance (less £15 that Lord Vivian allowed me towards my expenses).

As I wrote to *The Times* in 1949, my play is a serious work of art, which is sympathetic to Rossetti and his work, and draws carefully on very wide reading of all the recognized authorities—in 1945—on the Pre-Raphaelites. The incidents with which I deal all took place more than ninety years ago. I contend that, after such a time, relatives should not be allowed to destroy the work of playwrights. Such power is too great to be granted, through the Lord Chamberlain, just because people are born into the families of the famous.

My play is still banned. As you know, when a play misses its chance, it usually misses it for good.

* * *

It was over the open dramatization of homosexual love that the main battle against the Lord Chamberlain was fought in the 1950s. Although, as a *Guardian* journalist (John Rosselli) said with understandable exaggeration, the censor permitted in Christmas pantomime 'some of the most uninhibited homosexual behaviour to have been seen in public since the days of Heliogabalus', he vetoed the public production of a number of distinguished plays simply because they treated this fact of human personality without sniggers or subterfuge. They included Lillian Hellman's *The Children's Hour*, Sartre's *Vicious Circle*, Julien Green's *South*, and Arthur Miller's *A View from the Bridge*, and many more never submitted because the Chamberlain's ban was widely known. He carried his objections in the 1950s to the point of banning the words 'queer', 'camp', 'fairy' and even 'inversion'. Alec Grahame describes the Office's reaction to a sketch in the revue, *On the Brighter Side*:

> The final line of the song was, 'There are fairies at the bottom of my garden', at which point two boys came on dressed as a Fairy Snow packet and a Fairy Liquid container. The manager and I had to parade the costumes at St James's Palace to convince the military gentleman who had objected that it was a funny visual picture we were trying to create, and that homosexuality didn't come into it.[1]

When Henry Sherek applied to the Chamberlain to stage *The Children's Hour*, Lord Scarbrough called him 'a corrupter of youth'—and said no. Ronald Duncan's *The Catalyst* was banned because it included a Lesbian love affair between a man's mistress and his wife. When the

[1] In a letter to the author.

165

author went to Stable Yard, Sir Norman Gwatkin said: 'First of all, I should like to congratulate you. It's a wonderful play. But, of course, we've got to ban it.' Duncan asked if there was any revision he could make which would allow it to be passed. But Sir Norman replied, 'We wouldn't have you alter a single line. It would be like putting a red nose on the Venus de Milo. But we've got to ban it.'[1]

Inevitably, dramatists wrote between the lines, winking quite heavily at the audience; and on at least one occasion the ambiguity was deliberately retained by an author when, in an American production outside the Chamberlain's jurisdiction, he could have restored the situation he had originally conceived. When Terence Rattigan first wrote *Separate Tables*, the seedy Major Pollock's secret offence was accosting men in public lavatories; but when the management pointed out that the Chamberlain was not yet so liberal as *that*, Mr Rattigan changed the details and the major became addicted to accosting ladies in cinemas instead. And when the play moved to New York, the author decided that the alteration should stand, because restoring the original addiction would upset the balance by spotlighting one element in the story.

Not all authors, however, benefited from the effects of censorship in this way. Here are two very different examples. Some seventy cuts were made by the Chamberlain in Meyer Levin's *Compulsion*, a play about the two American homosexual murderers of the 1920s, Leopold and Loeb, when it was staged in Croydon prior to a London run. The result was, in the words of *The Times*, that 'the exact nature of the relationship between the two principals is unnecessarily obscure (ironically, more so than in the film, where one might expect to find pudency reigning supreme)'. The fact that the murderers were homosexuals had been widely broadcast in Mr Levin's own book, in many articles, on the radio and in a film; and yet the *theatre* was ordered, in effect, to suppress this fact. Again, in 1958 a new author, Jeremy Kingston, wrote a play, *No Concern of Mine*, which suffered from the censorship—indirectly. Robin Fox, who presented it, writes:[2]

> Like many plays which have been written on this subject it was really a cautionary tale and the one genuine homosexual whose 'friend' finally fell in love with and wanted to marry his sister, was driven to an attempted suicide—an attempt which was not successful. It was, as I say, impossible even to submit the play to the Chamberlain at that time,

[1] In a letter by Mr Duncan to the author.
[2] In a letter to Lord Willis.

and Robert Morley and I persuaded the author to rewrite the play eliminating the homosexual relationship. This rewrite left the character of the homosexual brother unmotivated and unprotected, and his jealousy for his friend and his sister, became petulant and unreasonable, and although the first act worked splendidly as it was indeed an extremely well-written comedy act, the second became thin and unreal.

Yet while the Chamberlain continued to ban the serious treatment of homosexuality in contemporary drama, he was obliged to tolerate the frank presentation of a queers' love-affair which went further in stage action than anything projected by Lillian Hellman or Tennessee Williams. Agamemnon and Patroclus could hug and kiss on the Old Vic stage as much as they and Sir Tyrone Guthrie, the director, pleased, because it happened in *Troilus and Cressida*, and was in the name of Shakespeare. This immunity from censorship of plays written before 1737 was an aspect of the system's anomalies glaringly emphasized in the 1950s by the revival of such Elizabethan shockers as *Titus Andronicus*, with rape, mutilation and cannibalism among its box-office attractions.

This prohibition of homosexuality in the drama led in 1956 to one of the milestones in the Chamberlain's retreat: his open defiance by the leading London managers, who had always supported him—as they do again now, and no doubt will hereafter. Hugh Beaumont and Donald Albery combined with Stephen Arlen, Ian Hunter and others to present plays banned by the censor under 'club' conditions at a theatre hitherto used for public performances, the Comedy. This was the first time that the device had been used for such a purpose, and it put the Chamberlain to the test. The club was already in dormant existence, the New Watergate; and the three plays of disparate merit which it announced for its occupation of the Comedy were all American hits and all touched, incidentally, upon homosexuality; so that all would have been banned by the censor, if the authors had refused to make heavy changes, as seemed certain. They were Arthur Miller's *A View From The Bridge*; Tennessee Williams's *Cat on a Hot Tin Roof*; and Robert Anderson's *Tea and Sympathy* (the *Young Woodley* of the 1950s).[1]

[1] One result was that provincial playgoers were penalized, for such plays could not be toured or staged by repertory companies. It was impractical for most provincial theatres to turn themselves into clubs in the Watergate style, as the incidence of bannable plays was not high enough to justify the additional expense, labour and difficulty involved.

167

The club's announcement helped to save the Chamberlain's face and its own bacon by insisting only that its purpose was merely to stage 'new and first-class plays which, because of their importance, could not be produced adequately and economically on small club premises.' Within two years, while the membership rose to 60,000, the supply of 'new and first-class' plays dried up, and the club label wore thin. When it peeled off in 1958 the members may have been disappointed, but the New Watergate had made its mark in theatrical history by helping to undermine the censorship, in extending 'private' staging to public theatres and recruiting the most powerful London managers against the Chamberlain. It seems doubtful whether he would have stood the evasion for much longer, for the Office has made it plain during the past year that club production is tolerated only as a loophole for minority plays in small theatres. But the New Watergate played its part in the change of heart announced in 1958 in an edict from St James's Palace, and the publication of this edict was, in itself, a startling precedent. In a letter to Mr Charles Killick, chairman of the Theatres National Committee, the Earl of Scarbrough, as Lord Chamberlain, informed him of 'a change of policy with regard to the censorship of stage plays concerning the subject of homosexuality. This subject is now so widely debated, written about and talked over that its complete exclusion from the stage can no longer be regarded as justifiable. In future, therefore, plays on this subject which are sincere and serious will be admitted, as will references to the subject which are necessary in the plot and dialogue and which are not salacious or offensive.' By a bitter irony for Jeremy Kingston, this announcement was made on the very day that his maimed play, *No Concern of Mine*, opened in London.

Another bulwark had been abandoned; another freedom was open. For the banned plays it was, on the whole, too late: they had missed their hour. But from 1958 onwards the inclusion of homosexuals among the characters of a West End play was no longer a subject for scandal and concern. They cropped up in the drama as they do in life, rather less frequently than in the theatre backstage. *Ross*, *The Collection*, *A Taste of Honey*, and other plays in the last eight years have made practical use of the belated liberty granted by the Chamberlain. Seriousness was the test—and sincerity, too. Yet this test, after all, was still put by the censor, and his application of it has kept off the public stage a play by one of Britain's leading dramatists, *A Patriot For Me* (see page 188). The new freedom, in fact, had a catch in it: the fact that it was given as a favour from St James's Palace, and that the dramatist was on parole.

Today the main battle between the censor and the dramatists—on the surface at least—is over words. In 1924 the Chamberlain banned the word 'hips'. Some years later 'impotence' was on the black list.[1] In 1949, there was trouble over *Pick-Up Girl*, described by Peter Cotes— then running the enterprising New Lindsey Theatre Club—in his autobiography:

> The script of *Pick-Up Girl* was submitted to the Lord Chamberlain, but he refused to grant a licence for public performance without certain modifications being made to the script. He demanded that the words *syphilis*, *abortion* and *miscarriage* should be deleted from the play. There was also a line of five words to which he objected. During the court proceedings the judge asked a question concerning the defendants. In reply the police constable said, *They were both wearing nothing*. This line was considered unfit for public performance and the Lord Chamberlain demanded deletion . . .
>
> While negotiations were in progress with the Lord Chamberlain, Queen Mary decided to see the play at the New Lindsey on her seventy-ninth birthday. Not a line or a gesture was cut for the royal visit. After the performance Her Majesty confessed that she had not enjoyed herself so much for years.[2]

Pick-Up Girl was later licensed, intact; but the subject of abortion was still a perilous one, as Alec Grahame and Peter Myers—authors of *For Adults Only*—discovered in 1958. One of the censor's main deletions from this revue was a song about a London debutante's coming-out season. It contained the lines:

> I am the doctor, now struck off,
> In my room above the appliance shop
> I used to perform an illegal op.

'The Assistant Comptroller demanded the removal of the word "illegal",' says Alec Grahame, 'and refused to accept the substitution of "appendix"—until I remembered that Noel Coward had used the same euphemism in a revue written in 1932. Thereupon permission was

[1] *The Surprise of My Life*, by Leon M. Lion (1948).
[2] *No Star Nonsense*, by Peter Cotes (1949).

grudgingly given.'[1] In another post-war revue by the same authors, *On the Brighter Side*, the censor objected to some lines in a song about the London boom in office-blocks:

> Going up! going up!
> In a space that once was green;
> A structure we call 'pencil-shaped',
> But others call obscene.

'The Lord Chamberlain wasn't having that—plainly a phallic symbol was being hinted at,' says Mr Grahame. 'Once again Noel Coward came to the rescue, as I was able to quote a much blunter line from *Design for Living*, which has been passed some twenty years earlier.'[2]

The new generation of authors in the 'straight' theatre have pressed hard for greater realism in colloquial idiom, with an alert ear for class and regional variations; and this has brought them, especially in writing about life in the ranks or the working class, to demand the freedom to use four-letter words. Sometimes they have demanded more than they knew they would get in a deliberate attempt to force the Chamberlain's hand, just as before the war—according to J. B. Priestley—dramatists would often insert more swear-words than they needed, in the knowledge that the censor's cuts would secure them the desirable quota. But those rationed oaths and epithets of the 1930s were child's talk beside the 'shit', 'turd', 'fuck', 'fart', 'cock' and other Anglo-Saxon monosyllables which sprinkle the pages of some contemporary plays *before* they are performed. There seems, at times, a self-conscious naughtiness in this insistence on words still not widely used in mixed society which often has the air of a determination to embarrass the censor, to spit in Nanny's eye. It is a far cry from the scandal of *Pygmalion*. According to Peter Fryer, in his history of Grundyism, 'bloody' was never used between the notorious cry of Eliza Doolittle in 1912 and Noel Coward's *Red Peppers* in 1936. But, be that as it may, it was still frowned upon by the censor after World War Two. Speaking in the Lords in 1966, Ted Willis said:

> I think that in 1948 or 1949 one of my first plays went to his office, and it came back with a long list of words which had to be omitted, including the word 'bloody', which it was requested should be removed, I think, fourteen times. Subsequently, of course, in 1956–57, I went to see a play called *Billy Liar*, which had that same word in

---

[1] In a letter to the author.   [2] Ibid.

170

it 249 times. I do not quite know what this proves: either I was ten years ahead of my time or the Lord Chamberlain was ten years behind it.

Yet the current agitation for greater verbal freedom is by no means a synthetic or pointless one, and the irritation of serious dramatists is understandable when they are forbidden to use a word like 'arse' on the directive of a Court official because it is indelicate. Harold Pinter, for instance, was not allowed to use it in *The Caretaker* in 1960, although it had been licensed in *My Fair Lady* the year before. 'Ah, but in *My Fair Lady*,' said the Chamberlain's men, 'there is a lot of noise on the stage at the same time.' And that was a musical, anyway.

Illustration of bannable words—and other difficulties with the censor —may be found in the next chapter. Here let John Osborne—as reported in *The Stage*, in 1961—put his case for verbal freedom:

> It would take a large number of theatrical productions and many more playwrights than we have to produce a comparable treasure of dirty words, obscene *double-entendres* and cheerful, ingenious and obsessive filth as that found spattered all over those two monuments of Eng. Lit., the King James Bible and the Works of Shakespeare.
>
> Partridge's *Shakespeare's Bawdy* has well over a thousand entries, nearly all of which Lady Chatterley and Mellors would hesitate to use in the presence of women and servants. As for 'bloody', Shaw killed that one for ever fifty years ago. Repeating it 153 times, or 1,053 times, makes it neither more nor less objectionable.
>
> Of course, there should be no limit to what is said on the stage, Good taste can only be involved as an aesthetic principle, and four-letter words or variations on them cannot, in themselves, be unaesthetic. Almost everyone over the age of seven knows the four-letter word for sexual intercourse, and a perfectly good and decent one it is too. I use it myself and so do most people I know. Only a fool could be shocked by it and only a lunatic could be corrupted by hearing it.

A crucial episode in the story of the censorship opened in June 1965 when *Saved*—a play commissioned from a new writer, Edward Bond, for the Royal Court's first season under William Gaskill—was submitted to the Lord Chamberlain. He demanded, apart from various small cuts and changes, mainly in the four-letter word area, the omission of two whole scenes. In one a baby in its pram is attacked by a gang of young yobs, who rub its face in its excrement, and then—seized by a psychopathic violence—stone it to death: it is the unwanted illegitimate offspring of one of the boys. In the other scene a young man darns a middle-aged woman's stocking, while she is wearing it, and they conduct a dialogue of sustained sexual *double-entendre*.

Saved aroused strong feelings in the press and the theatre, when it was staged in full—following the precedent of *A Patriot For Me*—as a club production at the Royal Court. J. W. Lambert in the *Sunday Times* declared that the play represented 'something of a crux in modern drama: a clear demonstration of what is permissible, what is not, and why . . . there comes a point when both life and art are irretrievably debased, and Edward Bond's play, in this production, is well past that point'. But was it ? Half the press shared Mr Lambert's sense of outrage, although no critic put the issue quite as trenchantly. Yet the other half praised the play highly, while criticizing its crudities and over-emphasis, and some perceived a deliberate didacticism which was lost on the opposition to *Saved*. The author—an embattled moralist—wrote a wordy and indignant letter to his critics; a 'teach-in' was held at the Court; and a good deal of cant on both sides was exuded, notably in Mr Bond's defence, by such champions as Miss Mary McCarthy, who praised the play's 'delicate escalation of violence'. This is not the place to pursue that debate: except to say that, in my view, the shock-effect of the sex and violence in *Saved* resulted not from deliberate pornographic titillation and sensationalism, as some leading critics seemed to believe, but from the fact that this remarkably promising young writer had not yet learned practical control and self-criticism. Far from representing The End, it was just the beginning. To judge the play from its descriptions in print—like the outline of the two key scenes above—would be to misunderstand its purpose and effect in the theatre; for although it can and does both shock and horrify, and although it is obsessively concerned with vernacular accuracy, it is a work of considerable spasmodic power which uses both horror and disgust for warrantable and indeed traditional artistic ends.

In December 1965, however, the Royal Court was visited several times by police officers, acting on behalf of the Chamberlain's Office, during performances of *Saved*. In March 1966 eighteen summonses were made against the English Stage Company, by the Director of Public Prosecutions, on the Chamberlain's instigation, because the theatre was not being run as a genuine club. After a three-day hearing in which Sir Laurence Olivier, among others, praised not only the Royal Court regime but Edward Bond's play in glowing terms, magistrate and prosecution agreed that it was, in fact, genuine; but the magistrate understandably ignored the Office's traditional but non-legal exemption of clubs and insisted that any performance 'for hire' exposed it to the censorship under the Act of 1843. A conditional discharge was granted on each summons, and the company was ordered to pay £50 costs, a token punishment for a technical offence, in what turned out against the Chamberlain's intention to be a test case. The Bow Street ruling clearly seemed to indicate—more ominously than the Unity case of 1951—that the club loophole for unlicensed plays could no longer be used with any certainty of immunity from prosecution.

The prime reason for the Chamberlain's action, it seems, was that the Royal Court was still used for several nights in the week as a public theatre for public performances of other plays in the repertoire: it was the mixture of public and 'private' that upset the Office.

Talking to J. W. Lambert in the *Sunday Times* in 1964, Lord Cobbold said:

So long as they are genuine clubs for a genuine purpose I am very much in favour of theatre clubs. They give selective and interested audiences a chance to see experimental work and I think they are very useful to the theatre. Whether or not they could strictly be brought under the Lord Chamberlain's jurisdiction—which has never actually been tested in the courts—my predecessors and I have never wished to interfere with genuine theatre clubs. Where a management uses them for a different purpose, e.g. to put on for a long run a play part of which has been refused a licence, I think rather a different position arises. The arrangement is then really being used more as an attempt to evade the law . . . I can think of circumstances in which the Lord Chamberlain as custodian of the Theatres Act would feel it his duty to challenge the arrangement and to test the law in the courts. I very much hope myself that managements will have the good sense not to force the issue to this point, which might well involve difficulties for all theatre clubs and which would, in my view, be harmful to the general interests of the theatre.

It may also have been prompted by the feeling that the Court was too persistent and aggressive in its defiance of the censorship and that this particular play was, in its entirety, unfit for public performance in what was still, in fact, a public playhouse. The result, in any case, was that champions of the common-sense empiricism of the Lord Chamberlain's rule were deprived of one stock argument—that a play could always be seen on a stage, if a 'club' would present it. The prosecution of *Saved* has closed, for a time at least, the gap through which, for nearly a hundred years, so much of the *avant-garde* drama of Europe and America has escaped the English censorship. It is characteristic of that institution's history that the Chamberlain's action in 1965 should have an effect so very different to the one which he intended, and that the club system may well end, as it began, by accident.

Meanwhile, a special committee set up by the Arts Council decided in the summer of 1966 to recommend the abolition of the censorship for a trial period of five years; proposed, once again, the safeguard against irresponsible Puritanical putsches by local watch committees—that prosecutions could be undertaken only after permission was obtained from a judge in chambers, as outlined in the Bill of 1949; and otherwise recommended adoption of this Bill, while deleting the clause which continued the ban on representing living persons on the stage.

*　*　*

And where are we now? Are all the battles over? Have the freedoms all been won? Has the Lord Chamberlain really abdicated already? It is true that in the last few years actors have been allowed to say—here and there—'arse' and 'piss' and a few other 'common' but useful monosyllables. Within limits, you can dramatize homosexuality (*The Collection*, *The Killing of Sister George*); abortion (*Saturday Night and Sunday Morning*); tranvestism (*The Anniversary*); incest (*A Bond Honoured*); and sado-masochistic fetishism (*Under Plain Cover*). You can mention menstruation (*Public and Confidential*). You can not only introduce the sound of a lavatory being flushed off-stage (prohibited as recently as *The Living Room*, although the Chamberlain could not prevent the audience from hearing the same sound-effect, unscripted, in the adjuncts of the auditorium), but you can also present a W.C. to the public (as in *Ubu Roi*). But is it all really necessary? And does it spell real freedom?

Meanwhile, behind the vaunted permissiveness of the new regime, the old royal, political and religious prohibitions are still stubbornly defended, in spite of some apparent retreats. And even in the sexual area strangely blimpish vetoes accompany the censor's concessions to the avant-garde. In 1965 the Chamberlain could still solemnly ban a line *in German*, spoken at the National Theatre, in the Berliner Ensemble production of Brecht's *Die Tage der Commune*. A woman says to a man, 'Zeigt uns die Kolben ... die Löcher haben wir', which means, roughly, 'Show us the piston ... we have the cylinders'. The double meaning is

174

plain enough, if you understand German; but to ban its delivery in a British theatre was surely one of the dizzier instances of censor-mania. In the same year the Chamberlain insisted that in a stage version of *Tom Jones*, presented at a provincial repertory theatre, Fielding's hero should not be seen in bed with Mrs Waters, even though she was almost fully dressed and Tom was 'out of bed again almost as soon as in', even though somewhat greater excesses in the hero's life were to be seen by millions in the nation's cinemas. Again, in 1964, the censor objected to several lines in 'I Sing of Olaf', a poem by E. E. Cummings in the Royal Shakespeare Company's anthology, *The Rebel*. The prime offence was the line, echoing an old-soldier maxim, 'There is some shit I will not eat'. The management decided to print the complete poem in the Aldwych programme, explaining that the offending words had not only been published in many books but had been spoken from the stage in two poetry 'festivals'—at the Royal Court and at Stratford-on-Avon—and on the television screen in 'Monitor', without one complaint from any member of the public. And so it goes on . . .

The situation, in fact, is still confused. It will continue to be confused as long as the Lord Chamberlain is obliged to reign over the English stage. And it will be just as bad, after he is allowed to abdicate, if he is replaced by a committee, a board, or another mortal man.

By order of the Lord Chamberlain . . .

It is understood that, wherever the word 'shit' appears, it will be altered, in every case, to 'it'.

Spare, by Charles Wood

The killing must be semi-hidden from the audience. There must be no severance of the head.

Afore Night Come, by David Rudkin

There must be no scratching of private parts.

Meals on Wheels, by Charles Wood

The Doctor's trousers must *not* be hauled down.

The Happy Haven, by John Arden

The huge Spanish Crucifixion must not be visible in the brothel room.

The Balcony, by Jean Genet

12

You cannot have any form of censorship without upsetting some people; and the censor, whoever he is, must always be, if anything, a little more behind public opinion than in advance of it.—VISCOUNT DILHORNE, speaking in the debate on theatre censorship in the House of Lords, February 1966

> When correctly viewed
> Everything is lewd.
> TOM LEHRER

*   *   *

WHAT do contemporary dramatists say about the censorship? Although most are in favour of its reform, and the League of Dramatists has voted for its abolition, a minority appear to have suffered from it directly *in practice*, whatever the majority's objections to it *in principle*; and some, especially among the older generation, prefer the Chamberlain's rule to the imagined perils of interference by Puritanical local authorities. (All the quotations below are from letters to the author, unless otherwise stated). Graham Greene, for instance, says:

> I have been harassed on certain occasions by the Lord Chamberlain, but I have always found a way round and I have always found his officers very ready to accept diversionary tactics. This would not be the case in a magistrates' court. I don't personally support the proposals for the abolition of the Lord Chamberlain's powers, as I can imagine nothing worse than dramatists being left at the mercy of police prosecutions and complaints from old ladies.

Again, Christopher Fry says:

> I don't think we should feel much bothered by the censorship if it would regularly overhaul its point of view instead of staying fixed in its views of ten, twenty, even thirty years ago. It is obviously ludicrous that (for instance) *Green Pastures* is banned. On the other hand, I'm not sure that legislation against Puritan prosecutions will take care of nuisances if the Lord Chamberlain is buried. Let him take a blue pencil to his own Index.

T. S. Eliot was of the same view. Some years before his death he said that he had 'never given very much thought to the subject of censorship', as so far none of his plays had been prohibited from appearing on the stage, and he was 'generally in favour of the existing situation until someone can convince him that there is a preferable alternative'. He had no trouble with the Chamberlain. James Bridie had only, his son recalls, 'one or two mildly flippant exchanges' with the Chamberlain over words. Noel Coward testifies:

> I cannot remember any particularly unwarrantable instance of interference: indeed, on the whole, I think that the Office has been fairly good to me.

J. B. Priestley, who advocates the replacement of the Lord Chamberlain by another kind of censor, says:

> I had occasional objections to bad language, but no other trouble with the censor. I would of course have had plenty of trouble if I had written a religious play, but I never wanted to write a religious play in the conventional sense of that term. I never had any trouble about sexual scenes because I have never enjoyed sexual exhibitions in the theatre and so did not want to produce any myself. In general I think I had little trouble with the censor not because I am a man who easily accepts authority, but simply because as a dramatist I never depended upon shock tactics as the dramatists of the Absurd and the Cruel seem to do.

Among the Chamberlain's opponents, the late John Whiting said that although the censorship gave him 'an inhibiting feeling', he had never had any personal trouble; to him it was 'a *bore* and an anachronism', rather than a menace, and it was the *idea* of censorship which he opposed. Peter Ustinov says that 'it inhibits you from the outset'; but his only quarrel in practice has been the deletion of half a dozen words. Robert Bolt, up to date, has had only one 'brush' with the Chamberlain, over a few lines in *Gentle Jack*: 'it was all as silly and fundamentally frivolous as a censorship is bound to be when it isn't actually sinister— as ours, thank Heaven, at the moment isn't.'[1] Arnold Wesker, too, has experienced no 'great battles', only 'irritating deletions': although some people would question this conclusion:

[1] In a letter to Lord Willis.

The important thing for me is that their censorship doesn't cover ideas. Consequently, a play like *Chips with Everything* which Harold Hobson said—mistakenly, of course—is 'the first anti-establishment entertainment of which the establishment need be afraid', is left untouched. For this reason I have never felt as strongly about the Lord Chamberlain's Office as other writers have. But I have every sympathy with a writer like Osborne, whose *A Patriot For Me*, dealing seriously with the disastrous results to both the State and the individual of an intolerant view of homosexuality, is pushed into the constricting form of club production.

Charles Wood has had more trouble with the Lord Chamberlain than any other dramatist: two of his plays—*Dingo* and *The Plastic Igloo*—are banned, at the time of writing, and others—notably, *Meals on Wheels*—have been heavily edited at the censor's behest, largely because of four-letter words and service slang of a kind still not generally heard on the stage. His own view of the Chamberlain is very different from that of the Edwardian crusaders, who might well have found it hard to defend Mr Wood's right to make his characters say, as they would in life (and do in Penguin print) 'tits', 'fuck', 'shit', 'turd', and other expressive monosyllables. He writes:

> I didn't expect any trouble from the Lord Chamberlain over *Dingo* and *Plastic Igloo* because I didn't expect them to be performed. When the National Theatre bought *Dingo* I thought they might be joking, and of course they were. The Lord Chamberlain is not to blame for the death of *Dingo*. It was dead before he got it.
>
> Actors are timid, managements are timid and we shall always have the Lord Chamberlain. I don't think of him much because I'm not timid. I don't have to earn my living from being loved or hated. That's for actors, and I don't envy them. His censorship hasn't put me off writing for the theatre. What has put me off writing for the theatre is the theatre, and the fact that nobody goes to see my plays when they are done.

Peter Shaffer, whose brushes with the censorship have been negligible, is more absolute:

> I am in favour of abolishing the censorship completely, entirely and with no reservation at all. I see no saving grace to it, and do not believe that it performs any function.

178

Henry Livings—'I've had the usual famous battles'—takes the same view:

One of the reasons I get at cross-purposes with the censor is the difference between us personally: words like 'bugger' being common parlance where I live, with friendly rather than offensive connotations; whereas 'bleeder' is sharply vituperative to me, and a lousy substitute. But, like 'U' and 'non-U', I can never remember which is which, so I just carry on, and continue to be amazed afresh each time.

I am heartily in favour of abolishing the Lord Chamberlain's Office, or anything or anyone else that comes between me and the public. I face the prospect of prosecution for indecency or offences against public morals or corrupting the young anyway, and must always be careful to know what I'm doing. The astounding human deviousness that is offended by a lavatory on-stage, yet calmly contemplates violent and cruel death, is one strand of a tightrope any playwright walks (Agatha Christie as well as me), and I'd be an ass to stand up and say they're wrong to be offended in so bizarre a way; all I can do is to take it into account and carry on telling the tale the way I'd like to be told it.

David Mercer—'I write exactly as I wish and then fight every inch of the way'—is another younger dramatist who is baffled by the current procedure, 'where a playwright is not allowed to use language familiar to (and used by) any school child'.

The humiliating thing is to have to go to St James's Palace and haggle—e.g. 'bugger' disallowed, but a 'fart' or two handed back by way of consolation. Perhaps most sickening of all—a scene in which a man beats his mistress, of which the L.C.'s representative said: 'We'll allow that if it takes place behind the furniture.' The final outcome is nearly always serious compromise on the author's side, and a few concessions by the other side to prove how reasonable and progressive they are. But they are, of course, quite inconsistent. I keep hearing words on the stage which have been disallowed in my plays—and I'm sure the reverse is also true. If it comes to a real impasse, the author must give in or be refused a licence. I wonder how many lawyers and doctors would feel if their professional practice were arbitrated by an authority with *no* professional knowledge or status.

Mercer, too, is in favour of complete abolition; 'the question of what the public will and will not tolerate should be tested in public'; though he recognizes that it is 'a very complicated issue, and the thought of innumerable expensive court cases is daunting', so that 'stringent safeguards' would be needed.

The case against niggling verbal censorship from the contemporary dramatist's side was put well by John Arden in this letter to Lord Willis, written early in 1966;

I am in principle opposed to theatrical censorship, but I do recognize the difficulty of abolishing the Lord Chamberlain and thus putting the theatres in danger of eccentric prosecutions by minority interests. I do feel, however, that it might be a lot better for the artist if this were the case. The Lord Chamberlain has become a sort of arbiter of standards which have little to do with art and equally little to do with the manners of individual people in our society. If writers are of any use at all to society they surely must examine such standards for themselves as freely as possible and, in their work, either throw them over or confirm them, according to circumstances.

However, I do recognize that such radical views may not be very helpful to you in your capacity as legislator: I have little knowledge of the law and can only write from my own experience of the censorship, which has not been a very favourable one. I have never had a play wrecked by the cuts imposed, but in nearly every piece I have had performed there have been a number of niggling impositions which have had the surely undesirable effect of making me say what I wanted to say in roundabout and weaker language. The fact that I have been allowed to say it at all may be taken as a tribute to the liberality of the censorship: but I do not believe this is so. I can see no reason for interfering with the actual words of a writer—which are his tools—while at the same time pretending not to interfere with the finished product. I am not incidentally referring to the question of 'swear words', which I do not personally find particularly necessary to my work.

The sort of thing I mean may be illustrated from *Armstrong's Last Goodnight*, where a sixteenth-century lowland Scot refers to a Highlander as a 'draff-black bare-arse horse-turd Hielandman'. 'Horse-turd' was cut by the censor, 'bare-arse' was allowed. Why on earth? The one referred to the man's kilt, the other to an old Scots legend that the first Gael was created by God out of a pile of horse droppings,

180

which, although not flattering, was a correct reflection of the racial feelings of the period, and unlikely either to deprave or corrupt, though it might have caused some degree of disgust. As I was endeavouring in this passage to illustrate the moral limitations of the speaker this seems to me a legitimate purpose. The poem which contains the original horse-turd legend was published some years ago in *The Penguin Book of Comic and Curious Verse* and was not censored there. I suppose that had this case been presented to the Lord Chamberlain's office they might have yielded the point, but we had a hanging in the last scene of the play which they were making dubious noises about, and it was felt by the management (Glasgow Citizens' —not a wealthy theatre, and not in command of a great influence in this direction) that we had better not prejudice an important stage effect for the sake of one phrase. Also, why was 'bare-arse' permitted, when only four years before it had been cut out in *Serjeant Musgrave's Dance*?

This sort of thing is so trivial and yet so annoying that whether or not the censorship can be entirely abolished, at least some form of X certificate might be introduced. I do not believe either play could have been prosecuted successfully had there been no Lord Chamberlain and had someone brought them into the courts.

Since Mr Arden wrote this letter, the Lord Chamberlain has changed his mind. In the 1966 revival of *Serjeant Musgrave's Dance* at the Royal Court, he allowed 'bare-arsed', together with the words 'randy' and 'pissed' ('I'm a bit pissed tonight'): although a few phases were still retained on the black list, including the soldier's oath 'You dirty turd'.

Does the case against censorship today, then, rest—after all the crusades for freedom—on the freedom to say 'turd', or 'shit', or 'fuck', on one hand; and 'Christ', or 'Jesus', or 'the Duke of Edinburgh', on the other? No, it does not, although you might get this impression from studying the files of a theatre like the Royal Court. It is worth recalling that less than twenty years ago the forbidden words included 'abortion' and 'syphilis', and twenty years before that they included 'hips' and 'breasts'. Yet it is true—and it should not be concealed—that for most dramatists the censorship, as it is today, does not appear to have been a serious deterrent: rather, an unpredictable and unreasonable nuisance. Most plays are left quite intact by the Chamberlain; mutilations—after polite discussion—are small and relatively infrequent; only one or two plays a year are banned. But the argument from statistics—like the

181

argument from progress—is irrelevant to the main issues: and it is unwise to presume that because the censor has moved forward, he cannot slide back, or to overlook the possibility that among the authors denied a public showing for their work are those who have most to give to the theatre, and who may be sidetracked or turned away because of their treatment by Stable Yard.

*　*　*

When I talked to Terence Rattigan some years ago about censorship, I remember him saying, 'Does Osborne have any trouble? If he does, then the censorship's wrong. That's the test.' Up to 1966, out of ten Osborne plays staged in London, only one was licensed by the Lord Chamberlain without any requests for cuts and changes—and that, surprisingly, was the last, *A Bond Honoured*: surprisingly, because it jumped into forbidden territory by representing incest (as an enjoyable act between brother and sister) and attacking Christianity (with a send-up crucifixion). But then it was an adaptation of a seventeenth-century play by Lope de Vega, and it was staged at the National Theatre, which perhaps made a difference.

Among the distinguishing marks of Osborne's work are its volcanic spurts of social criticism; its blaze of private feeling—personal obsessions, fantasies, guilts seem to pulse through the plays with a confessional intensity of contained violence; the sexual ambiguity of many of the relationships dramatized; and the isolation of a central figure, a lone outsider haranguing the smug, unloving world. All these characteristics suggest an unusually high probability of conflict with the Lord Chamberlain, and Osborne's clashes can hardly be said to be representative of the modern dramatist's situation. Yet their history, briefly noted here, illustrates the way that censorship operates today.

Trouble with the Office began for Osborne before he made his name at the Royal Court in 1956 with *Look Back in Anger*. One episode was described in a letter to the *Observer* in 1964, by Mr Patrick Desmond:

> In 1955 I was producing a play, *Personal Enemy*, by John Osborne and Anthony Creighton, at the Opera House, Harrogate. It dealt with a McCarthy-type witch hunt in Canada and the two young men accused of being 'Commies' (i.e. liberals) were also smeared with the homosexual brush. I had had considerable experience in getting plays licensed and had no fears about this one. I had seen a play a couple of years before, at the Criterion Theatre, in which the homosexual

theme was much more predominant, indeed the only reason for the story. And so I had put the play into rehearsal before getting the official O.K.

Four days before our opening night I was summoned by telephone to St James's Palace. I took Mr Osborne with me and we were, indeed, most courteously received and most comfortably seated. A gentleman, whom I understood to be the Lord Chamberlain's head reader, then informed us that his lordship would not tolerate perversion. We waited, with straight faces and the utmost possible respect, to hear what his lordship would tolerate. In regard to this play, it seemed, very little.

After the cuts had been made we were presented with a script that was largely unintelligible. There was no time to rewrite and re-submit, and the play had to be presented in that form. It is not surprising that it has not been heard of since.

Tantalisingly, the correspondence with the Chamberlain's Office over *Look Back in Anger*, in which some verbal changes of the usual kind were requested, has been mislaid. With *The Entertainer*, in 1957, however, Osborne was faced with a curious little list of prohibitions from Archie Rice's dialogue on and off the stage. Among the more understandable requests, by the censor's standards, were the omission of the words 'rogered', 'screwed', 'shagged', 'turds', 'balls' and 'had' (in the sexual sense); and 'the vicar's got the clappers' (as a substitute for which the censor accepted, 'the vicar's dropped a clanger'). But it seems bizarre that he should have taken objection to 'ass-upwards', 'pouff' and 'camp'; and it must have been the censor's sense of responsibility to the Church which dictated his demand for the omission from Archie Rice's routine of the scene where he holds up a brassière and says, 'Now what about this: "Lift Up Your Hearts" ', and then, producing a large pair of bloomers, says 'Sunday Half Hour?' Religious programmes were not, in 1957, to be mocked in a play.

In *The World of Paul Slickey* in 1959, the censor permitted the sex-change in the plot, but objected to the words 'crumpet', 'queer' and 'fairy', among half a dozen others. Osborne's solicitor pointed out that:

With respect, the expression 'crumpet' is now one in fairly universal use, and can be construed as referring to ladies or girl friends, and not as appertaining to any particular part of the physical anatomy. My client feels that 'fairy' and 'queer' have now become accepted expressions and that apart from this, these references are nothing

183

like as salacious or offensive as—which happens from time to time in revues and other productions—the depictions of effeminate gentlemen.

But the Chamberlain was adamant; so Osborne exchanged 'crumpet' for 'muffin', 'fairy' for 'swishy'; and 'queer' for 'queen'. Three weeks later the Chamberlain issued a warning—through the Assistant Comptroller—that as stage business was 'an integral and censorable part of the play', action could be taken against any interpolations not yet licensed: and that he could ban a play in toto at *any* time if it was produced in a way that offended against 'good manners, decorum or the public peace'; although he was not making any allegations about the current production. Early in May the Chamberlain informed them that, as the result of an 'inspection' he had ordered at Leeds, seven departures from the licensed text had been discovered. For instance: 'the banned line in the Income Tax Song, "He's almost definitely queer"'. This line must be totally eliminated and no substitute referring to the Income Tax Inspector as a homosexual will be allowed'. In Act 1, Scene 2,

'The stage direction at the commencement . . . are not observed. Jack is lying on top of Deirdre, instead of sitting on the bed. When he removes himself Jack's shirt is seen to be outside his trousers, and the later dialogue is punctuated by his stuffing it back. Deirdre's slip remains outside the whole time.
Requirement: Jack and Deirdre must sit on the bed as allowed. They may not lie. Jack must be fully clothed, not in déshabille, and Deirdre's slip must be inside her breeches.

Again, 'the reference to the Honourable Penelope Cumming, "Well, I suppose she's always worth a few inches", [by a gossip columnist, nominally talking about newspaper space] must be deleted. An acceptable substitute for "inches" would be "lines".' Moreover, said the Chamberlain, a line in the Income Tax Song, 'I'm sure he played with little boys', must be deleted. This 'inspection' at Leeds was made, according to the Office, because of the insistence of 'a considerable body who wanted the play banned in toto'. Among this 'body', it is widely believed, was the manager and lessee of the London theatre presenting the play— Emile Littler.

In May 1959, Osborne wrote a letter of remonstrance to Sir Norman Gwatkin at the Chamberlain's Office:

Dear Sir Norman,

I received your letter last night—delivered, incidentally, at my final dress-rehearsal. I take note of all your requirements, and undertake to make such modifications as consistent with your suggestions.

Before dealing with your specific recommendations, however, I should like to make some observations on general principle, which seems to me to be vital. I feel that in their dealings with myself, the behaviour of your office has been determinedly frivolous and irresponsible, and because of my past public opposition to the function of your office, it is difficult not to assume that the treatment I have received at your hands stems from a desire on your part to be wilfully obstructive.

In view of the undoubted policy of liberalization pursued by the Lord Chamberlain recently, I ask you, Sir Norman, does it not seem outrageous that I should be selected for this treatment? I am one of the few serious artists working in the English theatre, with a serious reputation in almost every civilized country in the world, countries have honoured me in various ways. And yet your office seems intent on treating me as if I were the producer of a third-rate nude revue.

What I find most bewildering is the lack of moral consistency and objectivity which seems to characterize your recent decisions—decisions which seem to be reversed and changed because of the whim of any twisted neurotic who cares to write to you and exploit his own particular weird sexual frustration or moral oddity. During the past three weeks something like 30,000 people have seen this play. Do you honestly believe that the proportion of those who walked out (not one in Leeds) or who wrote to you—all of whom cannot number more than a few dozen—fairly represents decent and informed opinion? In paying attention to what is without question an infinitesimal and lunatic minority, you are doing a grave injustice, not only to myself, but to the general public and your own office.

In view of your recent relaxation of policy, I cannot believe that you wish to encourage this appalling situation at the expense of the serious writer and his public.

I would also point out, in passing, that isolated members of the public continue to walk out of performances of all my other plays—all of which are performed with the benefit of your licence.

I have been entirely co-operative in this matter with you, and I do ask to be treated seriously and responsibly by your office. It is unquestionable that public opinion is in support of the liberality and enlightenment pursued by you on other occasions, and public interest in the matter is tremendous.

I have, for example, been approached by most of the national newspapers for the right to print the entire text of my correspondence with your office. This has seemed to me to be an invitation to sensationalism which could obscure a serious subject. Accordingly, I have tried to behave responsibly in a difficult situation which is trying for all concerned.

Therefore, I ask you most sincerely and urgently to be helpful and sympathetic. The difficulties, you will surely admit, are inconsiderable. Your licence should be a protection to me also. At present, I am not merely unprotected, but I am being exposed to every tide of individual malice, eccentricity and ignorance. I enclose a note indicating how I intend to comply with your recommendations.

In March 1961, when Osborne saw the list of the fourteen cuts ordered by the Chamberlain in *Luther*, he told George Devine at first that he refused to accept any of them *'under any circumstances'*, or to agree to any substitutions, because they were 'severely damaging to the psychological structure, method and interest of the play' and the principle involved was 'too important' for him to be influenced by the possibility that the English production would have to be postponed indefinitely. 'I don't write plays to have them re-written by someone else . . . I am quite prepared to withdraw the play from production altogether and wait for the day when Lord Scarbrough is no more', he wrote to George Devine. There were discussions at the time whether the Royal Court could be transformed into a 'club' theatre for *Luther*'s performance, and whether if it were transferred, the English Stage Company would turn the West End theatre into a club as well.

After George Devine and Oscar Lewenstein went to the Palace to discuss these cuts in *Luther* with the Assistant Comptroller, the Lord Chamberlain relented and passed all but four of the passages he had banned two weeks earlier. This left 'convent piss', 'monk's piss', 'piss-scared', 'crap' and 'balls of the Medici'. Helpfully, the Office suggested that 'testicles of the Medici' would be 'acceptable'. It was an unusually rapid retreat. On the remaining objections, Osborne pointed out that 'piss' was freely spoken in Shakespeare ('Master, I do smell all horse piss', in *The Tempest*): and that 'testicle' was less ambiguous, more clinical, and more absurd than 'balls', apart from the historical fact that balls were a Medici family symbol. He was over-ruled.

With *The Blood of the Bambergs*, in 1962, Osborne committed three tiny offences against the royal taboos, by referring to Prince William and Prince Henry (the names of members of the reigning house); to Commander Crabtree, which sounded—to the censor—perilously like Commander Colville, the Press Officer at Buckingham Palace; and to 'Gentlemen at Arms', because such a body existed at the Court. The Lord Chamberlain's Office carefully pointed out that the tune to which the Bamberg National Anthem was sung must *not* resemble 'God Save The Queen', either 'in notation or rhythm'; that the uniforms must *not* resemble those of the British Services; and that no living person must be impersonated. A film sequence was also examined and passed, with the warning that this, too, must not contain impersonations of living people—or, indeed, any photographs of them, either. After negotiations, Prince Wilhelm, Prince Gustav, Commodore Crabtree and Halberdiers at Arms were substituted for the offending names. What the Chamberlain refused to pass was the speech of the Archbishop in the second act: although 'straight' in itself, it was—in its satirical context—a direct mockery of the Church service, and somewhat close to Canterbury. All the censor would accept was a film in which the Archbishop was seen but could not be heard.

In *Under Plain Cover*—with which *The Blood of the Bambergs* was staged—seven passages were queried, apparently for reason of sexual candour, religious irreverence and direct allusion to the Royal Family. This was a short inventory of photographs: 'Lord Snowdon's own study of Princess Margaret and her baby. Also the Queen in Ghana, Princess Alexandra in Hong Kong, the Queen in Italy with the Pope.' Instead, with excessive caution, the Chamberlain allowed Osborne merely to say: 'A well-known photographer's study of a royal baby'.) Vetoed were brief references to having sex 'anally' and 'orally'; to somebody who 'likes to be crucified'; to a best man who 'might have felt a bit funny, standing up there at the altar—you know—when you've slept with the bride *and* the groom' ('Been on such intimate terms with' was 'accept-able'); to a 'plastic crucifix' (changed to 'plastic object or ikon'); to a crucifix 'as used by the nuns of St Bridget in Limerick' with a little battery in it which lights up ('nuns' was replaced by 'convent'); and, as usual, to 'Oh, Christ' (for which 'God' was substituted). Yet the central situation of sado-masochistic fantasy and clothes fetishism, happily practised by a married couple till they find that theirs is an incestuous union, was sanctioned by the Chamberlain. He had come a long way.

There was trouble again over *Inadmissible Evidence*, in which some twenty cuts and changes were requested. All were related to taboos on language and references to sexual practice. For instance, the Chamberlain objected to 'Do you have it off with that girl of yours ?'; but the deletion of 'off' made it, for him, innocuous; 'that beautiful arse' had to be changed to 'bum'; in 'Don't tell me you're short of crumpet', the last offending word had to be replaced by 'it'; even though the management pointed out that the term was 'often used in North Country comedy in a much less serious context'; 'half-arsed' was changed for 'half-baked'; and 'creep' replaced 'catchfart', in spite of Osborne's argument that the latter word was 'a vigorous expression of contempt, after all used frequently in Chaucer'. But on more substantial questions, the Chamberlain changed his mind. For instance, he allowed the author to keep the scene in which a homosexual in trouble tells the solicitor how he made love to a man in a car, while the man's wife was driving, without her knowledge that anything was going on, and that the man made a rendezvous with him for the next night.

The Royal Court told the censor that 'Mr Osborne's intention is to show, as seriously and trenchantly as possible, the extent of sordid furtiveness and guilt to which a man of this sort is drawn. He is very anxious, too, that we should not cut "and made me meet him the next night". It is difficult to see the reason behind this cut, and such incidents are well known to have happened.' The Chamberlain also sanctioned after some discussion a man's statement that his wife 'failed to reach satisfaction'. ('It is Mr Osborne's purpose', the Court explained, 'to show the humiliation involved in having to discuss such intimate matters for legal purposes.') But the Chamberlain still refused to license an allusion to enforced intercourse in menstrual periods as a ground for divorce, in spite of the theatre's explanation that the passages were deliberately couched in law report language, 'since it is Mr Osborne's intention to show the way in which intimate and personal problems are affected by coming into court'.

The biggest battle of Osborne's career to date, however, came in 1964 with *A Patriot For Me*. 'Like all serious plays', as Lord Annan said in the House of Lords in 1966, 'this centred on a number of themes, but one of the most important was that of homosexuality. The play was based on the life of an intelligence officer in the Austro-Hungarian Army before the first world war, who gradually discovering his homosexual tendencies, indulged them and was blackmailed by agents of the Russian imperial secret service. On being exposed, he shot himself. I cannot conceive of any play less sentimental towards homosexuality, more cold-eyed and ruthless in its exposure of the horror of life with a particular kind of homosexuality and less likely to induce anyone to go into this practice.'

In September 1964, however, the Assistant Comptroller notified the Royal Court that there were whole scenes in this play as it stood which the Lord Chamberlain could not license, 'on the grounds that they exploit homosexuality in a manner that may tend to have corrupting influences. He cannot allow such scenes as a homosexual ball at which some of the men are dressed as women (including one who portrays Lady Godiva dressed in a gold lamé jockstrap); and others in which men embrace each other and are seen in bed together.' There were also phrases and words which he 'disallowed', including 'clap' and the exclamation 'Tears of Christ' but mostly referring to homosexual love: for instance, when a man says to a woman of her husband-to-be, 'You'll never know that body like I know it.' In the protracted exchange of letters which followed the production, the Lord Chamberlain acknow-ledged the 'evident merits of the piece', and was prepared to review its licence 'with an open mind'; but the Assistant Comptroller pointed out that there were 'aspects of the play other than those' raised by the director, Anthony Page, about the disallowed parts', and these would have to 'weigh with the Lord Chamberlain when making his decision'. He refused, in effect, to accept the argument that in the ball scene Osborne aimed at showing 'the extremities of behaviour to which this minority of society can reach. The desperation and triviality are a very important part of it—Redl [the central character] sees the world, to which he feels he is largely condemned, presided over by the Baron, a figure whose homosexuality has made him increasingly snobbish, cynical and corrupt. At the end of the scene Redl, who has tried to integrate himself with society, is provoked into a physical assault by the homo-sexual mockery of institutions which he has respected up to then.'

The Royal Court decided, in view of the Chamberlain's refusal, that it would stage *A Patriot For Me* as a 'club' production. Only members of the English Stage Society would be admitted, on the lines adopted by the New Watergate Theatre Club when the Comedy Theatre became a 'club' in 1956. This was not planned as an act of defiance. On the contrary, the move was made without manifestoes, because the theatre

189

did not want to bring down the full power of the Chamberlain against it. But it was the only way of getting the play on to the stage. Even so, it involved the theatre and the author in a big financial loss. However successful it might be at the Court it could not, with so large a cast and so relatively small a theatre, hope to make ends meet, because the refusal of a licence made a transfer impossible; and it is on transfers (and film rights) that the Royal Court depends, to reinforce its State and civic grants. In fact, although *A Patriot For Me* was greatly acclaimed by the critics, was awarded the *Evening Standard* prize for the best play of 1965, and played to packed houses (ninety-five per cent capacity), it lost £16,500, and Osborne stood half the loss. 'Is this the way to reward one of our best playwrights?' as Lord Annan asked the House of Lords.

No critics said that they found the play obscene or corrupting; but Ronald Bryden said in the *New Statesman*:

> If anyone still doubts that art knows better than censorship, John Osborne's new play . . . should provide clinching evidence. With the excision of this ballroom scene for which it will clearly go down in theatrical history, the Lord Chamberlain apparently might have considered licensing *A Patriot For Me* for public performance. Apart from the fact that it is one of the best things Osborne has written, the deletion would have been ludicrously self-defeating . . . Without its climactic evocation of high Hapsburg queerdom at its annual drag ball, *A Patriot For Me* would be, more or less, a sentimental, high-flown piece of propaganda for the rights of a noble and oppressed minority. Osborne's ball scene is not only magnificently theatrical, the best thing in his play, but its centre, its validation, the image from which all else takes perspective and completeness.[1]

The case for licensing the play was supported by independent people outside the theatre such as Lord Goodman, Chairman of the Arts Council. The Royal Court received no complaints, by letter or in person, about the indecency of *A Patriot For Me*. 'If I did not know it to be untrue,' Harold Hobson began his notice, 'I should think that the Lord Chamberlain was mad.'

> One cannot protest too strongly against that double moral standard which prevails in the government of the British theatre, by which it is

[1] *New Statesman*, 9 July 1965.

permissible to treat a difficult and delicate subject frivolously, but of which any thoughtful consideration is almost automatically penalized.[1]

Seventy years earlier, Israel Zangwill had written of the censorship:

Seriousness is the unpardonable sin. Coarseness can be condoned, if it is only flippant and frivolous enough. [2]

Plus ça change, plus c'est la même chose.

[1] *Sunday Times*, 4 July 1965.
[2] *Without Prejudice*, by Israel Zangwill (1896).

13

If one were starting from scratch in 1965 I don't think one would invent this particular set-up.—The Lord Chamberlain, LORD COBBOLD; *Sunday Times*, 11 April 1965

What matters is not what the censor does to what I have written, but to what I might have written.—LEO TOLSTOY

* * *

HOW DOES the Lord Chamberlain's Office work today in its relations with the theatre? In the opening chapter Lord Cobbold made a brief personal appearance: the bizarre history of his inherited responsibilities has occupied the intervening pages. Now it is time for an outline of contemporary censorship, in which I shall have to recapitulate some facts already reported in order to fill a few gaps and dispel some of the fogs which surround the old house in Stable Yard—and its critics, too.

The Office is a small one: it is proud of this—and there is reason for pride in its claim that in the 220 years since the house was built the full-time working establishment has remained virtually the same. Dozens of royal posts come under the aegis of the Lord Chamberlain, but the permanent staff at the centre consists of no more than ten people, almost as in the eighteenth century, although the labels have changed; they are the Comptroller, Assistant Comptroller, Secretary, Assistant Secretary, and their clerical assistants and secretaries. (The Examiners or Readers work at home.)

The theatre claims only a small part of the Chamberlain's week; and, as we know, the licensing of *buildings*—as distinct from *plays*—is nowadays a largely nominal chore. Instead of an annual licence, the Chamberlain now issues a triennial one, against a bond of £200. The L.C.C.—now the G.L.C.—engineers inspect the London theatres, and the Chamberlain signs the licences, without a breath of controversy. He does, on occasion, have to act against offenders. Some years ago, for instance, he made a theatre-owner pay back £250 because on more than one occasion no fireman was on duty in his theatre and the exit doors were found to be locked, a mistake which the Chamberlain and the G.L.C., understandably, take very seriously. (In the event, the Office gave the man £150 back, on the assurance that he would mind his ways and presented the rest to reduce the National Debt.) Yet, although the Chamberlain's jurisdiction over London's theatres is supported by the managers, who like to retain the personal influence of a single, known umpire, it seems likely that he will lose this anomalous role in the near future, whatever may happen to his function as stage censor.

By Section 12 of the Theatres Act of 1843, as we have already seen, no new 'Stage Play' can be performed unless a licence has been issued by the Lord Chamberlain, if he is satisfied that it 'does not in its general tendency contain anything immoral or otherwise improper for the stage'. 'Stage Play' is defined as any tragedy, comedy, farce, opera, burletta, interlude, melodrama, pantomime, or other entertainment of the stage, or any part thereof. Music-hall sketches—defined as 'parts of plays'—have to be submitted, although extempore music-hall routines are free from censorship. Opera libretti are censorable, but ballets are not; although a judge's *obiter dictum* in Wigan v. Strange (1865) suggests that a ballet devoted to telling a story (*ballet d'action*) may be tantamount to a play in mime (which is the Chamberlain's business), while a *ballet-divertissement* is not. He ruled that 'the *ballet divertissement* involves no consecutive train of ideas, but consists merely of poses and evolutions by a number of persons, elegant in shape and graceful in action. On the other hand, the *ballet d'action* has a regular dramatic story which may give rise to all manner of emotions incident to tragedy, comedy, or farce, accompanied by elegance of form and grace of motion.' And the *divertissement* was distinguished, under the 1843 Act, as 'not an entertainment *of*, but *on* the stage'. Most of us have seen *ballets d'action* on the contemporary stage, but the Lord Chamberlain prefers not to. Sometimes he sends an emissary to check on doubtful cases. One of his aides was despatched, several years ago, to examine the Ballets Africains whose girl-dancers appeared naked to the waist—and *moved*. But after careful scrutiny the officer from the Palace decided that this choreography did not constitute a *ballet d'action*, and the girls continued to shake, uncensored. Although the Chamberlain's intervention is frequently sought by Puritans disquieted by the near-nudity, the homosexual kitsch, and the copulatory (and, in one recent case, masturbatory) mime of some modern *white* ballet, the Office firmly refuses to act. If ballet was *meant* to be in the Act, they say, it would have been specified

193

there along with opera and burletta. As it is not, it is no concern of theirs—and they say so with relief.

Plays written before Walpole's Act of 1737 may be staged without application to the Chamberlain. But he has the power—under Section 14 of the 1843 Act—to stop the performance of *any* play or any part of any play, licensed or not, if he thinks it necessary to protect good manners and preserve public peace, 'either absolutely or for such time as he shall think fit'; and this applies (it is understood) to pre-1737 plays and indeed to those which he (or one of his predecessors) has already licensed. He would certainly ban, wherever it was staged, a deliberately pornographic piece, like Rochester's seventeenth-century shocker, *Sodom*, if anyone should aspire to give it a public performance. In 1966 he even banned several lines in a *poem* by Rochester, read aloud in a poetry-and-jazz anthology presented in the Open Air Theatre, although the passage has frequently appeared in print without a hint of controversy. A young girl speaks to an old man:

> *Thy nobler parts, which but to name*
> *In our sex would be counted shame,*
> *By age's frozen grasp possessed,*
> *From their ice shall be released:*
> *And, sooth'd by my reviving hand,*
> *In former warmth and vigour stand.*

There is, however, no record of any open ban on English pre-1737 plays in the past twenty years, and during that period only two plays, to my knowledge, have had their licences withdrawn—*Felicity Jasmine*, a comedy staged at the St James in 1946, because of objections to its salacity and poor taste, and *A Pin to See the Peepshow*, a play about the Thompson–Bywaters murder case, because of the objections of relatives (see page 160). Lord Cobbold could also, as his predecessors did, veto all or part of any classic which has been newly translated. *Lysistrata* was heavily cut until recent years, and *Oedipus Rex* was banned altogether until fifty years ago. In *Miss Julie*, which was banned until 1939—over fifty years after it was written—the Lord Chamberlain continued until recently to insist on two deletions: the line where a maid says to Jean of Miss Julie: 'Oh, she's got her monthly coming on'; and the word *Merde!* which Jean uses against Miss Julie when she calls him a swine. (Strindberg used the French word, as it is part of Jean's character to show off his sophistication by using French phrases.) In 1964 Michael

194

Meyer, the translator, took up these points with the Assistant Comptroller, and some weeks later he received a revealing letter from Colonel Penn.

Dear Mr Meyer,

I write in continuation of my letter of the 15 April, and after having discussed the matter with the Lord Chamberlain who has only just come back from Switzerland.

I explained to him your view that the works of an acknowledged foreign master, in the hands of a translater of proven capacity, should, in the interests of the work and the reputation of the interpreter, be exempted from the normal requirements of the censor. The Lord Chamberlain asks me to explain in response that, whilst he can employ some universal measure in deciding upon the effect of phrasing or situation in a play, there is no measure known to him that would be acceptable to anyone where it was a matter of establishing the status of an author or an interpreter or producer. The matter is not so much one of being unable to establish the position of the topmost, as the utter impossibility of convincing anyone that he does not belong to that category. This being so and since justice must be *seen* to be done, the Lord Chamberlain feels that he must adhere to the proven system of judging each question on its merits.

Whilst he is unable, for the reasons stated, to accept your view as a matter of principle, he has considered the three specific requests made in your letter of the 15 January on their merits. In the circumstances which you set out and although the fact of doing so may cause him some embarrassment in dealing with other claims, he is prepared to agree to these three requests.

For the sake of clarity I recapitulate these decisions in the appendix to this letter, and I am having the records of this Office altered in conformity. If you are able to secure the original licence forms I will have them altered conformably.

The following dialogue is now allowed:

(1) *Hedda Gabler* (Licence No. 2665 of 19 June 1962), Act 1–22: 'Jesus'.
(2) *The Master Builder* (Licence No. 2987 of 15 November 1962), Act 1–39: 'Christ's'.
(3) *Miss Julie* (Licence No. 3497 of 5 June 1963), page 21: 'Merde'.

Mr Meyer says:[1]

> No reference is made in his attachment to the menstruation objection;
> I thought he might refuse to amend this, so made no mention of it to
> him and then simply used it without bothering. When the time came
> (a year later) for the National Theatre to perform my translation,
> we re-submitted it to him (as there had been some amendment in
> other respects) and it went through without comment.

★ ★ ★

The law provides no fixed code of rules. For most of its existence, the
Lord Chamberlain's Office has followed a personal assessment com-
bining custom, precedent and instinct in ways which have often proved
to be confusing and contradictory. One Chamberlain has not considered
himself bound by the decisions of another, or by his own, with dis-
quieting effects upon dramatists. The censors refuse to recognize
precedent as a rule or as a justification: they have been known to license
a number in one revue, and then ban it on its reappearance later, un-
changed, in another script. But the Office now uses as a basis the list
suggested nearly sixty years ago by the 1909 Committee investigating
dramatic censorship. As we have seen, it said that plays should be
licensed unless they were judged:

(a) to be indecent
(b) to contain offensive personalities
(c) to represent on the stage in an invidious manner a living person or
    any person within fifty years of his death
(d) to do violence to the sentiment of religious reverence
(e) to be calculated to conduce to crime or vice
(f) to be calculated to impair friendly relations with any foreign
    power
(g) to be calculated to cause a breach of the peace.

Although these proposals were never endorsed by Parliament, the more
recent Lords Chamberlain have—as Lord Cobbold said in 1966—kept
them in mind, 'in exercising our personal judgement, as the law requires
us to do. We have sought to interpret them in the light of changing
climates of opinion and of any advice on particular subjects or particular
plays which it has seemed appropriate to take.' Practice does change—
or *swerve*, to be more precise: sometimes, as in the 1960s, with relative

---

[1] In a letter to the author.

196

rapidity; seldom with any official announcement or codification.

About 800 to 850 scripts a year are submitted to the Lord Chamberlain: he personally reads only a handful of them—perhaps fifty.[1] They are the 'difficult' ones. But they—and all scripts sent to Stable Yard—are seen first by one of three or more Readers, part-time workers outside the Office whose identity is—like most of the mechanism of censorship—generally kept quiet. They are appointed by the Chamberlain; and are responsible to him and to the Queen. These Readers now usually have theatrical associations: in the past they have sometimes—like the Chamberlain and his deputies—stemmed from the military, upper-class tradition of public service. A recent Reader who united both qualifications was Lieutenant-Colonel Sir St Vincent Troubridge, a descendant of Nelson's admiral, who combined a distinguished army career in both world wars with a passionate, resonant interest in theatrical research (and fishing): his clubs were White's and the Garrick. Today one Reader is a former chairman of the Society for Theatre Research, a theatre historian and antiquarian bookseller, Ifan Kyrle Fletcher; and the senior Reader, who has worked for the Office for nearly thirty years, is Charles Heriot, a former actor, writer and producer.

The Readers can pass a play, without obliging their superiors in the hierarchy to read it; but if they are in doubt about its inflammatory or offensive potentialities, in any of the especially tender areas with which the Office is concerned, they refer it to the Deputy Comptroller or to the Comptroller. The Comptroller was defined in 1866 by Lord Sydney as 'a permanent under-secretary', who 'manages the whole of the detail of the Office'; and this definition still holds good. They have faced with apparent equanimity such incidental problems as the distinction offered in nude shows between an artistic pose and an indecent exposure; or the choice between 'balls' and 'testicles', 'arse' and 'backside'; or the possible degrees of phallic implication in the use of a plank, a fish and a banana. These officials, like the Chamberlain himself, are generally former Guards officers and members of the landed gentry who find a full-time job in the Office after a service career. They may, and often did in previous regimes, settle a play's fate themselves, without bother-

---

[1] This compares with as many as 1,310 in 1952, before the final collapse of the touring system, and with around four hundred a year in the 1890s. In the six months from October 1964 to March 1965 441 stage plays were submitted: of these 378 were licensed without reservation; one or two verbal changes were required in forty-five; 'a lot of verbal and business changes' were made in fifteen; one or more scenes were banned in three.

ing the Chamberlain; but if it is a matter of a veto on a scene or the play as a whole, then the Chamberlain will see it. He no longer consults an official advisory committee, which functioned—spasmodically, it seems—between 1910 and 1960. Instead, he takes personal and unofficial ad hoc soundings inside his wide circle of friends and official contacts, perhaps consulting as many as thirty people for 'top professional opinions' inside 'the responsible community', as one of his staff has described it. This flexible approach is advanced, with some justification, as one of the clear merits of the current system over, for instance, a formal committee, which would be bound by procedural rules in summoning expert witnesses, who might well be decidedly less helpful in the open testimony of a committee room than in the *tête-à-tête* privacy of a West End Club. In what he considers as borderline cases the Chamberlain can go to the summit: on religious problems the Office may refer to the Archbishop of Canterbury, and it sends Buckingham Palace all plays and sketches involving any members of the Royal Family. As Lord Cobbold said in 1965, 'there's a wealth of experience and technical advice available'.

Now, as a hundred years ago, the Office works on the principles set out in 1866 by the Examiner, Mr Pigott—'to act as much as possible by personal intercourse, or confidential correspondence with managers; and, in some cases even, unofficially, with the authors of plays; in short, to avoid all unnecessary friction'. Now, as then, it appears to believe that its mistakes are 'always in the direction of extreme indulgence, for the simple reason that if the reins were tightened, they would snap in his (the censor's) hands'. According to Lord Cobbold (in his 1965 *Sunday Times* interview), 'we always think of ourselves as a licensing authority rather than as a censoring authority. The bias is always to give a licence unless there is a very strong ground for objection.'

Most of the managements have been in touch with the people in my office for years and are on very good terms with them. They write in, and they come in, and explain and ask for reconsideration; and of course one is always ready to look at any arguments that are put up. There is a bit of gamesmanship in all this. Some managements, not all, put in a number of four-letter words and other things they know perfectly well will be cut out, possibly in the hope that we will cut them out and leave one or two borderline things in. And of course there is some advertising value in 'banned by the censor'. So there's a good deal of give and take on this.

198

When the Office decides that changes should be made before a licence can be granted, the manager—*not* the author—gets a letter, probably from the Assistant Comptroller, which runs something like this: 'I am desired by the Lord Chamberlain to write to you about "X". I am to say that the Lord Chamberlain cannot allow the dialogue contained in the appendix attached and this must be altered or omitted altogether. In the latter case an undertaking must be given to that effect. If you intend to substitute any new dialogue, then the alterations must be submitted before they can be used.' In the past, as we have seen, he has sometimes suggested that it would be better not to apply for a licence at all, in order to protect the author from the stigma of writing a banned play, to preserve some secrecy about the workings of the censorship, and to keep down the temperature of the opposition; but it appears that such discretion is seldom, if ever, practised today.

If the author agrees to make changes and the changes are approved by the Chamberlain, the manager finally receives the indispensable licence. It is a numbered foolscap sheet of blue quarto, headed by the royal coat of arms, running as follows:

I, the Lord Chamberlain of the Queen's Household for the time being, do by virtue of my Office and in pursuance of powers given to me by the Act of Parliament for regulating Theatres, 6 & 7 Victoria, Cap 68, Section 12 Allow the Performance of a new Stage Play of which a copy has been submitted to me by you, being a —— in —— Acts, entitled —— with the exception of all Words and Passages which are specified in the endorsement of the Licence and without any further variation whatsoever.

Given under my hand this —— day of —— 19——

Lord Chamberlain

On the back, if there is room, the offending Words and Passages are typed, usually in red ink; and another notice calls 'the particular attention of the Management' to five regulations.

Any change of title must be submitted for the Lord Chamberlain's approval.

No profanity or impropriety of language to be permitted on the Stage.

No indecency of dress, dance or gesture to be permitted on the Stage.

No objectionable personalities to be permitted on the Stage, nor anything calculated to produce riot or breach of the peace.

No offensive representation of living persons to be permitted on the Stage.

'The strict observance of these Regulations,' says the form, 'is to be considered as the condition upon which the Licence is signed.' Any deviation from the text is illegal. No improvisation is allowed. Ad libbing is breaking the law.

An author can discuss the cuts and changes proposed, by post and in person, with the Comptroller or his Deputy; or, on rare occasions, with the Chamberlain himself. But although he may—and often does—persuade them into greater permissiveness, and although they behave with courtesy and tact, there is still no appeal against their final verdict, if they decide against a particular passage or the play as a whole. The Chamberlain's official communication is still usually with the manager only. He is not *obliged* to give the author any explanation at all, and indeed he did so infrequently, if at all, in the past. A printed memorandum which the Chamberlain used to send to dramatists informed them that, 'The Licenser has no official cognisance of authors as such'. When a Victorian dramatist, Sydney Grundy, wrote to the Lord Chamberlain, to ask him why one of his plays had been banned, Grundy says he replied that 'his office did not recognize authors and he could take no official notice of my existence'.

Once the play has been licensed, how does the censor ensure that the cuts or changes have been made? This question has been asked in each committee of inquiry into the Chamberlain's Office and it has generally been met with some righteous indignation from the Examiners under interrogation. George Colman, for instance, said 'My duty is to object to everything immoral, or politically dangerous. When I have marked my objections, the play is licensed, subject to the omission of the passages objected to; beyond this I have nothing to do, or an Examiner would become a spy as well as a censor on the theatre.' William Bodham Donne, in 1866, said: 'I should be very sorry to pursue any manager with a sort of system of espionage. Indeed it would be impracticable, and I think worse than arbitrary.' Yet in 1853 the Superintendent of the Lord Chamberlain's Department, Mr Norman Macdonald, testified to the committee that 'the examiner' of plays is supposed not only to examine the play, but to go and see whether the manner in which it is put on the stage is proper and not offensive'. When Donne was appointed as Examiner in 1857, he was instructed that he should 'attend personally . . . in any case when important alterations have been made . . . or whenever any report has been made of impropriety either in a drama itself, or the mode of placing it on the stage'. In the Chamberlain's opinion, he was told, 'the duty of Examiner is not only to read plays submitted for licence and advise him thereon, but that he is responsible to him for seeing that the play when acted corresponds in every respect with the play as licensed by the Lord Chamberlain'. Moreover, in 1866 an official memorandum of the Department noted that 'the Reader of Plays . . . attends any performance when important alterations have been made in a piece submitted for licence'. And an official memorandum quoted at the 1909 Committee directed that, 'The Examiner is further directed to visit the theatre constantly, and to see that the rules of the Lord Chamberlain are carried out with regard to the pieces licensed by him'. But in a letter from the Office in 1959, the Assistant Comptroller informed me that: 'There is no statutory duty upon the Lord Chamberlain to attend at the theatre, his only duty being to consider the copies of the plays that must be sent to him. The Examiner of Plays is no more than adviser to the Lord Chamberlain with no statutory responsibilities and no authority.'

Certainly the censor has not—up till now—prevented the plays he has banned from being staged by club theatres; and he cannot prevent them from being published, or presented on television or the radio. He cannot, moreover, invigilate throughout the country: he relies on press reviews and public complaints; and he knows—from personal experience —that his instructions are sometimes ignored on the stage, and that unlicensed words and business are being used.

In 1965 Lord Cobbold explained that:

> If we've been doubtful about business, I get somebody to have a look and see if the stage directions we've authorized are being carried out accurately. Also, if we get two or three complaints I usually send somebody to have a look at it. And I might add that we get more complaints about what we pass than about what we don't pass.

One difficulty, of course, is that the 'business' licensed for one company —say, the Royal Shakespeare—might well look quite different a couple of years later in some other company's production. As the Lord Chamberlain said, in 1965:

There is a great problem here because we are dealing with highly reputable managements, highly competent producers, who come to us and say, quite properly and accurately, that they can put on a certain scene without giving the slightest offence to anybody. I accept that as absolutely true; but the same scene as produced by a less competent management with a quite different production might result in something being undesirable indeed.

On several occasions in the last five years cuts or changes ordered by the Chamberlain have, in fact, been restored in performance, for one reason or another—perhaps by accident, perhaps by design. This happened, in a recent play when one character talked about a girl 'parting her thighs all over the furniture' instead of the staider alternative 'having sex', to which the Chamberlain had agreed; and 'To you she was just meat', instead of the substitute line, 'To you she was just a convenient repository'. Usually, nothing happens—because nobody notices. Yet if some people complain, the Office feels it is bound to act. And sometimes the discrepancies between the licensed text and the words spoken on the stage have been too glaring for the Chamberlain to turn a blind eye. In the spring of 1965 there was a flurried crisis at the Royal Court over Charles Wood's *Meals on Wheels*, after a stern letter was received from the Assistant Comptroller, demanding an explanation of the theatre's apparent defiance of the Office.

'In consequence of information received,' he said, 'the Lord Chamberlain caused an inspection to be made . . . From the report submitted to him . . . it appears to the Lord Chamberlain that much of the play presented, including most of the penultimate scene and the whole of the final scene, is different from the submitted version of the play as licensed by him. It would seem, furthermore, that some of the Lord Chamberlain's actual prohibitions have likewise not been observed. In this regard I am to cite his refusal to allow the phrases "I'll have your cobblers" and "I'll have your taters", which on several occasions on the 24 May were replaced by the phrase "I'll have your 'ollies".'

A grave debate ensued over the frequency that the forbidden (and now suppressed) word 'ollies had been spoken. Only *twice*, said the Court; much more, said the Chamberlain's man; not true, retorted the Court. But it did not deny that other liberties had, apparently, been taken. Nine lines had been added to the last scene and thirty lines had been added to another scene without approval by the censor. There was clearly a feeling at the Chamberlain's Office that the Royal Court was going too far. Yet everything ended characteristically, if not happily. For it turned out that although a few of the smaller discrepancies were due to amnesia among the cast (like the utterance of the controversial ' 'ollies') and some were due to last-minute additions by the author, which the director had not sent to the Palace in time, the main trouble was that the typescript sent to the Chamberlain was short of five pages, which had been accidentally doubled in another copy. In the circumstances, the Chamberlain relented—especially as by the time the investigation was over the play was due to close; and the theatre was notified, with kindly menace, that 'action on this occasion will be limited to suspending the licence' after the last night; it would be renewed only when a full description of any 'action' or 'business' was given to the Office.

Although the Chamberlain's Office clearly cannot be sure that its instructions will be followed to the letter, a manager may find that it is dangerous—or, at any rate, inconvenient—to ignore them. To take an example from a different terrain, the *Daily Mail* reported in 1948 from Salford that a shorthand writer had visited a production of *Aladdin* there and taken down every word of the dialogue in his notebook, 'to decide whether it was one of the 136 versions already licensed by the Lord Chamberlain'. On examination at Stable Yard—and what a job of comparative Christmas scholarship that must have entailed!—the censor's men discovered that although two-thirds of the panto came from a version licensed in 1939, the rest was 'entirely new'. For this offence the director, the company manager and the manager of the show were fined £30 between them, while the theatre licensee had to pay £10 for aiding and abetting. It all scarcely seems to have been worth the trouble.

Up to 1925, a conviction under section 15 of the Theatres Act of 1843—for presenting unlicensed or banned material 'for hire'—automatically rendered null and void the licence of the theatre where the offence was committed. But section 43 of the Criminal Justice Act of 1925 gave magistrates the power to impose fines instead, on theatre licensees concerned in proceedings brought under the 1843 Act. In the twenty years from 1929 to 1949 at least one hundred prosecutions took place, resulting in over three-hundred convictions, most of them for unauthorized alterations in licensed scripts. Since then the number of legal actions appears to have dropped, but although no figures are available, I estimate that about forty cases have been brought in the past seventeen years—nearly all of them obscure offences in provincial towns—'*pour encourager les autres*'.

* * *

If the author does *not* agree to change the text, or if the play as a whole is vetoed, there is no appeal against the Lord Chamberlain's judgement. He cannot be called to account in Parliament, for he is answerable to nobody but the Queen, and his salary comes from the Civil List. In the Commons his conduct can only be challenged by a special, specific motion. In 1909 the Lord Chamberlain said that if he were attacked, he would answer questions in the House of Lords; but this appears to have been a purely private readiness. In the Memorandum of Appointment given to the Examiner of Plays in 1895, it stated that the Examiner acted 'on the part of the Lord Chamberlain, who is responsible to Parliament', but this appears to have been one of those misunderstandings which recur in Stable Yard's history. The 1909 Committee recommended that there should be the same opportunities for the Commons to review his 'general administration' as for other Ministers; but this was among the main recommendations ignored by the Government.

By what criterion does he judge plays? By rulings which 'simply codify the present and most of the past prejudices of the class he represents?' So it seemed to Shaw—and so it seems to many outsiders now, on much of the evidence. Today, the Lord Chamberlain defines his approach in a rational way: 'My personal objective is to try to assess the norm of educated, adult opinion and if possible to keep just a touch ahead of it. I find I have to make a positive effort to keep my own personal tastes, likes and dislikes right out of the picture. They are obviously irrelevant for censorship purposes.' (*Sunday Times*, 11/4/65.)

Inevitably, the Office is lobbied by diehard Puritans of all ages, classes and lunacies. Sometimes these fanatics are treated too seriously, but a special sense of humour is often in evidence. When one of these zealots complained about the use of the word 'maidenhead' in a revue in the 1950s, he received a letter from the Office beginning:

Dear Sir,

Maidenhead is a town in Berkshire, in which over 17,000 people contrive to live without embarrassment . . .

On another occasion, questioning the propriety of presenting a popular

French farce in the West End, one of the Chamberlain's men is said to have pointed out that English playgoers might object to the way in which the French dramatist conjugated the verb 'to violate':

I am violated.
Thou art being violated.
He, She, It is violating you.
We watch you being violated.
You seem to like being violated.
They discuss at great length your being violated.

★   ★   ★

Unlike all his predecessors, Lord Cobbold has talked candidly and informally about his job to the press and in the House of Lords. He speaks with practical common sense and disarming liberalism. 'I do not see myself as an arbiter of taste or morals on the stage,' he said in the Lords in 1966. 'Public opinion on these matters is not static, and my objective is to move . . . with the mood of the times and to keep as near as possible to the centre of public opinion.' When he accepted the job, he says, 'I think I had rather an open mind on the subject.' Three years in office almost closed it. He agreed in 1965 that 'there are some disadvantages in the connection with the Royal Household', but added, 'there's not much point is saying that unless one's got a constructive alternative.' Yet a year later, in the House of Lords, he suggested, in effect, a division of responsibility: 'I doubt whether it is wise, even if the two functions are generally recognized to be separate, that the person who for the time being is head of the Queen's Household should also bear these responsibilities.'

Is he the right man for the job? Giving his own opinion on that topic to J. W. Lambert, 'as objectively as I can give it', he said in 1965:

I would personally have thought that the main qualities required for the person at the top were wide experience, a knowledge of what is going on in the contemporary world, and the habit of sifting advice, reaching decisions and taking responsibility. If a person is appointed to be Lord Chamberlain, quite apart from his theatrical responsibilities, he must surely be presumed to have these qualifications.

In 1966, however, Lord Cobbold agreed with Lord Willis in a House of Lords debate that 'it is not in line with present-day thinking' that his powers and responsibilities 'should be entrusted to any one individual

205

without any form of policy supervision or any provision for appeal'. It sounded as if he had had enough.

He is, of course, a man of good will. So are his deputies. So, indeed, have all the censors been for the past eighty years. Each Lord Chamberlain in his turn has been acclaimed as a model of gentlemanly good sense, charm and progressive views. Back in 1892, William Archer—an opponent of the system—was assuring his readers that 'the censorship has never been better administered than at present', and that the Lord Chamberlain was 'a man of culture and liberality and certainly above any suspicion of any sort of personal motive'. Lord Cromer, between the wars, was estolled as a paragon of wisdom. In the 1940s Lord Clarendon received the homage of the managers. No Chamberlain, they said in the 1950s, could match the far-sighted flexibility of Lord Scarbrough. Yet each of these gentlemanly, open-minded Chamberlains, as we have seen, sanctioned and supported absurd acts of petty tyranny, obtuse bumbledom, and ignorant persecution. Lord Cobbold may seem to us far better than his predecessors. But who knows what damage he has already done? Who knows what the *next* censor will be like? It is the office, not the man, that is to blame. The job is impossible—and unnecessary.

14

All censorships exist to prevent anyone from challenging current conceptions and existing institutions. All progress is initiated by challenging current conceptions and executed by supplanting existing institutions. Consequently the first condition of progress is the removal of censorships.—BERNARD SHAW

* * *

Now is the time, in this final chapter, to summarize some large and recurrent questions, and to return some tentative answers.

1. Does the theatre need a censor?
2. If so, should it be the Lord Chamberlain?
3. What is the alternative?
4. If we abolish censorship, what would happen?
5. What is, in fact, *likely* to happen next?

First of all, what is the argument for imposing official controls upon the drama, alone among the arts? What is so dangerously different about the theatre, that such special safeguards are required to protect the public? A classic answer was given in the report of the 1909 Committee:

> Ideas or situations which, when described on a printed page may work little mischief, when represented through the human personality of actors may have a more powerful and deleterious effect. The existence of an audience, moved by the same emotions, its members conscious of one another's presence, intensifies the influence of what is done and spoken on the stage. Moreover, scenes in a play may stimulate to vice without falling within the legal definition of indecency; they may include personalities so offensive as to be clearly improper for presentation, which yet are not punishable as libellous; they may outrage feelings of religious reverence without coming within the scope of the Blasphemy Laws; and they may give occasion for demonstrations injurious to good relations between this country and Foreign Powers without coming within the purview of any law whatsoever. The performance, day after day, in the presence of

numbers of people, of plays containing one or other of these elements, would have cumulative effects to which the conveyance of similar ideas by print offers no analogy.

Part of the theatre's business is, after all, public exposure. If its purpose 'both at first and now, was and is' to show 'the very age and body of the time his form and pressure', then its official censorship seems—to some people—inevitable. They steadfastly believe that a policeman will always be necessary—in England at least—because there are words that must not be spoken, there are subjects and situations that must not be dramatized, there are ideas that must not be ventilated on the stage; and these are much more likely to be exposed in the theatre than anywhere else. They are unfit not only for young people, but also for older English adults of both sexes; and the only way of keeping these things off the stage is to put someone in authority over the theatre. To people who think like this, there are also manifest dangers in cinema and television, which count their audience in millions, not thousands; but the theatre is singled out for special anxieties because it is only there that living actors can connect with a living audience: the possibilities of infection from flesh and blood people are consequently much greater than from the mere images watched on cinema screens or TV sets. A live actor can, and does, *change*: he can respond to the events of the day, the stop-press news of both public and private life; he can talk directly to the audience; he could, conceivably, make *them* change, too; he is a disturbingly free element, fallible and unpredictable, with a magnetic field at his command in which he can kindle an instant collective response; while the potential dangers of a live *actress* are even more apparent. Many champions of censorship appear to be convinced that the theatre is always poised, slavering, for the chance of 'taking a liberty', in that revealingly pejorative phrase of this Freedom-Loving People. Explaining his function in 1832, George Colman wrote:

> Produce constantly before spectators nothing but fascinating *debauchées*, and heroic conspirators, and the weak part of the multitude (which is the majority) would, in time, turn profligates and rebels; they would 'Live o'er each scene and be what they behold'.

There is an underlying belief, in some quarters, that religion and politics, in particular, are too good for the theatre: it is the argument of Queen Elizabeth, four hundred years ago, that 'matters of religion or of the governance of the estate of the commonwealth' could be discussed only before an audience of 'grave and discreet persons' by 'men of authority, learning and wisdom'. And belief in censorship is reinforced by the English belief in *limits*: 'in every single phrase of activity, each gesture, each impulse is tempered by the idea that it is possible to go "too far" '; as Peter Brook says,[1] and the conviction lingers still that the theatre is one of the places where people are most dangerously inclined to do precisely that. 'After all, there *is* a limit', and 'you've got to draw the line *somewhere*'. These are two more national catch-phrases which, in themselves, may help to explain the survival of the Lord Chamberlain. We cherish an obstinate moral cartography which demands that the frontiers should be charted and mapped. *Somebody* should be keeping an eye open to make sure that the actors don't overdo it, don't get above themselves, don't go beyond a joke and overstep the mark. And there is a burning suspicion that, as the authors, managers and directors can't be trusted because of their collusion in the whole business of self-exposure and make-believe, this *somebody* up above should be a kind of umpire with a gun, outside the corrupting tradition of the stage, to make sure that nobody says Christ, takes off all their own clothes or somebody else's, or is rude about the Queen or the President of the U.S.A. Sixty years ago A. B. Walkley put the case when he said:

The present form of censorship represents the rough common sense of the great mass of the public, or, as the phrase goes, the man in the street. The censor is what we call a 'plain man', looking at matters in a plain way as, say, a common jury would look at them. He has a tendence to what Matthew Arnold used to call Philistinism, to a certain limited, narrow, conventional view of literature and life . . . But the world at large consists of such people, and the censor very fairly represents the world at large.

For generations, moral chaos was predicted if the censorship were abolished. In 1866, for instance, W. Bodham Donne prophesied

a period of license, which would shut the theatres against all decent and respectable playgoers, and would revive in more than their former intensity all the expiring prejudices against playhouses and players . . . the entertainments of theatres and music-halls would too frequently consist of more or less indecent dances, more or less obscene songs, and of occasional farces and opera bouffes, plentifully garnished with

[1] *Censorship*, No. 4 (1965).

scurrilous doggerel, sparing neither Church nor State, neither religious bodies nor political institutions, neither sex nor age, until the inevitable reaction set in; and pandemonium was cleared out by a succession of police raids, as in the U.S.

His successor, Mr Pigott, explained to the 1892 Committee that he tried to guard the honour of the stage by protecting it against unscrupulous managers who would turn the theatres into 'disorderly houses, if not houses of ill fame'. Another witness to the 1892 Committee, T. G. Fardell, predicted: 'Detectives in disguise would be quartered about, the stage would fall into serious disrepute, and English liberty would be in real danger of serious abridgement'. Somewhat less sensationally, a former Lord Chamberlain, the Earl of Scarbrough, suggested in 1966 in the House of Lords that the outlook—not only for the theatre but for the Government—would be black if his old job was liquidated:

I believe that there is quick money to be made from obscenity, from indecency and from representation of cruelty on the stage, and although I would not for a moment suggest that the theatre, in its fullest sense, would be lured by that, I have little doubt that some persons would be so lured. And what would be the result of that? Strong public reaction. Most Governments have a great many things which bother them and which seem to be inescapable, and I do not see any Government adding to their inescapable troubles a further one which might easily rouse the sleeping conscience of the nation. For this what might be termed political reason I think it unlikely that censorship will be entirely abolished; and on broad grounds of public and national interest I do not think it should be. I would call to aid that view one sentence from the Report of the Joint Select Committee of 1909, of which the Chairman was the then Mr Herbert Samuel: 'There are few things more harmful to a community than the influence of a licentious stage.' That was written in 1909. Is there anybody who will say that it is any less relevant today?

A more realistic argument against abolition today is that, as Philistines and embattled Puritans abound in the provinces, waiting their chance to beat up the theatre, a *central* censorship, however bad it may be, is bound to be better than a series of *local* censorships. If there were no Lord Chamberlain, it is argued, then local authorities would apply their own vetoes. Moral standards vary so widely from one part of the

210

country to another[1] that far worse anomalies than the current set would spring up, everywhere. The list of prohibitions mentioned above would be lengthened to include, for instance, unfavourable references to the Roman Catholic Church or the police; or to sexual relationships between white and coloured people; the discussion, or even *acknowledgement*, of prostitution, venereal disease, and sexual deviation. Common informers might induce the police to bring prosecutions or issue injunctions.

The immediate result of abolishing the Chamberlain's powers would be to make the theatre *less* adventurous than it is now; because managers would be far more cautious in choosing a play. The official licence granted by the Chamberlain 'provides the manager, at the negligible premium of two guineas per play, with an effective insurance against the author getting him into trouble, and a complete relief from all conscientious responsibility for the character of the entertainment . . .'; and it protects the author, too, against the pressure groups of moral, religious and political interests.

Moreover, if a central censor is essential, then there are advantages in retaining the Lord Chamberlain's Office. The case is:

1. The Chamberlain has done the job for over two hundred years, and an office with such a long tradition and wide experience is preferable to a new body.

2. It is both small and flexible, as it is not tied down by committee red tape; it is outside the vogues and vendettas of the theatrical world; it aspires to reflect majority common sense; and it is not linked to a party or a Ministry.

3. Although anomalies and inconsistencies still exist, these are inevitable under *any* form of censorship; and, in spite of past blunders, the system now works well enough with a high degree of permissiveness. In practice, authors and managers are given a good deal of rope, not only before production but after it, too.

4. The Chamberlain brings national prestige to the theatre by his association with the throne, and his judgements have all the more weight with local authorities because they emanate from a royal palace.

5. He costs the public very little, far less than any new body, as the overheads of censorship are included in the Office's total budget, which is borne by the Civil List.

---

[1] 'When the British Board of Film Censors refused a licence to *Fanny Hill*, eighteen authorities gave it an X certificate, forty-four an A certificate, four a U certificate, and a considerable number banned it'—Lord Annan, speaking in the debate on theatre censorship, in the House of Lords (17 February 1966).

6. He can move with greater freedom than a committee in seeking advice on, for instance, allusions to domestic celebrities or the heads of foreign states, because of his special access to top people and because of his unique status above warring sects and vested interests.

7. As the Office has other jobs to do, it does not depend on censorship for a living, or for a reputation. It can surrender without worrying about loss of face or power. It can, and does, turn a blind eye.

8. Only a handful of writers are affected by the Chamberlain's vetoes and interventions. Fewer than three plays in every thousand are banned, and probably about fifty in every thousand authors are obliged to make extensive changes and cuts. Far more interference would be endured if the Chamberlain was evicted from the theatre.

* * *

The case against the Lord Chamberlain and the current system is, as we have seen, formidable: with some of the charges the Chamberlain himself is in agreement. It may be recapitulated and summarized as follows.

1. It is anomalous, unfair, undemocratic and inefficient that one man should be put in absolute authority over the drama, without being officially responsible to Parliament, or to any other body or person but his royal employer. He is omnipotent, and presumed to be infallible. It is irrelevant that he and his staff often defer to other opinions, and compromise with the author. Although he does not behave like a despot, his *power* is despotic—and he uses it to enforce his verdict where no compromise can be reached.

2. Although the area of forbidden territory has been drastically reduced in the past decade, the vetoes surrounding it are inconsistent, unpredictable and sometimes incomprehensible. A word is permitted in one play, prohibited in another. The dramatist is penalized for an offence before, perhaps, he knows what it is.

3. It is a *private* censorship, and there is no appeal against its decisions, except to 'public opinion'. This means that a writer's work may be tried in secret and sentenced to death, for a 'club' production, when it can be arranged, is no substitute for public staging. His property can be destroyed without recompense, for he has no redress in the courts.

4. The current system maintains an exaggerated and unhealthy insulation of the Royal Family, past and present, from criticism and discussion on the public stage: this protectiveness is inevitable when the censor's prime responsibility is to Her Majesty, and the Royal

212

Household. Not only are the Queen, Prince Philip and their living relatives taboo topics, but the dramatist and lyric-writer are also prevented from putting on the stage any English monarchs since Victoria. Even the Widow of Windsor and *her* relations are still, as we have seen, often shielded from legitimate theatrical use. At the same time the association of censorship and throne involves the royal family unnecessarily in miscellaneous controversy

5. The Lord Chamberlain's association with the throne makes his Office exaggeratedly alert to the possibility of offending the feelings of 'friendly' foreign powers, whose representatives are attached to a Court which he helps to run. This scrupulousness restricts unnecessarily the dramatist's freedom.

6. Whatever the safeguards, the system gives one man immense *political* power. This point is generally overlooked because of the absence of political drama (partly due, itself, to the censorship) and the concentration of the debate on issues of sex and violence.

7. The role of the Queen as Defender of the Faith and head of the Established Church obliges the Lord Chamberlain—or so he seems to believe—to enforce an excessively rigid and unrepresentative check, in a dominantly secular country, on outspoken criticism of Christianity, and even incidental irreverent allusions to leading characters in the Christian myth—and the Established Church.

8. The tradition of the Office restricts its staff (though not its Readers) to a military, upper-class background, which appears to the outsider and what *The Times* calls 'the outdated popular imagination' to restrict their understanding of, and sympathy with social, sexual and theatrical changes outside the Palace and the Guards, especially in judging criticism of the Queen and the armed forces.

9. Although the gentlemanly common sense in personal negotiations of the Chamberlain's men, which has now apparently persisted for two generations, is frequently cited as one of the prime assets of the system, it obscures the facts of autocratic power, and it cannot be taken for granted as a permanent feature of the Office. A sudden withdrawal to the era of Redford and Brookfield is improbable, but there is no guarantee that future Comptrollers and Lords Chamberlain will be as relatively impervious to extremist demands as the current establishment. The fact that the censors are now nice men makes the system bearable: it does not make it right.

10. Pre-production censorship makes the Chamberlain more susceptible to the demands of pressure groups, including the relatives of the

recently and even more remotely dead; because the onus is on him to detect and eradicate offensive passages, whereas if he was obliged only to do his censoring *after* a play reached the stage, he could not be saddled with any responsibility for passages at which somebody, somewhere, had taken umbrage.

11. It is plainly absurd that if there *is* to be any censorship of the stage, it should be conducted in complete isolation from television and the cinema; that language and themes should be allowed in one play and banned in another, simply because of the date at which they were written (i.e. before or after the Act of 1737); that ballet-dancers should be free to mime in a way forbidden to actors; that music-hall comedians in seaside concert parties and working men's clubs should tacitly be permitted liberties that sometimes go far beyond the dramatist's reach; that a play which is unfit for consumption in a public theatre has been, in effect, purified for a playgoer who pays, say, five shillings for membership of a 'private' society; that plays and sketches—including directly personal political satire and religious 'heresy'—can be easily seen by millions on television when they are banned for thousands in the theatre.

12. This kind of censorship, in fact, does not work—from the point of view of those people who believe in the necessity of its protection. Not only are we all, *outside* the theatre, exposed to continual shock and humiliation—by the Lord Chamberlain's standards (and our own, too) —in print, in the cinema, in the press and on the TV screen; but *inside* the theatre there is no kind of consistency about sexual and verbal frankness, which is what the champions of a national theatrical nanny are usually talking about. This variation is partly due to the censor himself; partly due to the law (in an English classic or an English music-hall, you can say and do almost anything); and partly to the fact that actors unofficially restore banned words or music-hall comedians may carry the craft of *double entendre* into regions of extreme smuttiness. In performance, censorship is very difficult to enforce. As William Archer said, 'it can suppress a play which touches upon an ethical problem, but it cannot prevent an indecent "gag" or an immoral double meaning conveyed by the actor's look or gesture; so that its survival depends upon a curious form of moral humbug or confidence-trick'.

13. The loophole of freedom—the 'private' production of banned plays at 'club' theatres—has always been a small one, and has been largely used for foreign drama. No dramatists can afford to write for 'club' productions only, unless public theatres can turn themselves at

214

will into clubs for the duration of the play's run. But now it seems likely, from the case of *Saved*, that this will no longer be allowed; and club performances, in general, will (for a time) be dropped by such theatres as the Royal Court. The loophole has been closed.

Here is Benn Levy to sum up:[1]

Had the Office been in less civilized hands, as often it has been in the past, then the sense of grievance would not be confined to that tiny minority of the population whom nature has foredoomed to the writing of plays. It would perturb all those who feel passionately on the subject of civil liberty. For them . . . it matters enormously if even one man's work and property can be destroyed without recompense, without so much as the opportunity of protest, at the whim of another man set above him, answerable to no one and administering no law but his own passing judgement and prejudices. To them it matters enormously if even one man's right to speak his mind, in whatever form he chooses, is restricted by the arbitrary fiat of a fellow-citizen who may dissent from him. It matters enormously if one man is penalized for an offence before he has committed it, it matters that he should have no appeal against this punishment, that the offence be nowhere laid down in the law of his land, that he should be refused the opportunity of trial and that Her Majesty's Courts of Justice should be inaccessible to him. He who argues that victims are few and far between, that only a small minority suffers, demonstrates merely his ignorance of the meaning of freedom, his ignorance that the good faith of a democracy is to be judged by the jealousy with which it protects its minorities and guards the rights of the individual. Discard that yard-stick and popular government is as tyrannical as any other.

Who, then, could—or should—replace the Lord Chamberlain? It seems unlikely that the theatre will ever follow the film industry's lead by appointing its own trade board. The views of managers, actors and authors—and, in particular, of their professional organizations—are too sharply divergent on that score to offer any rosy prospect of workable co-operation on a standing committee or agreement on a permanent official; and the managers will never go it alone, by setting up an autonomous official censorship of their own. They have no need for it. At the moment they are, almost unanimously, satisfied with the Lord Chamberlain, as indeed they have always been. If his powers over the

[1] *Theatre* (1 March 1952).

theatre are abolished, against their advice, they will fall back on their own ad hoc censorship, playing for safety in the provinces.

Is the answer, then, a body answerable to Parliament but appointed by, say, the Arts Council—as an earnest of independence from Government and party ties? This would include, no doubt, representatives of the Minister for the Arts, the League of Dramatists, the Theatre Managers Association and British Actors Equity, plus a lawyer, a bishop and a psychoanalyst, together with the inevitable spokesman of public opinion: all under the chairmanship of some national symbol of judicious fair play and non-specialist common sense? Perhaps: faith in the committee system dies hard. And, to be sure, it would eliminate some of the flaws in the current set-up: the element of anachronism, the social restrictiveness, the excessive devotion to Crown and Church, the invulnerability and impossibility of public appeal. Yet a body of this kind would bring its own fearful disadvantages: notably, red tape and slow motion, apparently inseparable from group decisions on matters where art, morality, politics, religion *and* money may all be confused. Verdicts on a play's fate might well take longer than those of Stable Yard, and they would often turn on skilful chairmanship. As this partly depends upon keeping a middle course, and ensuring that both right and left wings are satisfied, the judgements of the new censors might prove—in the short run—to be little more consistent or reasonable than those of the old ones. Censorship by committee is no solution for the drama, or for the champions of control.

Should the Lord Chamberlain, then, be followed by a Lord Protector: an ombudsman life peer, with all the qualities of the chairman specified above, but with responsibility only to the theatre, the law and the Prime Minister, free from the compromises of the committee game? His duty would be to license all plays, and to consider pre-censorship only where he recognizes serious problems of libel, pornography, sadism, and the provocation of public riots or international incidents, *not* the mere possibility that words or phrases will shock some members of the audience. Such a licenser must have a special status above the political battle, endowed with such personal and public authority, and monumental patience, that he can resist the pressure groups of both militant wings: the Puritan blimps and the extremists who want to put *everything* on the stage. And who is this paragon to be? Neither a politician nor a clergyman, nor a man of the theatre: in the current climate, all these professions would be ruled out. After the experience of the Lord Chamberlain's Office, ex-officers would also be opposed. A lawyer,

216

perhaps? But legal expertise is often irrelevant to the complex and changing dilemmas of the theatre in day-to-day practice and personal relationships. And would an appeals committee not be needed, still, whoever was appointed to the job?

The problem of the successor to the Lord Chamberlain is, in fact, one which has been curiously neglected, partly because its giant difficulty is recognized, and partly because the debate on censorship has usually resulted in four proposals only: either the retention or the liquidation of the role of the Lord Chamberlain; or the institution of an optional system, or the creation of an appeals committee. Should we, then, follow Hilaire Belloc's advice (recalled by Lord Annan):

> *Always keep a-hold of Nurse*
> *For fear of finding something worse.*

My answer is NO. *Nor* should we try another Nanny. Because it is not just the *present* form of censorship that is wrong.

There are several objections to *any* kind of institutional theatrical censorship in a free society. First of all, it contravenes the dramatist's right to free expression. A man who writes a play should be subject only to the laws of the land, the hazards of commerce and his own censorship—like other kinds of writers. In an age of television, the argument that the theatre is uniquely *dangerous* is anachronistic. What *is* unique is the channel it keeps open for individual vision, discovery, heresy and synthesis, for the exploration and interpretation of the realities outside the theatre. In the increasingly conformist, mechanized, pre-packaged, deodorized world of show business and mass communications the theatre needs *more* freedom than television and the cinema, not *less*. The law, under the controls defined in any worthwhile Act abolishing censorship, can deal with any mobsters selling open pornography, sadism and libel. There are more than enough checks already on the theatre's freedom, imposed by the hard facts of economics, architecture and the national emotional climate. As Lord Annan said, in the 1966 Lords debate on the censorship:

> We notably extend less tolerance to the artist than do some other Western countries where the theatre is concerned. In my view, the serious author must be given freedom of choice as to what to say and how to say it. I am afraid this means that the language or the theme or the treatment may very well shock. But can one have art without

217

shocks? This is one of the things that art does: it makes us see life in a new and disturbing way . . .

The real question seems to me to be how far should we go, over and above what the law lays down, to protect the sensibilities of all sorts of different people from shock? . . .

Why should any *special* protection be necessary, in an open, secular and stable society, which has laws to deal with offences against public decency and public order? Why should any additional limits be imposed on the theatre? Parents find it almost impossible to conceal 'unsuitable' television programmes and newspapers from their children; but there is no *need* to expose children, or the young in mind of any age, to any theatre which is presenting plays for adults; and no special protection is consequently needed. If a parent is not sure whether a play is 'suitable', he can always *ask*. But for the more stupid, idle, bigoted, and frightened parents, it may be desirable—without embarking on the institution of a grading system, like the one operated by the film censorship—to require theatre managers to label appropriate productions as 'not for children', and to refuse admission to under-16's. This diminishes the mild, if obvious, risk that a showman will try to whip up excitement by the exploitation of an X label. The decision to label should be left to the managers—and the public.

There is no uniform standard, no moral Mean Time, by which to measure the propriety of the theatre and any other art. A big slice of society no longer accepts its tone, manners, and loyalties from the top layer, and it questions the habits, codes and institutions which it once took on trust, for better or for worse. A large sector of the other ranks don't salute the flag, stand for the Queen, or go on church parade any more; they also don't go to the theatre. Playgoers who see the old certainties in ruins are naturally disturbed. Naturally, some of them turn their backs on the hard facts which have helped to destroy the traditional picture—the facts of politics, physics, history, psychoanalysis, sociology, anthropology, and the rest—and they want the theatre made safe for them against the mob.

This is a small but very articulate minority inside a minority. Its cries of outrage—and it is easily outraged—are heard in high places, and will be heard much more often if censorship is abolished. But why should this fraction of the public be allowed to set the standards by which another minority, in the theatrical *avant-garde*, is regulated? The *derrière-garde* of the public doesn't *have* to be offended by the

218

theatrical *avant-garde*'s work: it can just stay away. The *avant-garde* has no power—and indeed no chance—of monopolizing the theatre now. But it should have the freedom to work as well as it can, within the law and within its budgets. Special protection is needed for neither group, if the law abolishing the censorship is framed as proposed in the 1949 Bill (as amended by the 1966 Arts Council Committee). As Edward Garnett said fifty years ago: 'There are many publics each wanting a different drama on a different level; and they have no right to interfere with one another, or suppress one another's drama.'

One alternative to complete abolition, often canvassed since its proposal by the 1909 Committee, is *optional* censorship: that the Lord Chamberlain or another body should issue licences, as before, to all managers wishing to submit plays to him; but that a manager should be permitted to stage plays *without* a licence, and take his chance. This compromise might prove tempting to the latest committee of inquiry, but that seems unlikely: because although it has the recommendation— to the British appetite to settle for half—of leaving things as they are, while giving the appearance of reform, it also has the drawbacks of tilting the balance heavily in favour of the status quo, while destroying some of its practical advantages. Plays *without* a licence, and otherwise unprotected, would at once attract the attention of the militant zealots, who would not be deterred from challenging either established dramatists of the recent past—Strindberg, say, or Wedekind—or classics such as *Lysistrata*, or even English classics (immune *de facto* if not *de jure* under the present system) such as *The Country Wife* or *Titus Andronicus*. The militancy and power of these objectors is usually exaggerated: they would probably lose, and they would certainly be pilloried and ridiculed. But the unpalatable fact is that their intervention could be so expensive for the kind of management putting on unlicensed plays that it would soon go out of business. In what the court might regard as borderline cases, the prosecution would use the invaluable weapon that the manager was *afraid* to submit the play for a licence; or, perhaps, that he was the kind of manager who *never* submitted plays for a licence. Only one or two 'commercial' managers would, in fact, risk this procedure, and then revert to the old habit of submitting plays to authority. But, meanwhile, it also seems likely that the censorship would become less liberal. If an alternative route was available for the author, the censor would stretch a point less elastically and put more rigidly the orthodox case for cuts and changes: even if the Lord Chamberlain were replaced by an official under authority, with a fixed and open code. The

State-aided theatres might venture more, but if they ventured too far and too often, the cost of legal proceedings—and of postponed productions—could not be met out of their subsidies and would certainly not be paid by special Government grants. If the National and the Royal Shakespeare, let alone the leading reps, made a point of staging unlicensed and controversial plays then there would certainly be political pressure on their governing boards. And the rows and resignations and recriminations that might follow would not, in the end, help the dramatist—or the theatre in general. The repercussions might be far more damaging than in the present system, or after complete abolition.

Moreover, optional censorship would not meet the need for special safeguards against offending the royal family, heads of friendly states, or relatives of the recently (or remotely) famous (and infamous) dead. This is, I believe, an illusory need, but it is one which many supporters of censorship fervently maintain. Why *should* reverence for the President of the U.S.A., for instance, be enforced in the theatre, when any TV satirist, newspaper columnist, or novelist can lampoon the White House? Why *should* a dramatist be denied liberties which are taken for granted by any self-respecting biographer, historian, and writer for television and the cinema? Why should the Chamberlain anticipate the laws of libel? 'Common law provides a perfectly effective remedy for royalty, as for anyone else', as Lord Goodman has said of the threat to privacy—plus common sense. It all comes back to that fallacy that there is something specially dangerous about the living theatre.

No, abolition is the only possible solution. And the best way of achieving it is through a measure along the lines recommended by the Arts Council Committee (see page 174), for a provisional period of not less than five years. If the country can risk a temporary abolition of capital punishment for this length of time, it can surely venture a suspension of the Lord Chamberlain's censorship.

The dangers of complete abolition are obvious, but they have usually been exaggerated. If the dormant fury of Puritan resistance were quite as strong as the prophets of woe suggest, we should have seen more eruptions of it by now. After all, the approval of the Lord Chamberlain is not—and never has been—a guarantee of immunity from prosecution. Moreover, the pro-censor Jobs tend to overlook the virtual extinction of the old-style touring system in the past decade: with it has gone one of the most powerful arguments for Safety First.

There is no danger to the general public. Our traditional self-protective Puritanism and the caution of managers will take care of that. If there is a danger, it is to the theatre, and it may come from some of those impatient authors and directors who believe that the main role of the modern stage is deliberately to disturb people. In their eagerness to extend the frontiers of the theatre, to bring it into closer touch with both social and psychological realities, they will stage as much as actors will agree to speak and do, and as the police tolerate; and although that point of tolerance—in the absence of a Lord Chamberlain—is unknown, it may well be lower than that observed in St James's, and can only be discovered by experiment. This experiment is likely to stop short of sexual intercourse, although the Literary Manager of the National Theatre has suggested—in a matadorish way—that this, too, may be part of the theatre of tomorrow. But attempts would probably be made to achieve a more complete *verbal* freedom; to attack national figures, in *Private Eye* style; to develop the 'documentary' news theatre: to open up religious, sexual and political polemic; and (most explosively) to carry further the exploration of violence—all subject to the laws of the land. Such challenges might well stir up to a new fever-pitch the anti-theatrical Puritanism of the provincial Roundheads; and, whatever the safeguards written into any legislation, there may be a brief flurry of legal action and counter-action. This will affect, however, only a tiny sector of the public. The experiments will not last if that fractional audience rejects them, if only because the subsidies on which most of the *avant-garde* depend will then be withdrawn if they play to empty houses—and, indeed, they may be withdrawn if the writs start flying.

Economic censorship, inevitably, is likely to become even more important than it is today. The partisans of the theatre of embarrass-ment—as distinct from those more concerned with the theatre of surprise, delight, fun, instruction and illumination (to name a few other useful aims) may succeed in holding a public and keeping their play-houses open. But all dramatists who favour abolition must not only be prepared to face controversy, even prosecution, if they are to justify their freedom and achieve parity with other writers. They must also face the certainty that, for a while, there will be *less* chance of getting adventurous, controversial and experimental plays on to the 'commer-cial' stage. And the main 'non-commercial' theatres will have to tread warily if they are to keep their grants—for the politicians will be ready to pounce on 'scandals' paid for out of public funds, and scandals will undoubtedly be discovered or invented, with the eager assistance of some sections of the press.

It may well be true, as Lord Goodman said in the Lords debate in 1966, that we have had a more liberal stage in the last few years, under the Lord Chamberlain, than we might have had if he had been abolished. It seems probable that for a few years after his abolition we will have a *less* liberal stage—in the majority theatre of comfort, at least. But that risk is the price of freedom: and that cliché is, like the eventual abolition of official censorship, unavoidable. In the words of John Mortimer, 'Once the Lord Chamberlain has been abolished, the really interesting problems of censorship will have to be faced.'[1] How free will the managers, the theatre and society, allow the theatre to be?

> Censorship is like the god Proteus, guardian of the answer to certain questions, who eluded the grip of the questioner by ceaseless metamorphoses. . . . censorship never gives ground, but only shifts it . . . Nor is the ground apparently yielded necessarily finally won . . . No subject will be altogether immune from automatic censorship, until all subjects are. The censor guards the vast and intricate mechanism of society, in which the parts are all interconnected in a puzzling network . . .
> We should not be too exclusively obsessed with formal legislation. Ambiguous as it often is, it is in the open; informal censorship, subtle and pervasive, is hiding all around us, permeating even the figures of everyday speech. In the exploration of informal censorship lie the greatest perplexities and the greatest potential rewards.[2]

[1] In *Censorship*, No. 4 (1965).
[2] 'The Natural History of Censorship', by Claire Russell and W. M. S. Russell, in '*to deprave and corrupt* . . .', edited by John Chandos (1962).

POSTSCRIPT

To keep the story of the Lord Chamberlain within the bounds of one book I have had to cut it short and to postpone my original plan of presenting a *sottisier* of censorship in action, now reserved for separate publication. This cannot be a complete record or a completely fair one; but it is intended to be up to date.

First of all, my thanks are due to the many people who have helped me to write this book by their refusal, over the centuries, to acquiesce in theatrical censorship and their determination to ventilate their grievance, however trivial the immediate cause may seem in the perspective of world drama. I owe an especial debt to those writers who have allowed me to quote from their letters to me (and, in some instances, to Lords Cobbold and Willis): John Arden, Noel Coward, Ronald Duncan, Christopher Fry, Alec Grahame, Graham Greene, Benn Levy, Henry Livings, David Mercer, Michael Meyer, T. B. Morris, John Osborne, J. B. Priestley, Harold Pinter, Peter Shaffer, Arnold Wesker, Sandy Wilson and Charles Wood. For their assistance or advice on detail I am deeply grateful to Charles Landstone, Norman Marshall, Ted Willis and Hugh Willatt; to the many printed sources acknowledged throughout the text, especially the 1913 work of Frank Powell and Frank Palmer; to Helen Dawson, for her critical encouragement; and, in particular, to the Royal Court Theatre and the Lord Chamberlain's Office, which has shown me exemplary, unrewarded courtesy.

For permission to quote extracts acknowledgements are due to: Her Majesty's Stationery Office (the Hansard report of a debate in the House of Lords on 17th February 1966); Routledge and Kegan Paul (*Early English Stages* by Glynne Wickham); Souvenir Press (*to deprave and corrupt . . .* edited by John Chandos); Curtis Brown (*Vale of Laughter* by Ben Travers); Jonathan Cape (*The Unexpected Years* by Laurence Housman); Rupert Hart-Davis (*The Letters of Oscar Wilde*, edited by Rupert Hart-Davis); Ernest Benn (*About the Theatre* by William Archer; and *The Censor and the Theatres* by John Palmer); Heinemann (*Not in Front of the Children* by Henry Sherek); Hutchinson (*The*

Theatre in My Time by St John Ervine); A. D. Peters (*Such Were Those Years*, by Ruby Cromer); The Estate of the late Leon M. Lion and Messrs Hutchinson (*The Surprise of My Life* by Leon M. Lion); Peter Cotes, Benn Levy, Norman Marshall, Henry Sherek; the editors of *The Stage*, the *New Statesman*, the *Observer*, the *Sunday Times*, and *The Times*; and the Public Trustee and the Society of Authors (for various excerpts from the work of Shaw).

BOOK LIST

MAIN SOURCES AND WORKS OF REFERENCE

FOWELL, FRANK, and PALMER, FRANK. *Censorship in England.* 1913.
KNOWLES, DOROTHY. *The Censor, the Drama and the Film 1900-34.* 1934.
Scouten, Arthur H. (ed.). *The London Stage 1660-1880.* 1961.
NICOLL, ALLARDYCE. *History of the English Drama 1660-1900.* 1952-5.
PALMER, JOHN. *The Censor and the Theatres.* 1912.
Report from the Select Committee on Theatrical Licenses and Regulations. 1866.
Report from the Joint Select Committee on the Stage Plays (Censorship). 1909.
Hansard

GENERAL READING: A SELECTION

APPLETON, WILLIAM H. *Charles Macklin.* 1961.
ARCHER, WILLIAM. *About the Theatre.* 1886.
—— *The Theatrical World* for 1893, 1894, 1895 and 1896.
BAGSTER-COLLINS, J. F. *George Colman the Younger.* 1946.
BEERBOHM, MAX. *Around Theatres.* 1953.
BRIDGES-ADAMS, W. *The Irresistible Theatre.* 1957.
BUNN, ALFRED. *The Stage.* 1840.
CHAMBERS, E. K. *The Elizabethan Stage.* 1923.
Chandos, John (ed.). *'to deprave and corrupt . . .'* 1962.
CIBBER, COLLEY. *An Apology for the Life of Mr Colley Cibber.* 1739.
COCHRAN, C. B. *The Secrets of a Showman.* 1925.
CROMER, RUBY. *Such Were Those Years.* 1939.
DAVIES, THOMAS. *Memoirs of the Life of David Garrick.* 1780.
DUDDEN, F. H. *Henry Fielding, his life, works and times.* 1952.
ERVINE, ST JOHN. *The Theatre in My Time.* 1933.
FITZGERALD, PERCY. *Samuel Foote.* 1910.
FRYER, PETER. *Mrs Grundy: Studies in English Prudery.* 1963.
GENEST, J. *Some Account of the English Stage.* 1832.

8—B

GILDERSLEEVE, VIRGINIA. *Government Regulation of the English Drama.* 1905.

GLOVER, J. M. *Jimmy Glover His Book.* 1911.

Hart-Davis, Rupert (ed.). *The Letters of Oscar Wilde.* 1962.

HENDERSON, ARCHIBALD. *George Bernard Shaw.* 1911.

HIBBERT, H. G. *Fifty Years of a Londoner's Life.* 1916.

HOUSMAN, LAURENCE. *The Unexpected Years.* 1937.

Johnson, Catherine B. (ed.). *William Bodham Donne and his Friends.* 1905.

LION, LEON M. *The Surprise of my Life.* 1948.

LOFTIS, JOHN. *The Politics of Drama in Augustan England.* 1963.

LOW, RACHEL. *The History of the British Film*: Vol. 1. 1949.

MANDER, RAYMOND, and MITCHENSON, JOE. *Theatrical Companion to G. B. Shaw.* 1954.

MARSHALL, NORMAN. *The Other Theatre.* 1947.

NICHOLSON, W. *The Struggle for a Free Stage in London.* 1913.

ORME, MICHAEL. *J. T. Grein.* 1936.

PEARSON, HESKETH. *The Life of Oscar Wilde.* 1946.

PHILLPOTTS, EDEN. *From the Angle of 88.* 1951.

PURDOM, C. B. *Harley Granville Barker.* 1955.

SHAW, GEORGE BERNARD. *Our Theatres in the Nineties.* 1938.

—— *Prefaces.* 1934.

SHEREK, HENRY. *Not in Front of the Children.* 1959.

TRAVERS, BEN. *Vale of Laughter.* 1957.

West, E. J. (ed.). *Shaw on Theatre.* 1958.

WICKHAM, GLYNNE. *Early English Stages.* 1959, 1963.

INDEX

229

235

237